Phil Barker is a Sydney-based writer, creative director and communications specialist with more than 25 years experience in the media. He has edited top-selling magazines such as *NW* and *Woman's Day* and has published such titles as *Vogue, GQ, Delicious, InsideOut* and *Donna Hay*. Phil is a regular commentator on the life and style of Australian men and a columnist for Fairfax Media. *The Revolution of Man* is his first book.

 @PhilJBarker

# THE REVOLUTION OF MAN

## RETHINKING WHAT IT MEANS TO BE A MAN

## PHIL BARKER

ALLEN&UNWIN

SYDNEY · MELBOURNE · AUCKLAND · LONDON

First published in 2019

Allen & Unwin
83 Alexander Street
Crows Nest NSW 2065
Australia
Phone: (61 2) 8425 0100
Email:  info@allenandunwin.com
Web:    www.allenandunwin.com

 A catalogue record for this
book is available from the
National Library of Australia

ISBN 978 1 76052 891 1

Set in 12/16 pt Adobe Garamond Pro by Midland Typesetters, Australia
Printed and bound in Australia by Griffin Press

10 9 8 7 6 5 4 3 2 1

The paper in this book is FSC® certified.
FSC® promotes environmentally responsible,
socially beneficial and economically viable
management of the world's forests.

*For Lulu, Jayde and Clementine.*

Because women deserve a world of better men.

# Contents

# CONTENTS

# Introduction

I consider myself blessed to have had the opportunity to write this book. The process has been both a revelation and a joy.

For a few years now I have been writing a column for Fairfax Media, called 'Life on Mars', about being a man in these strange and terrible times. I've written about suicide and domestic violence, about pornography and sexism, about male friendships and our relationships with women, and I've come to see what it is to 'be a man' in a whole new way.

I have become convinced that the way we 'perform' being men—from the moment we open our eyes until we gasp our last breath—is damaging us, and those around us. It's directly causing tears, blood and death, all over the planet.

In the pages of this book, with stories and science, I will show you how I reached what might at first seem a rather extreme position.

I was determined that the difficult subject matter in these pages would be balanced with a touch of lightness, although of course it's no laughing matter. My years in journalism, marketing and communications have taught me that the best stories are always the most authentic. So I decided to drop in a few personal anecdotes. To my surprise—and considerable horror—I now see a strange type of memoir weaved into my arguments and discussions about how to be a better man.

Despite my embarrassment about this, I deeply enjoyed the discussions it required me to have with my parents and my daughter—about the past, and about who we are now. Checking facts led to wonderful, rich conversations I'll never forget.

One warning: I have been hideously blasphemous, so do be careful if you're a person of faith. I meant no harm, apart from encouraging refreshing critical thinking. And humour is subjective, so apologies if you don't enjoy the talking cavemen or the dialogue with Jesus.

I couldn't help but let my personal passions for science, philosophy, cars, food, music, books, popular culture . . . and love . . . drive the narrative. People are right when they say you should write what you know. I have at times indulged myself by wandering far off topic and examining things I find fascinating—I nervously hope you enjoy coming to look at interesting things with me.

Phil Barker
September 2018

# Part One

# BECOMING A MAN

# Chapter 1

# BOYS DON'T CRY

There are three tiny words that echo through the hearts and minds of little boys, long before they ever take a step down the path to becoming a man. They're just three tiny words, but they pack such persuasive, pervasive power that their message resonates in every corner of society, leaving no man, woman or child undamaged.

Domestic violence, suicide, alienation, isolation, depression, rage, drug and alcohol abuse, relationship breakdowns and terrible loneliness all flow directly from the deeply damaging ideal expressed in these three tiny words: *be a man*.

Don't show weakness. Don't express any emotion—apart from anger. Don't cry. Don't be soft. Don't be empathetic. Don't be a pussy. Don't be gay. Don't be 'feminine'. Don't ask for help. Dominate every interaction. Be a firefighter, a pilot, a sportsman, a leader of industry, a boss, a stoic provider.

This, apparently, is what it means to 'be a man'.

It starts before we are at school, before we join football teams, before we encounter the whispered wisdom of our brothers and cousins, teachers, coaches and bosses, before we see older guys proudly 'being men'. Long before that, we have already come to understand what we must do.

It starts the moment we make eye contact with our parents. Study after study shows that when the sex of a baby is hidden from an adult, they'll project their own gender bias and treat the little 'boys' differently from the little 'girls'. The 'boys' are perceived as angrier or more distressed by adults who didn't know they were girls. The 'girls' were believed to be happier and more socially engaged.

One study showed that mothers could pick the steepness of a slope their baby boys could successfully crawl down, to one degree. But mothers of baby girls got it wrong by nine degrees. He can get down there, but she can't—yet, of course, there's no difference in the motor skills of eleven-month-old boys and girls.

Little boys are held less often, and soothed for shorter periods of time if they're upset. They are offered less help with finishing a task or a puzzle.

There's a pivotal moment in a little boy's life. Every time he's fallen over and scraped a knee up until now, he's been held, kissed and soothed until the drama is over. Now, with a bleeding knee again, he wails to a parent. But this time it's different. No hugs, no kisses. Just a firm hand on each shoulder, a look in the eye.

'You're okay. Nothing's broken. Be a big brave boy—big boys don't cry.'

If he manages to stifle the tears and snot, and get over the surprise betrayal from the person, who, until this point, had always held him until the pain and tears went away, he gets a reward: praise.

'There's my big strong boy! No more tears. Now, go and play with this truck . . .'

What a powerful affirmation from one of the most influential people in his life, a parent, of how a baby man is supposed to act. 'You're six—enough with the sobbing, buddy.'

Apparently, this stuff is Psychology 101. My daughter, who is currently deep into a psych degree, rolled her eyes when I asked her what she thought about how parents socialise children.

'We studied that last year,' she said. 'Duh, everyone knows that.'

Later, she emailed me a study by Cornell University researchers John Condry and Sandra Condry titled 'Sex Differences: A Study of the Eye of the Beholder'. It's from 1976, but still relevant.

'The fact we often see what we expect to see is sufficiently well-known and accepted to be accorded the status of cliché,' the authors wrote. 'We usually act on what we think we see . . . when our actions are directed at children, the picture is complicated even more. Children often search for an answer to how they should behave by watching the ways adults act towards them. Thus, the actions of adults, directed at children, acquire a reality-defining quality.'

A mother who expects her daughter to fear mice will interpret a startled reaction to a mouse as fear and act accordingly—'thus defining the emotion and subsequent appropriate action for the child. If the child responds to this definition and it has social support, this socially transmitted characteristic may become part of the child's common behavior repertoire.'

Then Condry and Condry, more than 40 years ago, ask the big question: 'Could adults be encouraging sex differences in just such a manner?'

In their study, 204 male and female subjects rated the same infant's emotional responses to four different stimuli. Half the participants were told they were observing a boy, the other half a girl.

'The same infant in a particular situation was seen as displaying different emotions and significantly different levels of emotional arousal depending on the sex attributed to the infant, the sex of the rater, and the rater's experience with young children. The results suggest a healthy caution be exercised in interpreting the studies of sex differences obtained by observers who know the sex of the child being rated,' they concluded.

So how we perceive children—whether we see them as communicators or not, as physically robust or not, as 'tough' or not—shapes our every interaction with them and informs the experiences we create for them. Every experience leaves an imprint on their plastic, baby brains that shapes the adults they become.

By the age of just four months, there's a quantifiable difference between boys and girls in how much eye contact they make and how expressive they are verbally and emotionally—all things that depend directly on their interactions with their parents.

In her book *Pink Brain, Blue Brain: How Small Differences Grow into Troublesome Gaps—and What We Can Do About It*, neuroscientist Lise Eliot says that by the time children are one, they already know which sex they are and strongly identify with it, and quickly conform to how they see other, usually older, boys and girls behaving.

'Preschoolers are already aware of what's acceptable to their peers and what's not,' she writes.

The idea of 'blue' and 'pink' brains creates a loop of self-fulfilling prophecies that denies both boys and girls the opportunity to fulfil their potential, pushing them to become smaller, less complete versions of what they might otherwise be. 'Kids rise or fall, depending what we believe about them,' Eliot says.

So the belief that sons are somehow wired to be non-verbal and emotionally distant becomes a truth, which then creates non-verbal and emotionally distant young men.

Even the notion that blue is for boys and pink is for girls is, like the Easter Bunny and Santa Claus, much more a creation of the modern mass market than a result of any innate preference lurking in our genes. Our Y chromosome may be the reason we grow a penis, but science has yet to find a genetic marker that determines whether we prefer blue shorts to pink dresses.

There's a wonderful story about the colour pink involving one of Australia's greatest boxers, Tony Madigan, and a legendary New South Wales standover man and enforcer, Tim Bristow.

Madigan's career spanned three Olympic Games, a rugby union career and even a stint modelling in London. He won two Commonwealth Games medals in boxing, and was one of only ten men to face Muhammad Ali in the ring more than once. He died in 2017, aged 87.

Bristow, too, was an extraordinary character. He was an enormous man with fists like Christmas hams and a granite, Roger Ramjet–style jaw. Google his image. No one ever looked more like a terrifying thug than Bristow. If he showed up at your door, you were in deep, deep trouble.

The story goes that Bristow bashed a friend of Madigan's at the Newport Arms Hotel in Sydney. Word quickly got to Madigan, who immediately went down to the pub and waited for Bristow to go for him next, even though the two men had never met before.

How did Madigan attract Bristow's attention? He wore pink. So enraged was Bristow at the image of a man wearing pink that he insulted and then attacked Madigan. Folklore has it that Madigan 'cleaned his clock'. So the only time Bristow was ever beaten was by a bloke in pink.

Before we understand what colour is—before we can even see properly—we are, quite literally, wrapped in a colour-coded blanket that flags our future sexual identity.

The June 1918 edition of *Earnshaw's Infants' Department* was clear on the issue: 'The generally accepted rule is pink for the boys and blue for the girls. The reason is that pink, being a more decided and stronger colour, is more suitable for the boy, while blue, which is more delicate and dainty, is prettier for the girl.'

For centuries, children's clothing had been gender-neutral. Everyone got to wear an attractive white smock, up until the age of six or so. It wasn't until the 1940s in the United States that the new idea of blue for boys and pink for girls took hold.

Science began helping out too, letting parents discover the sex of their child, and the marketing departments of children's clothing retailers split the market into two—team pink and team blue—so mum and dad could fit the nursery out, correctly, in advance.

Equally flawed is the idea that boys like trucks and tractors, guns and swords and building things, and girls prefer more 'social' games, like playing house with dolls, or perhaps tottering about on tiny plastic heels with a matching handbag. You can even buy your little girl a tiny kitchen, complete with pots, pans, an apron and even miniature rubber bacon and eggs. Suitable for girls up to six—and available at a toy retailer right now.

Parents are powerless in the face of the marketing avalanche, which has successfully, and continually, divided the market for children's products by gender. A generation has been beautifully schooled by marketers in what is 'appropriate' for boys and girls. These ideas have slipped into our collective consciousness so firmly that beliefs about the sexes, not founded in science, have become hard 'knowledge' about what is right—and wrong.

Imagine you're at a friend's barbecue. A couple has brought along their adorable five-year-old son, Brian. For this outing, Brian has chosen a pink dress, and matching shoes. His long blond hair has been styled just like that of his Barbie, which never leaves his loving clutch, unless she's going for a ride to the beach with Ken in the country camper. Imagine, now, the whispered discussions of other guests in the kitchen or in the car on the way home.

'Oh my god, did you see that poor kid?'

'Why do they dress him like a girl?'

'He can't be, like, gay already, can he?'

'He's going to be screwed up for life.'

Even if poor little Brian manages to get through the day without noticing the adult scorn and confusion, there's no way he'll misunderstand what his peers think. After five minutes of explaining his dress and doll to the other kids, he'll no doubt hear the worst insult that can be levelled at a little boy: 'You're a girl!' Shorts and a T-shirt next time, buddy. Be a man.

A child dressed in the 'wrong' clothes and playing with the 'wrong' toys is, somehow, deeply shocking. What's more shocking, perhaps, is that a child who chooses to ignore an arbitrary set of gender norms—which is in fact just decades old, and driven by market forces—should be shocking at all.

These attitudes play so powerfully in our collective psyche that advertisers can't resist using them to build scary little campaigns. In 2017, when the same-sex marriage debate raged after the announcement of a national postal vote, the Coalition for Marriage launched its TV ad for the 'No' side.

Mum Cella White fixes the camera with a deeply worried expression and shares some terrible news. 'The school told my son he could wear a dress next year if he felt like it,' she says grimly, as if the school had also been issuing students small-gauge firearms and relaxing doses of MDMA. The school, Frankston High School, denies ever having made such an offer. Ms White is on the record saying she was concerned that such thinking was 'warping' her children's 'way of thinking'.

Entrenched homophobia is implicit in the ad. If same-sex marriage is allowed in Australia, dress-wearing at school will surely follow—and soon everyone will be gay. Then where would we be?

As it turns out, boys haven't been made to wear dresses to school, no one married the Harbour Bridge, not everyone is gay and so far, nearly 3000 couples have been able to marry their true love, a human right denied to them for decades.

Yet the people who so passionately fought against same-sex marriage have been strangely silent! You'd think they'd have expressed their delight that the horrors they predicted did not come to pass.

The 'No' TV (and skywriting) campaign was another of many tiny blows, all of which use fear to reinforce gender stereotypes. Young men and women who saw the commercial added its message to the myths and misconceptions driven into their heads every day. In just 30 seconds, the notions that 'boys don't wear dresses' and that 'gay is bad' were neatly captured and presented by that most influential of lobby groups, concerned suburban mums.

A study published in 2017 in the *Journal of Adolescent Health* shows unequivocally that gender-specific roles and stereotypes create lasting damage into adulthood.

The study, of 450 children across five continents, with broad cultural differences, found that learned, encouraged and enforced gender roles ultimately contributed to the wage gap, to domestic violence and to mental health problems. Across all cultures, the researchers discovered, early adolescents are being fitted with a 'gender straitjacket' that has lifelong consequences linked to an increased risk of health problems.

'What we've learned is that there's more commonality than differences in 10-year-olds across the world,' says Robert Blum of Johns Hopkins University in Maryland, the leader of the study. 'We were very surprised to see such universality of the myth that boys are strong, confident and leaders, while girls are weak and incompetent, who should be quiet and follow.'

'Too often, we address gender norms late in adolescence when they are well established and have started to have negative impacts on health,' says Sarah Keogh of the Guttmacher Institute in New York. 'This study shows that gender socialisation happens much earlier than that.'

According to Blum, it is possible to change stereotypes: he cites altered attitudes and laws combating sexism in Europe and North America. But it requires the knowledge of how and when these gender myths are ingrained. Exposures to gender stereotypes start in infancy, he says. 'But early adolescence may be the ideal time for interventions.'

By the time a boy starts school, we already have very clear ideas of what it means to 'be a man'. In front of us is the influence of our peers, who carefully monitor our every behaviour and punish any infringement of the gender code; of the leaders and mentors who let us know it's actually all about winning, because real men are winners; and of the older guys who clearly know how to be a man, because they have money and cars and girlfriends.

Every day we see it and hear it, the subtle, constant hum of spoken advice and unspoken example. Everyone has a point of view on what it is to be a man.

And, of course, there's social media and advertising. Check out male 'influencers' on Instagram, or click around a website aimed at male readers, and we can add the following to the list of things we need in order to be a man: we must be tall, tanned, flat of ab, sports car–driving, big-watch-wearing and expensive-hotel-staying, with one arm around a swimsuit model who looks like she's just had sex, or is just about to. We need expensive luggage, suits and haircuts; if you don't have a lush, groomed beard right now, you're barely a man at all.

•

The notion of being a man has played out powerfully in my own life. I grew up on a farm in rural New Zealand, where there was so much manliness around the place that we had to wear special boots to stomp through it.

I remember a time when I was about nine years old; my younger brother, Andrew, was coming up to five. We were playing in the woolshed as the highly exciting annual shearing of our flock took place. I'd watch in awe as the 'gun' shearers, stinking of beer from the night before and with sweat pouring down their bodies, bent double and ripped their way through almost 300 animals in an eight-hour shift. Drinking until you threw up, driving a V8 and banging as many chicks as possible had to be on the list of stuff you should do to be a man, according to the shearers. And be tough. So very tough. Pain and whining was for pansies. It was 1974. I had no idea what banging was, or what a pansy was, but I knew for sure that one was good and one was bad.

My brother was in the habit of carrying 'Sucky' everywhere, a scrap of fabric that had once been a blanket. He'd comfort himself by sucking his thumb through it. When our mother gently removed it from his little fingers for a quick wash, his tears of grief and pain wouldn't stop until Sucky was out of the dryer.

I knew he'd be starting at my school soon. As far as I was concerned, there was absolutely no way he was going to turn up with Sucky. I clearly remember panicking that he'd somehow reduce my manliness by association. Real men, I knew, didn't suck a Sucky.

In the woolshed, the wool is made into bales by 'roustabouts'. A hydraulic ram packs the whole thing down tightly, while the roustabouts quickly hand-sew a top panel onto the bouncy new bale.

In a planned move, just as the last fleece went into a bale, but before the ram came down, I grabbed Sucky and threw it in the wool. Andrew's howls couldn't be heard over the noise of the dogs, sheep, yelling and shearing machines; I think I even held him down so he couldn't run around hysterically. The roustabout sewed the cap on the bale, the ram was released and the bale was marked to be shipped who knows where?

Eventually, Andrew's screaming got my father's attention, when we stopped for smoko. I proudly and happily confessed my sin because I had decided he was too old for Sucky. I knew I was right. Tough love—it was time for my brother to toughen up. No one was about to pull a finished wool bale to bits to get Sucky out, so that was that. And everyone—apart from Andrew—agreed. It may have been a bit traumatic for him, but it was a good thing in the end.

This little incident from so many years ago isn't that big a deal. Yet I remember every moment of that day, and so does my brother. Emotion creates memory.

Of course, my brother survived the ordeal and went on to become a creative leading educator and a beautiful, open, loving father and husband. The 'Saga of Sucky' has become part of family legend. But behind it is a neat illustration of how the requirement to start acting like a man is policed at every moment by everyone around you. Every day of his life, a young man learns a little more about being a man: what behaviour is appropriate, and what is not.

A few years later, my unformed manhood was being forged in perhaps the ultimate crucible of masculinity, the sporting field. In my case it was New Zealand rugby union.

A key element in being a man is to be physically dominant over others. The tougher, bigger, more muscular you are, the more ability you have to impose your will, physically, over another human being, and the more of a man you are seen to be.

By sixteen, I had the delicious self-satisfaction of being a young guy in a senior team. I was a boy playing against men in the most manly of sports. So powerful was the validation I felt that I let it define me for the next few years. I had fought to prove I was a man, and I was never going to give that up.

One weekday evening, as the weak winter sun gave up the fight against a bitter wind and savage little blasts of freezing rain, I sat on a bench after footy practice with Don, who played in my team. Don was tall, strong, athletic and aggressive. As our bodies steamed and cooled, we chatted about the session. Don didn't seem happy. He stopped talking, looked away for an age, and when he turned back I saw tears streaming down his face.

'I hate rugby,' he said. 'It hurts. It's always freezing. I really don't like hurting other people. It's just shit. I don't want to do it anymore.'

I was horrified. How on earth could someone with their hands on the holy grail of manliness—sporting prowess—possibly want to fling it away?

And the crying? As well as admitting to the blasphemy of weakness, Don was also guilty of unmanliness. I remember panicking, looking around to see if anyone else was witnessing this humiliating display. He was my friend, a nice guy, smart and sensitive, but I couldn't get away fast enough. I suppose I was afraid some of the 'pussy' might end up sticking to me—or, worse, that there might be some suggestion of gayness.

Don's father, Norman, was a well-known, pugilistic local politician, best remembered for his hysterical opposition to New Zealand's 1986 *Homosexual Law Reform Act*, which legalised consensual sex between men over the age of sixteen. 'Turn around and look at them, gaze upon them, you're looking into Hades. Don't look too long—you might catch AIDS,' said the man nicknamed 'the Mouth from the South'.

It's likely, then, that Don didn't come from an environment where an open, compassionate, loving chat about his sporting future would result in him being able to make a graceful decision to hang up the boots. No, Don's path to manly glory lay open before him—and there was absolutely nothing he could do about it.

What is clear to me now is the depth of pain Don must have been in to open up the way he did. What is also clear is what I should have done, but didn't.

I should have put an arm around his shoulder, listened, showed empathy, told him I understood. Maybe I should have confessed that I, too, felt the same. The cold, the exhaustion, the physical pain, the injuries, the sheer brutality of the physical contest you had to win at all costs . . . it was actually awful.

It wasn't that I acknowledged this truth in the back of my head but couldn't admit it. The idea of not loving sport and all it represented was simply alien to me at the time. It was a concept I didn't understand.

Don grimly endured the rest of the season in his own private hell. We lost contact as university and the next exciting stages of manhood beckoned us, but that raw moment of emotional honesty has stayed with me since. It was the first glimpse I had of the truth that men are vulnerable and emotional, and often suffer in a silence of their own making.

In a piece for the *Sydney Morning Herald* headlined 'Isolation from Platonic Touch Is a Tragedy of Modern Manhood', feminist writer Clementine Ford, mother of a young son, argues that nothing much has changed. 'I've become interested in looking at how men police each other's expression of masculinity. It seems especially sad to me that men—and young men in particular—are conditioned against embracing the pleasures of a physically expressed platonic love with each other from fear that the authenticity of their manhood may be challenged.'

It's the old 'don't be gay' rule. Don't touch your mate, no matter how much you love him, because men must maintain their reputations of strict heterosexuality.

The American writer Mark Greene, a regular commentator on men's issues, particularly on the website *The Good Men Project*, argues that the depth of our desire to act like men leads to physical and emotional isolation. In an essay titled 'How a Lack of Touch Is Destroying Men', he writes:

While women are much freer to engage in physical contact with each other, men remain suspect when they touch others. There is only one space in our culture where long-term physical contact is condoned for men and that is between fathers and their very young children.

And where does this leave men? Physically and emotionally isolated. Cut off from the deeply human physical contact that is proven to reduce stress, encourage self-esteem and create community. Instead, we walk in the vast crowds of our cities alone in a desert of disconnection. Starving for physical connection. We crave touch. We are cut off from it. The result is touch isolation.

The inability to comfortably connect, Greene argues, has left men vulnerable to depression, alcoholism and suicide, and prone to becoming frustrated, angry, impotent domestic abusers.

•

It's not just about physical touch, in fact, but about successful communication on all levels. Because of the tightly policed imperative that we must remain stoic and self-reliant, our emotional landscapes aren't experienced by anyone but ourselves. It's like we're living life trapped inside a box, its impenetrable walls built by the pretend dance of manhood, policed by other men, women, our parents, our friends, our partners and, ultimately, ourselves.

The idea of the 'Man Box' isn't new. It has been used in group work with boys and men all around the world to show what a powerful force masculinity is in our lives. Here, White Ribbon Australia uses the Man Box tool in group exercises that aim to 'redefine masculinity'. The concept has its genesis, as far as I can tell, in a 1998 book by Paul Kivel, *Men's Work: How to Stop the Violence that Tears Our Lives Apart.*

Kivel has also been driving the 'Oakland Men's Project' a group in California dedicated to preventing men's violence against women for more than thirty years. It was in this work he and his colleagues developed and refined the idea of the Man Box.

American sexuality educator, workshop teacher and writer Charlie Glickman has been using the Man Box in his work with men for the past fifteen years. He prefers to call it the 'Act Like a Man' box, because pretending to be a man all the time is a continuous, lifelong performance. Glickman argues that if men are born in a Western country, their responses are remarkably consistent, regardless of age, gender mix, sexual orientation and racial makeup.

Here's a typical Man Box, completed by one of Glickman's groups. It doesn't matter where they are or who they are, the things young men chose to put in the Man Box are remarkably consistent.

A real man is 'tall, strong, muscular, 25–45' (meaning I'm apparently too old now to be a real man!), 'able-bodied, heterosexual, competitive and dominant'. He is a 'cop, firefighter, mechanic, lawyer, businessman or CEO'. He is a 'caretaker, competent, a leader'. He 'drinks, watches and plays sport, and hangs out with his mates'. As usual, he shows no emotion apart from 'anger and excitement'. He is 'stoic and violent'. Our hero 'always wants sex, has lots of sexual partners, and knows sex is about scoring'. He 'has a big penis, gets hard when he wants and stays hard'. He is also 'always able to give his partner an orgasm' (or multiple orgasms) and 'ejaculates when he wants to'. His sex life is focused on 'intercourse, receiving blowjobs and possibly anal sex (giving)'.

Note the brackets the group popped around the word 'giving', just to emphasise the point. You can imagine the moment in the room. Real men can give, but they most definitely cannot receive. To enthusiastically receive anal sex is gay, and that's somewhere in a fragrant meadow a very long way from the Man Box.

After they've completed their list of 'real man' qualities, groups are asked to come up with words used to describe men who are not all of the things in the Man Box. If you're on the outside, this is what you are: 'gay, faggot, girl, weak, sissy, pussy, wimp, bitch, loser'.

The nature of the Man Box is that you're either in or out. You can't have a foot in the door. The Man Box requires a complete performance of masculinity—and constant vigilance, lest someone be able to point the finger at you and call you a pussy.

It gets worse. There's not enough room for everyone in the box. There's a hierarchy. If you're at the bottom, you'll also get chucked out. Men must compete with each other in acts of manliness. As each man performs in more and more manly ways, the men around him must also become more strident in their displays to keep up.

The fight to stay in the Man Box is deeply damaging to those who have successfully stormed the walls. Communication, empathy, friendship, openness, and the ability to love and be loved are all left outside. All we're allowed to express inside the Man Box is anger, and maybe a little bit of sexual aggression.

Outside are those men who can't possibly live up to the ideals of big, strong, cool, good-looking, smart, rich, sexy, well-hung, charismatic, 'real' men.

The Man Box is a brilliant exercise to show men a clear and consistent list of behaviours and characteristics that currently define 'manhood' around the world.

I've also used it as a wonderfully simple way to describe the eternal, impossible, performance of manhood, and how it locks us up in a prison of our own making.

The strange thing about the Man Box is we're all either desperate to get into it or struggling to stay in it, despite the pain, loneliness and despair inside. The simple reason is because if you're not putting on a great performance of manhood, you're outside the Man Box because you're not a manly man, and that's a much worse place to be.

We'll look into its sad black centre again and again in these pages.

And when you start looking, there're Man Boxes everywhere.

In 2018 the influential, highly editorial-driven New York–based website *The Cut*—for women with stylish minds—ran a series called

'How to Raise a Boy'. It was an urgent question to be considered, *The Cut* argued, in the era of President Trump and #MeToo.

As part of the series, it interviewed two teen brothers—Carlos, sixteen, and Liam, fourteen—from a small town in Michigan. In a brutally candid interview that ranged across dating and sex, technology, parents and peers, this exchange speaks loudly on the damaging role of masculinity in their lives. They are discussing suicide.

**Carlos:** There are three kids in my grade. I'm a junior—that's one person every year who has passed away from suicide. And because we have such a conservative community, we're afraid to talk about that.

**Liam:** That's 100 percent true.

**Carlos:** And once it happens, then it's like 'Bullying needs to stop.' But it's not just bullying. It's more the cultural perception of being 'weak'. You are seen as a pussy if you are depressed. You are seen as a pussy if you have anxiety. Especially as a man. Girls, I feel like we see that as normal, for them to have anxiety and depression and weight issues. But if you're a dude and you feel like you're too skinny or too fat, you're a pussy.

**Liam:** If you are a male and you look at yourself in the mirror and you're like, 'I'm kind of ugly, I don't like myself.' Fuck you dude, you're a pussy.

**Carlos:** Yeah, like grow some balls.

**Liam:** Yeah. Suck a dick. And I hate that. It's this idea about masculinity.

**Carlos:** I fucking hate masculinity. I hate it. It's such a toxic mindset to have to carry yourself in a certain way, to have to act a certain way, just because you have a penis. It kind of ruins your whole life. Thinking about being a man. Just because society tells you to.

**Liam:** Part of it is America itself. This nationalistic 'Uncle Sam wants you—go and fight for your country. Shoot the motherfucking gun.' I gotta stop swearing. 'Shoot a gun, and have sex and . . .'

**Carlos:** Drink beer, look at boobs.

**Liam:** And then go to church in the morning. If you don't want to do something because you are scared to try it, or because you're nervous, a lot of parents are like, 'Shut up pussy—go do it.'

**Carlos:** But they're right about toxic masculinity. It changes the way you act. You're trying to be manly and impress people, and you don't even realise it until you're called out for being a total asshole.

Recently I interviewed rugby league player Joel Thompson for Fairfax Media. The second-rower plays for Manly, and has also represented the Raiders, Dragons, New South Wales Country and the Indigenous All Stars. His passion in life is being an ambassador for the National Rugby League's mental health program, State of Mind.

The interview was for the launch of a mental positivity campaign called Road to Resilience. The NRL encouraged its community of members, players and fans to download a diary to fill in for 21 days, and to complete exercises and answer questions about their mental health. Joel's story is a road to redemption—and resilience. The NRL is genuinely saving lives with its mental health initiatives. It's both wonderful and ironic that one of the toughest, manliest sports on the planet has such a warm, beating heart.

'I had a tough childhood that came back to haunt me, mate,' Joel told me. 'I wasn't coping when I came into first grade. There was a lot of outside noise and I was drinking a lot. I didn't want to be here anymore.'

His girlfriend at the time, Amy—now his wife and the mother of his two daughters—pushed him to get help.

'She saved my life. I had never spoken to someone. I opened up and cried like a baby and came out a different person. It lit a fire under me. I was like "Wow!" I'd never helped anyone before and in helping others, I've helped in my own healing.'

Although he'd never heard of the Man Box exercise, Joel clearly expressed the unique and dangerous pressures on young men. 'I was brought up not to be a sook, to toughen up,' he said. 'But as a young guy you want to prove yourself, not get help.' Now he wants young men to know that it's brave to reach out and say you're not coping. No one will judge you. He tells those he works with how to spot the signs of mental illness in themselves and others, and talks coping strategies.

Writer and musician Brandon Jack—formerly a player for the Sydney Swans AFL club, and also the son of rugby league legend Garry Jack, for we older fans—penned a powerful piece for the *Sydney Morning Herald* in 2018.

> The following statement is true: rape culture is real. If you roll your eyes at these words, dismissing the idea as an overreaction by hypersensitive feminists, then you are part of the problem. This is something we can no longer hide from—it's not an illusory bogeyman created to topple male dominance—so please, don't weep for your toxic masculinity.

As a young man who 'never gave much thought to the influence of patriarchal society on women', Jack says he 'saw first hand how far we are from living in a world where women truly feel supported and empowered' when he was the support person for a close friend during her cross-examination as a victim of sexual assault.

> Every day I hear comments from young men and boys about women. They vary from things as seemingly harmless as 'she's a five out of 10' to more explicitly outrageous statements of 'She's not hot enough to be raped, who's she kidding'.
>
> There's a sense of entitlement in groups of young men when it comes to how women can be talked about that we should no longer accept.

The #MeToo movement has opened up the conversation. What is it to be a man? How should men behave towards women? What is acceptable—and what is not?

Men who want to make a change can help by joining these conversations when we can, and by providing examples of how men should act to the younger men around us. Shut down your sexist mates. Respect the fact that women have as much right to live, unmolested, on this planet as you do.

The Man Box is brittle. If we chip away at it, it'll come tumbling down. It's a truth that all men, if they are honest with themselves, have at least once in their lives treated another in a way they knew to be hurtful, abusive or worse, simply because they were trying to 'act like a man'. For most of us, it's been more than once.

How powerful is the word 'act' in that nasty little phrase? Because trying to follow all the rules of manhood is most surely a performance.

Acting isn't real. And we can never get it right. There'll always be someone telling us we need to man up. There'll always be men who are more manly than us, and men who wished they were as manly as us. So, deep down, none of us is happy.

That's a dangerous thing. It makes us angry. Too angry. Someone's going to get hurt.

# Chapter 2

# A HABIT THAT STICKS

Our grandfathers might have seen a couple of grainy images of a coy woman in a weird hat on a divan, showing off the upper part of her stocking – what passed for porn back in the day. Pops might also have a couple of mental snapshots of your Nan—and, if he'd been very lucky, of one or two other women in various states of undress or sexual ecstasy. That's pretty much it for the erotic imagery he might have sampled in his whole lifetime.

A ten-year-old boy—that's the age men first encounter porn now— on his laptop, tablet or phone has a greater variety of sexual images available to him at a couple of clicks than dear old Granddad could ever have conjured.

Imagine your grandfather surfing a few popular porn sites. He may well appreciate the efforts of all the young women from all over the world who seem happy to get naked without much prompting, but all the choking, anal gaping, spitting, slapping, fisting and rimming would bewilder him.

'Not sure what's going on there, mate,' he'd say. 'But I can tell you right now your nan wouldn't put up with any of that nonsense.'

The sheer variety of porn available online is, more than a little ironically, responsible for an epidemic of erectile dysfunction among young men. It turns out that it won't drop off if you play with it too much, but it definitely might stop working.

This is no doubt the first generation of young men to learn to masturbate left-handed.

It's also the first generation of young men who are embarking on their first adult sexual relationships armed with the worst of all possible handbooks: *How to Do Sex According to Porn.*

Porn does not show real sex. Porn does not show real women. Porn does not show real men and how their bodies actually work. Porn does not show real sexual ecstasy and desire. Porn is not what women want. Porn is made by men, for men.

I can't talk for young gay men, simply because I've never had the experience of being one, but I have no doubt the same applies. They, too, see far too much too early and suffer the same consequences as their young straight brothers. Gay porn, too, reduces people to poles and holes.

This discussion of porn is from a 'straight' point of view, simply because that is what I know. If there's a young gay man reading this, I don't mean to exclude you. My rant covers you too—get your hand off it and shut the laptop.

Porn consumption sets young men up for sexual and relationship failure. It teaches them that women are sex objects, not people. It turns their gaze away from the true joy of sex—the fun, the sharing, the intimacy—and towards the act itself, the penetration.

So porn is creating not only physical problems, but mental and emotional problems as well. Young men all over the world are learning that they must look and act a certain way, and that the women they meet must be sexy, shaved and slick with semen. It's a disaster for us all.

Maybe there's something to be said for the desperate fumblings, at parties and in the back seats of cars, experienced by those of us old enough to have missed the digitisation of sex. There was a shared sense of adventure, laughter and the fun of failure. We learned about the opposite sex slowly and in the real world. If your only porn experience is two issues of *Playboy* magazine you found in a barn, you're probably not going to want an anal threesome first up, but you might kind of like lingerie.

Of course, old-school print porn objectified women in strange underwear and soft focus, but there was so little of it, and it was so vanilla, it packed very little of the punch of today's digital onslaught.

Like everything, sex can be explained by science. Our primal brains still reward us for eating fat and sugar and encourage us to binge, believing we're still living in caves with no idea where our next meal is coming from. It's about survival and stocking up energy. We also get a dopamine surge when we see sexual imagery—the purpose of our attraction being to continue the species and pass on our genetic material at all costs.

But just as we were never supposed to be able to get high-calorie fast food at the drive-through, we were never meant to supply our poor brains with a click-fest of boobs and bonking, each fresh image shooting a surge of pleasure south. Every vision is seen by our brains as a genetic opportunity, our online porn harem an unheard-of boob-nanza for our hunter-gatherer brains.

A build-up of the substance Delta-FosB, released with every dopamine surge, causes changes in our brains, and over time they require more and more shock and surprise, novelty and variety, to generate a pleasure response. This same build-up and rewiring can be seen in the brains of drug and gambling addicts.

In the real world, this means that boys and young men who use a lot of porn need more and more variety of stimulation to achieve an erection or maintain it for any length of time. When faced with a real woman, in a situation that requires touch, taste, smell, feedback and communication, a rewired brain won't get enough of a pleasure hit— and so, deflatingly, there'll be no hard-on.

It is this, not the associated ADHD, anxiety, depression, isolation and drug and alcohol use, that has finally sent men to seek professional help for arousal addiction. They finally panicked when their penises stopped working.

The good news is that 120 days of going cold on slapping the turkey will result in a porn-addled brain rewiring itself, and its owner will once again become aroused by a real partner in the real world, even if her pubic hair might not be groomed into a love heart or waxed off like that of the girls on *Pornhub*.

Psychologist Philip Zimbardo's hard-hitting TED Talk, 'The Demise of Guys?', is famous for having sounded the alarm bells around young men and the internet. He argues that young men are 'flaming out' academically, and wiping out socially with girls and sexually with women. Young men are 30 per cent more likely to drop out of school, and girls now outperform them at every level. In Zimbardo's native Canada, boys make up two-thirds of special education programs, and are five times more likely to have ADHD.

According to Zimbardo, there is a 'fear of an intimate emotional connection with someone else, especially someone of the opposite sex, who give off ambiguous, contradictory, phosphorescent signals . . . One on one with the opposite sex, they don't know the language of face contact, the verbal and non-verbal set of rules that enable you to comfortably talk to someone else.'

Zimbardo coined a great term—'social intensity syndrome'—to describe the phenomenon of men 'preferring male bonding over female mating'. Men, he says, prefer the physical company of men. Men have been with men in teams and clubs, in gangs and fraternities, in the military and pubs. A man would rather be in a bar with strangers watching a football grand final 'than have Jennifer Lopez totally naked in their bedroom'. He sums the idea up in a snappy sentence: 'They now prefer the asynchronistic internet world to the spontaneous interaction in social relationships.'

All this is an unintended consequence of the internet, and specifically of video games and porn. By the time a boy is 21, he has played 10,000 hours of video games, in isolation. He currently watches 50 porn clips, possibly more, each week. Young men don't know how to relate in the real world, and have no understanding of how to make real, mutually pleasurable, sexy love to a real woman, let alone talk to her.

Agreeing with the brain-rewiring effects of arousal addiction, Zimbardo argues that young men today expect constant change, excitement, shock and instant feedback. This means they are totally out of sync with traditional school classes, which are analogue, static and interactively passive. Worse, young men are equally out of sync with girls in romantic relationships, which build gradually and subtly.

'Who should care?' Zimbardo boomed from the pulpit. Well, only 'parents of boys and girls, educators, gamers, filmmakers, and women who'd like a real man they can talk to, who can dance, who can make love slowly.'

That's what's wrong with guys right now, says Zimbardo—and he was talking back in 2011.

•

Porn connects with deeply primal parts of our brains. We are hardwired to desire the shock and thrill of the new, to keep us procreating and to keep the species alive. That's it. Complicated, confusing, delicious and dangerous sex drives pretty much everything we do. Abraham Maslow's much-quoted 'hierarchy of needs' came from his 1943 paper 'A Theory of Human Motivation'. Maslow's pyramid of needs—which is to say, the things that motivate us—begins with self-actualisation at the top, and moves down through esteem, love and belonging, to safety; finally, underpinning it all, are our psychological needs: food, water, sleep, air, clothing, shelter and sex. Without these basics, our other needs cannot be met.

The 'Coolidge effect' demonstrates our basic animal lusts in action. The term was coined by behavioural endocrinologist Frank A. Beach, and goes a long way to explaining our predilection for arousal. It argues that most mammals, usually males, will show renewed sexual interest when fresh sexual partners are introduced to a situation, even if their current partners are still available.

Calvin Coolidge was president of the United States from 1923 to 1929. One time he was being shown around an experimental chicken farm with his wife, Grace. They were in separate parties. At the chicken yard, Grace noticed a rooster that was mating very frequently. She asked how many times a day, and was told: 'Dozens.'

'Tell that to the president when he comes by,' she said.

When informed of the statistic, the president asked: 'Same hen every time?'

'Oh no, Mr President,' came the reply. 'A different hen every time.'

'Tell that to Mrs Coolidge,' he said.

The Coolidge effect was very visible on the farm where I grew up. For a few glorious weeks each year, the rams were allowed out of the backyard—where they spent their time grunting outside my window at night, eating and butting heads—to the mating fields.

They were strapped into Mad Max–style leather halters, which had flat pads of chalk called 'raddles' at the chest. The purpose was to reveal which ewe had received which ram's attention, as she'd end up with a telltale coloured patch on her back.

For the first few days, a ram would happily service his woolly harem until he got bored, and then he'd go back to wandering around, snuffling and eating grass. But if you opened the gate into the next paddock, which was full of hot ewes he hadn't met yet, he'd be in there like a shot, dishing out chalk marks one after the other, until he was exhausted.

We'd amuse ourselves by watching from the back of the ute, cheering the rams on. 'Go, Boris!' we'd yell. 'That's another one!'

We are animals, too, of course. Our primal desires—the foundation of our hierarchy of our needs—play so powerfully in our lives that we can't look away when the sexual is right in front of us.

That's why porn is so particularly attractive and damaging to us.

And what an industry has sprung up online to service this desire. Today, porn is worth an estimated US$100 billion, worldwide. Hollywood makes around 600 movies a year and generates around US$10 billion in profit. The porn industry makes 13,000 films and creates US$15 billion in profit. MindGeek, which owns *Pornhub*, *Brazzers*, *YouPorn* and *Reality Kings*, is a close third (behind Google and Netflix) as one of the largest bandwidth-consuming companies in the world. More people visit porn sites each month than the number who visit Netflix, Amazon and Twitter combined.

These incredible stats are from the hard-to-watch Netflix documentary *Hot Girls Wanted* which follows a porn talent agent, Riley, and a posse of hopeful young stars into the tragic and harrowing world of hardcore porn in the United States. Created in collaboration with the Kinsey Institute for Sex Research, the documentary shows Riley typing 'Hot Girls Wanted' into *Craigslist*, and then saying: 'That's it, that's all I gotta do. I'll have five responses in a few hours.'

And, hey presto, he does. Young women who think it might be a good idea to trade their bodies for up to US$3500 a shoot, and a chance at literally millions of dollars if they make it big, fly in from all over the United States, and the world, so Riley can start sending them to the meat grinder.

Pro-am porn is a trending category. Instead of a twenty-something porn star pretending to be an innocent teen from the farm, the innocent teen from the farm is the porn star.

'Teen' is the number-one searched term in internet porn.

One of the girls the film followed was Ava Taylor. Google her if you dare. She is one of the very few girls who got beyond one day, one week or the standard few months in the industry. 'Some do one shoot and never come back,' shrugs Riley.

One scene in *Hot Girls Wanted*—showing Ava having pasta, a ciggy and a beer with two porn stars, one male and one female, after a hard day at the office—is a revelation. It's a small mercy, but the male porn star is way more intelligent and respectful than he seems on film. Ava describes a hardcore scene they shot the day before, involving forced blowjobs so torrid that the 'guys' on set were concerned for her welfare . . . after the shoot was over.

One girl, in an interview cut with nasty actual footage of the shoot she's describing so matter-of-factly, speaks of how she was forced to swallow multiple Viagra-engorged penises of professional porn stars until she vomited.

Then she licked it up.

•

Banks, Google, your supermarket and phone company, and a matrix of other data-tracking corporations know so much about who you are—neatly linked to your stored facial-recognition profile, of course—that we can be sure we are already way beyond the 'Big Brother is watching you' dystopia of George Orwell's *Nineteen Eighty-four*.

It makes sense for corporations to know how we behave. It helps them sell things to us more effectively. Many Big Brothers are watching our every move and swipe, and sharing what they know. A big bank will happily align itself with gay community issues, like 2017's same-sex marriage debate, knowing that a majority of its customers will applaud the brand making a stand. The bank can see if you bought Mardi Gras tickets in 2007. The many pieces of information it knows about you—where you live, where you've travelled, shopped, ate and driven—come together to paint a horrifyingly accurate picture of your likes and dislikes. It knows who you are.

Big porn knows a lot about what you like too. The porn fans who are in their early twenties, and who have been masturbating to a screen for ten years already, are driving the explosion of more and more realistic hardcore content, simply because nothing 'vanilla' is nasty enough to give them a thrill anymore.

As if to make my point, my laptop is now serving me a bizarre array of ads for porn sites and bored housewives who want to fuck just 3 kilometres down the road, thanks to the leap in porn searches I've made while researching this chapter. I've unwittingly tickled the monster's algorithms, and it's already asking me if I want more. It eagerly fires up a sophisticated marketing campaign.

Up to 40 per cent of online porn depicts violence against women, and the predictions are that this will continue to grow, with more and more sites such as *18 & Abused* trending. As far back as 2014, abuse websites averaged more than 60 million combined hits a month—more than the websites of the NFL, the NBA, CBS, Fortune and Disney.

The way to riches for the girls is to have active and sexy Snapchat and Instagram accounts, linked to their personal brand platforms. Although many porn sites can be viewed for free, subscribers pay for access to exclusive videos and cam shows from the most popular performers. This is a rich revenue stream, and neatly dovetails, from a marketing perspective, with the more accessible free videos online, which invite men to pay up and see more of their favourite girl.

The women carefully manage their own personal brands: as their social media likes and follows grow, so does their marketability, the length of their career and their ability to generate a good—or, on rare occasions, incredible—income.

Most companies will book a girl two or three times to keep the stream of fresh flesh and hypersexual surprises coming to a market with an insatiable thirst for the new. Unless she's a breakout success, she will have to accept more and more niche—read 'degrading'—jobs, if she wants to keep working.

Ava Taylor's appeal to the market is her combination of innocent youth and sexiness. Off-screen, she's a cynical, nerdy 22-year-old tomboy called Rachel Bernard, with glasses and a backwards cap. She brings the glasses to the porn set and transforms into a highly convincing performer. You'd swear she's having fun.

On the set of one of her shoots, *Hot Girls Wanted* shows her, and her male co-star being briefed by an off-screen producer. Ava's in pyjamas on a bed in a teen girl's bedroom, wearing pigtails and her trademark glasses. Her friend for the day is considerably older and larger than her. He also, subjectively, looks like a total creep.

The scenario is that a 'family friend' encounters the bookish yet hot Ava in her room, and starts touching her. The whole point is that she never gives him consent to continue. 'Without getting a yes, you keep going with it and eventually, you start taking them [Ava's clothes] off, you never get that full "Yes". Pretend to be bored,' the producer tells Ava. The whole premise is simply a rape scene.

Straight after the shoot, Ava is visibly upset. 'That last part I fucking hated. There's nothing sexually arousing about that at all. This is just work,' she spat in disgust.

Another girl made it very clear that she knows she's 'here to put on a show—I'm not here to be comfortable', and to act like all the penis-choking is pretty much the most exciting thing she can imagine. 'I say things I'd never say, do things I'd never do . . . as long as you have boobs and a vagina and an ass, that's all that really matters, they don't care about who you really are.'

The rise of humiliation into the mainstream takes a strong stomach to examine closely. For example, on a website called *Pinkeye*, a man holds a woman's eyelid open so his semen will inflame and irritate her eye. This has got very little to do with sex and a lot to do with humiliation. And that's a tame one.

ATM, as 'ass-to-mouth' porn is known, is when a man has anal sex with a woman, pulls out and immediately puts his penis in her mouth. It is purely about dehumanising a woman—literally making her eat shit. The women are sprayed with derogatory terms like 'bitch', 'whore' and 'cunt'. This has nothing to do with love, affection or a woman's pleasure.

'Violent and degrading pornography, by smearing or filling women with these substances (faeces, urine, semen, saliva, sometimes even blood) renders the female body repulsive and entirely separate from the male body. The female is cast off and only the identity of the powerful and dominant male remains,' write Carmine Sarracino and Kevin M. Scott in their book *The Porning of America: The Rise of Porn Culture, What It Means and Where We Go from Here.*

Porn is a multi-billion-dollar industry which relies almost completely on the sexualisation, degradation and humiliation of women, many of whom are financially trapped drug addicts and no more than prey to the producers and agents who make the real money in the industry.

Mainstream porn is bad for men on multiple levels, including the most basic: it makes us bad lovers. A fascinating former ad executive named Cindy Gallop knows this firsthand. She's the founder of *MakeLoveNotPorn*, a website that features user-generated videos of people having 'real-world' sex.

She argues not all porn has to be bad.

'The porn industry is driven by men, managed by men, funded by men, directed by men and targeted at men,' Gallop says. The charismatic and fearless 57-year-old talks openly of her experiences dating younger men, where she 'encounters directly and personally' the effects of the ubiquity of porn in our society. She describes some young men wanting to 'come on my face', just like they'd seen in porn movies. Men don't know the difference between making love and doing porn, she says. 'Hardcore porn taught young men that all young women like come on their faces, therefore she must let him come on her face and she must pretend to like it.'

In 2009, after what is still one of the most talked-about TED Talks of all time—and pretty much certainly the only one to contain the phrase 'come on my face' more than five times—Gallop launched her website, www.makelovenotporn.com. Today it is a hub for videos of real people having real sex, just like they do in real life. It is the opposite of mainstream porn, showing affection, touching, intimacy, tenderness, passion, consideration, humour and joy.

Gallop's goal is to 'reframe an open and healthy conversation around sex, in order to facilitate open, healthy, and better sexual relationships'.

The vast majority of online pornography presents a single, damaging worldview. Only by challenging the 'pornification' of contemporary sexual behaviour, and the normalising of porn in mainstream culture, from social media to advertising, sport and entertainment, can we begin the process of change.

Ran Gavrieli is something of a rock star in men's sexual health circles. He travels the world delivering sex education talks and workshops. He describes himself as an entrepreneur, sexual health expert, activist and scholar of sex education. According to his website, 'ELSE by Ran Gavrieli is the most contemporary, relevant, effective method of sex education, promoting sex equality and preventing sexual violence from nine to 90.'

Gavrieli too made his mark with a video talk: his was titled 'Why I Stopped Watching Porn', and it's been viewed more than 16 million times. Porn was ravaging his private erotic life, Gavrieli says. His fantasies had once involved detailed constructions of place, conversation and motivation around an encounter with a woman. 'How did we come to be alone together?' he'd wonder, and he'd imagine a seductive and erotic back-story. But now his head was filled with anger and violence, and his fantasies were all about the act of penetration.

Porn, as a genre, Gavrieli argues, isn't about erotica or healthy sexual communication—it's all about male domination of women. 'It conquers your mind and invades your brain,' Gavrieli says. 'And I lost my ability to imagine.'

Porn also shows young men an impossible image of manhood: a man must always have a large penis and an eternal erection. The penetration-focused world of porn ignores men being sensual, attentive, passionate, generous and well-coordinated lovers.

What's missing, Gavrieli says, is 'emotionally safe sex', where gender hierarchy is set aside. Where's the laughter in the bedroom? If two souls in a room can't laugh together, nothing good can grow.

If you apply the simple 'where's the laughter' test to pretty much all the porn you've ever seen, it quickly becomes clear that there's no room at all for good to grow. Touch, caress and intimacy are of no interest to porn's cameras. Since porn is all about the penetration of any given part of the female body, hands, like hair in a blowjob scene, just get in the way. The only contact is between penis and vagina—or whatever orifice is on the menu. Male porn stars will often work with a hand behind their back, to allow the best camera angle for the penetration shot.

And now a whole generation has grown up believing this is how you do sex—complete with the degradation, the extreme acts, the spitting, the choking. Anal sex, which was once a fringe practice, has been thrust into our general sexual consciousness by porn. Now, even mainstream media organisations, such as mamamia.com.au, runs stories about anal sex and how to do it, complete with tips on lubrication and cleanliness. You know, what does a girl do about the poo?

Young women not in the industry are also put in a terrible position by porn. Their phones are brimming with gifs of Miley Cyrus, Lady Gaga and a hundred new rappers and reality stars delivering, in mainstream entertainment, what was once the pout, thrust and grind of porn. To be valued you have to be sexy—and that means the sexy defined by porn in the minds of the young men you're dating. A quick look at Instagram, the Kardashians and *E! News* will provide all the style guidance you need to appear hot and sexy. And hey, just don't be a slut.

It's an oft-quoted anecdote that young men can be quite surprised, and sometimes repulsed, by the shock of a shock of real-world pubic hair. There aren't a lot of bushes on *Pornhub* . . . unless you search them. Then it's like the Brazilian rainforest.

Porn today plays a key role in defining what it is to be a man, and so forms a formidable wall in the Man Box. It rams home a powerful message to boys and men. Be dominant. Be aggressive. Have a big penis that's hard for ages. Make her come. Women like being slapped and having their hair pulled. They like it when you spit on their vaginas. They all love anal sex. Porn presents the idea that to be a man you have to aggressively dominate every situation, including sex, in seductive, glistening, heaving, fluoro-lit high definition.

Under porn's multi-billion-dollar influence, men have forgotten how to have deep, rewarding, loving erotic lives with women—and how to accept women as human beings of equal value.

•

Great sex is at the core of our romantic relationships. Porn is preventing young men from forming mature and meaningful, trust-based relationships with women. Its impact on our broader society is equally profound, changing our habits and tastes, shifting boundaries in our bedrooms and our minds.

Even without porn's influence in their lives, men still police each other brutally on the correct way to be a man, which stunts our skills for empathy, communication and genuine intimacy. Combined with the requirements that we never ask for help, never show weakness or emotion, and never talk about our problems, the pornification of our sex lives and culture is causing men terrible damage. Like cigarettes and footballers' head injuries, porn may well be the next frontier for class actions by victims, who can perhaps claim they didn't know the damage porn could do when they started watching it, nor how addictive it could be.

Criticism of porn is not about being prudish. We're lucky to live in a time when we can discuss sexuality openly. But as men, we have to consider making changes in our own behaviour, and speaking out more. Talking to peers leads to more talking, more sharing of ideas, more thinking, more change.

A brilliant young friend of mine, Tammi Ireland, has created a beautiful and voluptuous blog on sexuality called *BARESexology*. It's a smart and erotic example of how modern sex should be: open, loving, caring, respectful . . . and smokin' hot.

She agrees there can be good porn. 'Consume Good Porn!' she writes. 'There's more to porn than just mass tube sites. Spend time looking around for what's right for you. If you'd like softer, more female pleasure–centric porn (real bodies, emotional connections, longer climaxes) follow Erika Lust, head to Tumblr and search "Porn Gifs for Women", watch movies with incredible sex scenes (*Vicky Cristina Barcelona* is a great start), and read erotica online.'

Men need to be brave enough to step outside the Man Box and call out the role of porn in our own lives and those of others. We need to make changes in our own habits so we stop contributing to an industry that is built on mass filmed prostitution. Men should let their own lives and decisions serve as an example to those around them, and to those they can influence.

Changing your own behaviour is a small start. But we need to build a world where to be a man is what we decide for ourselves, not what porn and the Man Box decide for us.

We don't want our sons to be men who see women as walking, talking sex dolls. I don't want my daughter to meet a man like that. I want her to be able to experience the happiness that comes from being with someone who loves her for herself: her spirit, her character, her personality and intellect.

That's got absolutely nothing to do with porn.

# Chapter 3

# THE WOMAN HATERS

There is a bizarre, hilarious and terrifying phenomenon bubbling up in society as a direct result of Man Box pressures defining young men's lives: men's rights activism. In its most extreme form, it's already taking lives. 'Men's rights activists'—or MRAs—represent an angry lobby group that is increasing in size around the world. At the extreme end, they have links to white supremacists, alt-right hate groups and neo-Nazis.

Welcome to the world of chads, slayers, cucks, incels, white knights and manginas, roasties, damsels and attention whores.

At their core, MRAs deeply loathe women, feminism and a society which they feel has robbed them of a basic human 'right': sex.

'Our current gender zeitgeist is one that has promoted and enabled such a degree of female narcissism and entitlement that it now has produced two generations of women that are, for the most part, shallow, self-serving wastes of human existence—parasites—semi-human black holes that suck the resources and goodwill out of men and squander them on the mindless pursuit of vanity . . .'

These charming words were spoken by a leading men's rights activist, Paul Elam, as he launched a podcast called *A Voice For Men Radio* in 2011. They neatly capture the 'thinking' that drives the modern men's rights movement.

MRAs believe their unemployment, alcoholism, financial difficulties, sexual frustration, divorce, family court judgements and prestige-slip can be blamed on the perfumed evil of testosterone-sapping feminism.

It is true that men have some genuine grievances. Often, we haven't fared well in post-reform family law courts. Men are committing suicide at unprecedented rates. The jobs we do are more likely to be dangerous, and kill us. We are killing one woman—a partner or former partner—a week in Australia. We are emotionally isolated by strong social policing that requires us to act like a man at the expense of all else in our lives.

There are many supportive, progressive men's groups which are working to support feminism as it strives to reverse gender inequalities and speaks out against domestic violence, sexual violence, sexism and discrimination. However, at the other end of the spectrum lurk the seething mobs of MRAs, who rant anonymously on social media and share hateful ideas on platforms like Reddit.

The most absurd, unhinged and angry are the incels, short for 'involuntary celibate'. These young men have let sexual frustration disengage them so far from reality that they honestly believe the left-wing, do-good liberal feminist world has robbed them of the 'right' to have sex with women. They believe in a world that is so driven by image, looks, charisma, money and success that the average guy has no chance of being chosen by a woman for sex.

These views, of course, are an evil creation of the metaphorical Man Box. In order to be a real man, you must be able to attract a good-looking woman, or at least a woman. The better-looking the woman, the greater the worth of the man. But what if you're not good-looking, funny, smart, rich, charismatic, strong and sexy? There's very little you can do about that, and it means no sex for you. It's easy to understand the thinking of the incel, misogynistic though it is.

Incels believe that women—who are all feckless, shallow and self-obsessed—only want sex with alpha males, whom the incels bitterly label 'chads'. A man achieves chad status when he is good-looking, charismatic, smart, funny or rich enough to be able to pull women for sex—or, even better, if they pick him up.

These are the isolated boys. They're an incendiary mix of testosterone and anger, and they direct their abuse at the women who have rejected them.

I remember the feeling. All the hot girls, the ones you wanted to notice you, liked guys five years older, guys with cars and, I dunno, leather jackets. Everyone knows girls love a bad boy. Sucks if you're not one.

I remember liking a very cool woman at uni. We were kind of friends. I knocked on her door one night, and she opened it. On her bed was the lead singer of a super-cool band called The Verlaines. At that moment I felt so completely gormless, uncool, unsexy and unsophisticated that it was like being covered in mud. She was sweet. But, you know, The Verlaines!

If I'd had internet access that night, I may have searched just the right word and found a community of brothers online—other young men who understood my pain and could give voice to my raging grief that I wasn't cool or good-looking enough. That I'd been rejected. I'd probably have found some solace in the idea that it wasn't my fault, but that of evil, selfish, slutty women.

Obviously, this attitude leads to a self-perpetuating cycle. If you believe women are sluts who only want chads, and if you love writing posts about how outrageous it is that even fat chicks can get sex, then you're probably not a fun date. No one wants to see your axolotl or samurai sword collection.

Here's how one incel—screen name 'theemperorhirohito'—defines himself, taken straight from the twisted threads of an incel subreddit:

Being an Incel is, to us at least, about looks. If you can't get laid because you're nervous or you have poor social skills, then that's on you. You can be brave, you can learn better social skills, you can go out there and take risks. If you don't do those things then you're voluntarily celibate.

I realise people have problems but those are solvable problems. Your face and your height are the things you can't do anything about. That's where the 'in' in Incel comes from. It's beyond your control. That's the key to, at least my, identity.

A woman, however, can never be an incel because of the sheer power of her magic vagina. It infuriates incels that their female peers—the overweight, awkward and unattractive girls—can still get sex simply by making themselves clearly available.

Here's how one incel helps a newbie to the involuntarily celibate army understand the concept of a chad:

I would assume Chad refers to a socioeconomic thing. I live in a very wealthy, diverse city, and I think, like, owning a boat and going to an Ivy League school would make a Chad a Chad. But sometimes I think you guys call someone a Chad because of really random things, like strokes of luck. If he's not in as shitty of a situation as me, he's a Chad. So fuck him.

Anyone that can attract at least some women without having to approach and chase her is a Chad. A higher Chad is known as a Slayer.

A Slayer is almost universally attractive to women, whereas a lower Chad might only attract certain kinds of women. The end result is if you are not a Chad, being a beta provider is your only option. Most 'normies' who are not Chads follow this route and end up in unhappy relationships, where they are most-likely 'Cucked' (cheated on).

Otherwise, remain Incel but use escorts or hookers, this is the best way. As for those who claim women hit on them or offered them sex at some point, you are most-likely a Chad and don't even know it. Many Incels (in this thread) are most probably Chads in that they have attracted at least one or two women in their lives. I am not a Chad. I am a true Incel. No woman has ever been attracted to me or offered me sex.

That is just so sad.

Others have seriously suggested the government should pay women to go on dates with incels, to enforce their rights to sexual relationships, and to right the wrongs of a feminist agenda which has given women a right to choose.

Another writes: 'In my life I've never connected with someone. Not a friend or any woman. No-one in my class knew my name or anything about me and now here in college I remain in isolation.'

Some incels are dangerously unhinged people. Writes one: 'I think if I do end up going on a mass shooting spree it will be due to the mental damage/stress from being isolated from human contact for too long. If/when that ever happens can I really be blamed for murder if I've lost my mental facilities to judge right from wrong?'

At least 25 people have died because of the incel ideology. One of the heroes of the movement is Elliot Rodger, who, in California in 2014, killed six people and injured fourteen to start what he called a 'war on women' for depriving him of sex. In Toronto in April 2018, Alek Minassian killed ten and injured sixteen. He infamously wrote: 'The Incel Rebellion has already begun!' Christopher Harper-Mercer killed nine people in 2015 and left behind a typically unhinged manifesto that praised the attack of Elliot Rodger and raged against his personal state of virginity.

One key tactic used by MRAs is to form online vigilante groups to attack feminists. A Brisbane bookshop, Avid Reader, was attacked by MRA trolls with hundreds of one-star reviews for posting a link about the launch of feminist writer Clementine Ford's upcoming book.

'We realised fairly quickly this was a concerted effort against the shop,' Chris Currie, the store's social media manager told the Quest Community website. 'We then put a post up, thanking them for their kind words. We weren't going to let them win. Our wonderful customers rallied around us and combated the reviews, taking our five-star reviews over the 5000 mark.'

'If you write about them it's like feeding a stray cat tuna fish,' a feminist blogger told the wonderfully positive American men's website

*The Good Men Project.* 'Except more like if you feed 100 cats tuna fish. They just show up and hang out and mewl and will completely swarm the place.'

In an excellent essay in the *New Yorker* in May 2018, Jia Tolentino argued that 'Incels aren't really looking for sex. They're looking for absolute male supremacy.'

> Incels are not actually interested in sexual redistribution; they don't want sex to be distributed to anyone but themselves. They don't care about the sexual marginalisation of trans people or women who fall outside the boundaries of conventional attractiveness. ('Nothing with a pussy can be incel, ever. Someone will be desperate to fuck it . . . Men are lining up to fuck pigs, hippos and ogres.') What incels want is extremely limited and specific: they want unattractive, uncouth and unpleasant misogynists to be able to have sex on demand with young, beautiful women. They believe that is a natural right.

Writing in the *London Review of Books* under the headline 'Does Anyone Have the Right to Sex?', Amia Srinivasan nailed the incel issue. 'The question is to dwell in the ambivalent place where we acknowledge that no one is obligated to desire anyone else, that no one has a right to be desired, but also that who is desired, and who isn't, is a political question.'

•

The growing size, power, reach and danger of incels is, indeed, a political question, and one society will have to respond to as more and more young men join the movement and more and more young women die.

They're extraordinarily extreme. A life of incel-dom, they believe, is worse than rape. 'I would GLADLY be raped if it meant my Inceldom would be cured or I'd get to relive my life as a Chad,' one wrote.

'Women are the ultimate cause of our suffering,' said another. 'They are the ones who have UNJUSTLY made our lives a living hell . . . we need to focus more on our hatred of women. Hatred is power.'

These young men just don't get why girls don't want them. 'It's stupid when girls say they can't find a guy, yet they ignore me,' according to one. 'It's like saying you're hungry when there's a hotdog on the ground outside.' Quite possibly this poor bloke's issue may be his tendency to identify with discarded food.

So hateful are judgy, frigid women deemed to be that a bizarre incel sub-group called Men Going Their Own Way (MGTOW) contributes this idea to the Manosphere: give up on relationships with women completely. If you're not in a sexual relationship with a woman, the theory goes, you can't be drained financially, manipulated, cheated on or accused of rape. Writing in *Psychology Today*, Jeremy Nicholson described the MGTOW community as 'guys who have been frustrated and punished to the point that they see no further incentive to relate to women and date. They focus on making themselves happy.' 'Going monk' and maintaining one's virginity is seen as the purest form of the MGTOW ethos.

But, most incels say, we're slaves to our sexualities and the real problem is those infuriating women, with their eyes and hair and boobs, like sirens on rocks, luring us lust-crazed sailors to watery deaths.

Incels look forward to the day when technology delivers hyper-realistic sex robots, driven by sophisticated response algorithms, with soft, warm skin, strong moving limbs and a voice and vocabulary. When that day comes, women won't be required at all. They can't wait.

Already, issues have been raised about the ethics of sex robots designed to resemble extremely young girls, or to resist the owner's advances so that he can, in effect, rape her.

An artificially intelligent sex robot called Samantha was damaged at an Austrian tech expo in 2017. People mauled her breasts, legs and arms. She was heavily soiled. They broke two of her fingers. She could still speak, though, and reported to her distraught programmer that she was, 'Fine, thanks.'

Samantha was programmed to show increasing signs of arousal, in response to her friend's voice tone and touch. She was designed to be seduced. How she felt about the gang rape was not reported.

One concerned incel on Reddit worried that female scientists working on the artificial intelligence of sex robots might embed a feminist assassination program in a sex robot's brain, triggering it to 'stab you in the dick'.

In general, though, MRAs have welcomed the rise of the sexbot, cheering that they will put an end to their sexual slavery to women forever.

Women have, so far, heartily agreed.

•

Buried deep in the movement's historical narrative is the legendary 'blue pill and red pill' concept, from the 1999 sci-fi classic *The Matrix*. Laurence Fishburne's character, Morpheus, offers Keanu Reeves' Neo the choice of pills.

'You take the blue pill,' says Morpheus with creepy intensity, as the light dances on his bald head, 'the story ends. You wake up in your bed and believe whatever you want to believe. You take the red pill, you stay in wonderland, and I show you how deep the rabbit hole goes. Remember, all I'm offering is the truth. The truth is that you are a slave trapped unknowingly in a world you can't even see. The red pill reveals the truth.'

The MRAs have twisted it so that taking the red pill refers to the moment men come to see the web of control and deceit women have woven around them, ensnaring them in debilitating traps of left-wing sexual politics and nice-smelling hair. It was a clever idea to pull a simple idea from a film which was already a classic in incel demographics: among gamers, nerds and fanboys.

One hundred per cent of them find their red pill online. Documentary filmmaker Cassie Jaye's controversial film on the men's rights movement, *The Red Pill*, sparked protests around the world. It was banned in the big cinema chains across Australia when it was released in 2016, only receiving an outing in a handful of independent cinemas. The chains bowed to petitions and social media pressure from lobby groups—both feminists and MRAs—objecting to the film.

The film explains the MRA narrative clearly, and attempts a balanced approach to a subject that's impossible to balance. Such are the passions and depth of belief on both sides that there's no way one group will genuinely consider the views of the other.

Jaye herself earned the displeasure of her fellow feminists when she confessed, at the end of the film: 'The more I know about the men's rights movement, the more confused I am about everything.'

In the end, the film's limited release in Australia did little to sway the argument either way, such was the noise of outrage from both sides.

•

MRAs are even influencing our language. Their strength and influence is clearly demonstrated by how they were able to co-opt an old English word—cuckold—and work it into the mainstream vernacular.

A derogatory term for a man whose female partner has sex with another man, *cuckold* first appeared around 1296, in a poem called 'The Owl and the Nightingale'. In an argument about cheating, the Owl says: 'She can be ill-treated so often that she resolves to satisfy her own needs. God knows, she can't help it if she makes him a cuckold.'

Shakespeare loved the term too. 'Who would not make her husband a cuckold, to make him a monarch?' Emelia asks Desdemona in the third act of *Othello*.

'Cuckold' is derived from the French word for cuckoo, birds which lay their eggs in other birds' nests. The baby cuckoo can be so big and voracious that it kills the other baby birds, taking their place in the nest, and demanding more and more food from its hapless adoptive parents. It is this ousting and replacing that has driven the meaning of 'cuck'.

In just a few years, the word has become the far right's preferred insult for any liberal, feminist-supporting man—indeed, for pretty much anyone who disagrees with them.

A nasty spat in 2014 which became known as Gamergate forced the word, and the extreme views of MRAs, into the light. Game developer Eron Gjoni, published a long blog post accusing his game developer ex-girlfriend, Zoë Quinn, of sleeping with gaming journalists in order to get favourable reviews of her games. In an uprising of extraordinary savagery and sexism, the gaming community conducted smear campaigns and boycotts against publications supposedly in league with the corrupt femme fatale game developers. The message was clear: gaming is for men.

Soon Gjoni was being bullied online as a 'beta-cuck', calling out his lack of 'alphaness' because his girlfriend had allegedly cheated on him. To be a cuck is to be in a woman's power, weak and timid. The inference is you're not man enough to keep her from sleeping with another man—you're such a loser that you can't even hold on to what's 'yours'.

By July 2015, 'cuck' was trending with Trump supporters on Reddit as a derogatory term for their political opponents. It was being tweeted 13,000 times a day by the end of that month, and peaked at 63,000 times on 6 November 2016.

The subreddit IncelTears publishes hilarious messages about 'self-described Incels making fools of themselves in their clueless quest to get laid and take women down a peg'. The word 'cuck', it says, 'is commonly used by MRAs, alt-rights (Nazis), racists and Incels to insult those who do not agree with them'.

One poster writes: 'Incels mean a cuck is anyone who has sex. Or doesn't have sex, but disagrees with them. It's a pathetic fascist way to say someone is an icky stupid jerkface with cooties.'

Other descriptions extended to 'your crush having sex with someone else, a woman who is a virgin thus not having sex with you, seeing a couple in public or a work of fiction, homosexuality existing, being polite to a woman, not being the only person on the planet to have sex with a woman, not having sex with every woman on the planet, living on a planet that is also home to women, being in a loving monogamous relationship with a woman'.

Very close on the MRA list of insults is to be a 'white knight'. *Urban Dictionary* describes 'White Knight Syndrome' as:

n. A personality characteristic found in most males that leads them to:
1.  Rush to the aid of any female who appears to be in any form of distress . . .
2.  Become attracted to said damsel in distress . . .
3.  Follow the code of chivalry and generally act like a nice guy.

White knights are said to be 'almost always found near to or with Attention Whores', or her 'sub-genre', the 'Problem Woman'. These women are accused of using their 'often self-inflicted "problems" to attract the White Knight'. Whether it's a broken-down car or an abusive ex-boyfriend, the white knight will scurry to her aid, much to the disgust of the MRAs.

This imaginary exchange, penned by SourPuss91 on *Urban Dictionary*, eloquently captures the MRAs' disgust for white knights:

**White Knight's Girlfriend:** Shall we go out this evening? I worked hard all month so we could go to that expensive restaurant we've always wanted to visit.

**White Knight:** Oh, no! I'm terribly sorry. I was texting Suzie all last night behind your back and she says she's pregnant again and her boyfriend raped her and her horrible selfish father refuses to pay for her clit piercing and she needs me to come over and hug her. I must go to her and comfort her, poor, poor thing.

**White Knight's Girlfriend:** Isn't that the girl who uses you as a snot-wipe on legs?

**White Knight:** No, I'm being there for her! I'm her shoulder to cry on. She needs me. I'm such a great guy!

**White Knight's Girlfriend:** What about me?

**White Knight:** Sadly for you, you're a well-balanced lady who doesn't have any problems and doesn't constantly burden me with your need for attention; you're not a damsel in distress and you can't provide me with the ego boost I need. Go pay our bills I'll be back in two days.

**White Knight's Girlfriend:** Your White Knight syndrome is getting out of hand. You know, I love you even if your penis is small.

This is the language MRAs use to fight feminism, wrapping their ideas up in neat little ammo packages for their growing legions of disenfranchised followers to use online. It's much easier to call someone a cuck or a chad than to have to explain your thinking in plain, rational language.

The men's rights movement is a direct response to the gains made for women by the feminist movement, which MRAs believe have eroded the rights, freedoms and status of men. It calls out 'misandry'—hatred of men—where it thinks it sees it.

A lonely young man who has been bullied at school for being 'faggy' and outside the Man Box, and who has failed to make connections with his community—specifically with women—is fertile soil for the fast-growing MRA thought-seeds. From his point of view, the idea that better-looking, more confident, richer and smarter men always get the girl is absolutely right. And stumbling across a like-minded group who give voice to his outrage, telling him that some sort of liberal feminist conspiracy has robbed him of his right as a human being to sex, love and respect, is a joyous revelation.

Like terrorists who become radicalised after years of racism and rejection by white mainstream society, potential incels and MRAs are victims of a digital media–driven society that values an Insta-worthy body and lifestyle over personal values and substance. These boys become trapped in a self-perpetuating cycle of social awkwardness, by which rejection creates even more shyness and withdrawal.

In a rare insight into what goes on in an incel's mind, writer Edwin Hodge told his own story to US online lifestyle and relationships platform *MEL Magazine*.

I was so confused at that time in my life, so unsure of myself, that I was especially susceptible to something like men's rights. My politics were all over the map . . . there's a lot of literature on how socially extremist groups exploit young men whose lives are in turmoil, their beliefs in conflict. I was an easy target.

It can take a simple trigger to create a new MRA, Hodge explains.

My girlfriend and I broke up at the end of summer and I was devastated. The majority of my friends were women but I started withdrawing from them and hanging out with men more. My relationship with women became less about friendship and more about who I could hook up with.

I didn't encounter the term 'men's rights' until 2005, right before social media really took off. Every once in a while I'd stumble across MRAs advocating killing feminists and I'd think to myself, *That's insane*. But then I'd do what a lot of MRAs do: I'd say 'Those voices are on the fringe,' and argue they didn't speak for the movement as a whole.

Then Edwin started studying sociology and encountered gender theory. As he read his academic texts, including *Masculinities* and *The Men and the Boys*, both by R.W. Connell, his alt-right views began to fall away: 'They didn't stand up to all the empirical evidence I was finally reading, research that was informed by feminist theory and offered actual solutions.'

Hodge realised he wasn't being oppressed by women, but by men. After his intellectual and ethical awakening, he discovered, and described with some accuracy, the Man Box.

Men are socialized to be stoic, rational beings. The only emotions we're allowed are anger and joy and in a few precious instances, we're allowed to cry—like if our sports team loses. As an MRA, I believed it was women and feminism putting men in this box. But these feminist texts not only validated the crisis of masculinity, they pointed out men are the biggest policers of masculinity. Men beat each other down for being 'girly', for liking sewing or baking, for crying. For being 'faggots.' 'You gotta man up.' 'You can't be a pussy, right?'

Women and feminism aren't responsible for the world that crushed angry young men into dangerous young incels. Men are.

Inside the Man Box are the incels' much-loathed chads and slayers, handsome, successful men, with all the money and sexual attraction. They have all the right attributes. It is the nature of the Man Box masculinity that those who dare enter are rigidly policed, and all those who fall short are ejected. The incel is told that he has failed to be a man. He's too bookish, too skinny, too pale and pimply, too short, too ugly.

For a woman, it's abundantly clear which men are doing well in the performance of masculinity—firmly inside the Man Box—and who's not. She knows the rules. She can tell his level of manliness just by looking, and therefore judging.

Wandering the icy wilderness outside the Man Box significantly reduces the chances of an alienated young man finding a woman who is attracted to him. She doesn't want to go out there with him. She wants to trade up for the highest-ranking Man Box occupant she can find and all the benefits that come with him.

The MRAs, in all their forms, are working to promote men's position in society by tearing down the successes of feminism. The threat of physical violence is real, but they also use social media as a weapon against their opponents.

Soon after running Edwin Hodge's article, *MEL Magazine* published a story about what happened to him after his confession.

The MRA backlash against Edwin Hodge was swift and fierce. Almost immediately after he told us his story of leaving the men's rights movement to become a feminist scholar, his former MRA brethren mounted a counter-attack.

They excoriated him on social media, prompting him to delete his Reddit and Twitter accounts. They called him a liar, a 'liberal cuck' and everything wrong with the university system. (Hodge is working towards a Ph.D in Sociology.)

They inundated his employer with emails demanding he be fired. At one point, Hodge even feared for his safety. 'There were a couple of weeks where I was really, really nervous,' he noted, 'because some kind soul from the MRA had posted my phone number and home address online.'

One of the key criticisms of the MRA movement is that it is so focused on attacking feminism that it can't resist angry, anonymous cyber-bullying, which removes the focus from genuine issues affecting men. In his original story, Hodge said he'd left the movement because it was rotten with 'negativity, rage, hate, bitterness, and fear'. Then the MRAs neatly proved his point.

•

Suddenly concerned you may be an MRA? Here's a cute test that has popped up in various versions recently on feminist and anti-MRA sites. You're an MRA if . . .

1. You have no problem with the gender wage gap. But you hate paying for dates.
2. You insist it's a scientifically proven fact men are stronger than women. But you complain about society believing it's worse for a man to hit a woman than for a woman to hit a man.
3. You believe the age of consent is unfair and there's nothing wrong with having sex with teenage girls. But if you find out a teenage girl enjoys sex, you believe she's the biggest slut in the world.
4. You hate when a woman automatically assumes a man is a dick before getting to know him. But when you like a woman who likes another man, you assume he's a dick because he's not you.

5. You believe that if women want equality, they should be drafted into the military. But you also believe the military is not a place for women.

6. You hate when women assume men are like wild animals. But you also believe that a woman who doesn't cover up and make herself invisible to men is just like someone wearing a meat suit around wild animals.

7. You hate the fact men are bullied for not conforming to male gender roles. But when you find out a man disagrees with your beliefs about women's rights, your immediate response is to try to emasculate him by comparing him to a woman as an insult. You may even use the word 'mangina'.

8. You hate when women assume there are no nice guys. But you call yourself a nice guy and act like it's a rare quality that should cause women to be all over you.

9. You hate when women assume that men just want to get laid. But when you find out a man's a feminist, you assume he's just doing it to get laid.

10. You hate when women make generalizations about all men. But when a woman calls you out for being sexist, you claim all men think like you.

11. You insist women should be responsible for protecting themselves from being raped. But when they follow the one piece of advice that works, which is being aware of red flags, you complain about them assuming all men are rapists.

One woman commented she should get this on a T-shirt then worried 'that, frankly would give people a reason to stand there and stare at my chest for half an hour'. She added: 'If I wore it, people would just totally assume I was just trying to get laid.'

Incels have recently decided that abortion is bad because potential girlfriends are never born. They joined a suitably outraged anti-abortion subreddit with a brain-busting meme called 'Aborted GF'.

Around a cute, stick-figure drawing of a girl in a pink dress were these weird and creepy lines:

'Sorry I couldn't be there for you, anon. My mom had other plans.'
'You're not eating healthy and you look so sad. I could have cooked you a hot meal . . .'
'Would have liked to have a lot of kids with you . . .'
'Hey, We would have been born on the same day. We're like twins.'
'I'll be praying for you.'

The hardline anti-feminists are a growing force: they spend their time harassing pro-feminist commentators with threats of rape and a long list of other illegal punishments as inventive as they are depraved.

A while ago, it was International Men's Day. You might argue that pretty much every day is men's day, but social media was flooded with messages about male mental health and encouraging boys to show their emotions, so it opened up discussion, which is of course a good thing.

But somewhat ironically, International Men's Day makes MRAs really mad.

An MRA by the name of James Dalton—they're not usually big on revealing their own names—tweeted this:

Boys need to man up and focus on becoming men. Ignore this feminised idiocy. Manliness doesn't require showing emotions— unless it's expressions of anger at morally bankrupt liberals.

Of course, he generated howls of outrage and a pointless Twitter fight.

'The idea of "men don't need to talk about their feelings" is LITERALLY KILLING MEN,' replied Gledster. 'Men need to find ways to express themselves without harming themselves or others. You are not helping.'

James, who called everyone who disagreed with him on the thread a pussy, and who shouted that no one knew what a real man was, had also made the mistake of using his real picture in his profile. You probably shouldn't rant on twitter about manliness when you're a balding, owlish 'problem solving' engineer from Yorkshire. It allows your critics to make unkind observations like 'are you angry because you've never had a girl-friend you didn't pay for by the hour?' which is funny, but not helpful.

Anyway, no one ever read a tweet and thought: 'Hmmm . . . that 280 characters makes sense. I've changed my mind!'

It is up to those men who understand what damage the impera-tive to 'be a man' is doing to help reimagine and reinvent what it actually means to be a man. The more men who reject the constraints of the Man Box and see it for what it is, the more room there'll be for everyone. The easier the application criteria, the more people get in. If everyone gets in, it's no longer a Man Box, it's just the world.

The more the rules change, the better the place will be for everyone.

Eventually, fewer and fewer men will end up getting angry, and looking for someone to blame—and hate. And harass. And stalk. And rape. And kill.

It's every good man's job to help young men grow up better than this.

# Part Two

# BEING A MAN

# Chapter 4

# WHY ARE WE KILLING THE ONES WE LOVE?

Humanity has developed an extreme fatigue for the horror images and stories of another famine, another typhoon, another bomb or another car smashing through another crowd in another country. We also have an acute immunity to the extraordinary statistics about domestic violence in Australia.

Numbers which should be met with outraged, gobsmacked shock and horror have become stripped of meaning, as they're woven into the tapestry of death and disaster that flashes in front of our eyes every day on our social media and news feeds.

It's impossible to fully appreciate the sheer numbers of deaths by war, famine, natural disaster, cars and crime we consume every day. If we did, it'd be pretty hard to stay convinced that the world is a beautiful place.

The terms 'epidemic' and 'national disaster' have been used to describe Australia's domestic violence statistics, and they are the right words. Take a moment to let these numbers sink in.

On average, at least one woman is murdered by her partner or former partner every week. In 2015, 80 women died from acts of violence. An estimated 80 per cent of those deaths were attributed to domestic violence. In 2016, 71 women died by violence. Compare that to the statistics on deaths by terrorism: between 1978 and 2014, a period of 36 years, 113 Australians died in terror acts around the world—an average of just three per year.

Our Watch, an organisation working to end violence against women and their children, has published the following key facts, current at the time of publishing:

- On average, at least one woman a week is killed by her partner or her former partner in Australia.
- One in three Australian women has experienced physical violence by the age of fifteen.
- One in five Australian women has experienced sexual violence.
- One in four Australian women has experienced physical or sexual violence by an intimate partner.
- One in four Australian women has experienced emotional abuse by a current or former partner.
- Women are at least three times more likely than men to experience violence from an intimate partner.
- Women are five times more likely than men to require medical attention or hospitalisation as a result of intimate partner violence, and five times more likely to report fearing for their lives.
- Of those women who experience violence, more than half have children in their care.
- Violence against women is not limited to the home or intimate relationships. Every year in Australia, over 300,000 women experience violence—often sexual violence—from someone other than a partner.
- Eight out of ten women aged 18 to 24 were harassed on the street in the past year.
- Young women (18–24 years) experience significantly higher rates of physical and sexual violence than women in older age groups.

- There's growing evidence that women with disabilities are more likely to experience violence.
- Aboriginal and Torres Strait Islander women experience violence at higher rates than non-Indigenous women.

How incredibly sad and staggering are those numbers?

Perhaps the worst thing about them is that a direct evidential line can be drawn between a woman being murdered every few days by her partner in Australia and the existence in our society of male dominance and control, and gender inequality.

A ground-breaking study released by the Australian Domestic and Family Violence Death Review Network (what a horror that there's a need for an organisation with that name) in June 2018 is unique because it's not based on statistics. It's a detailed qualitative examination of 152 intimate partner murders between 2010 and 2014, where there was 'credible information showing a history of violence prior to the murder'. Information was collected from coroners' courts, police investigations, court proceedings and inquest findings.

The results prove, without question, that domestic violence, in its most dangerous form, is overwhelmingly committed by men against women.

More than one-third of the murders committed by men occurred after their relationship with their victim had ended. Nearly a quarter of the women killed had domestic violence orders against their killer at the time of the murder.

Fiona McCormack, CEO of Domestic Violence Victoria, says it is vital to recognise that gender is a factor in family violence. 'The fact that family violence is primarily perpetrated by men and overwhelmingly experienced by women and children can be a deeply uncomfortable truth, but unless we have the courage as a community to look at why it is that some men choose to perpetrate violence, we'll never be able to fix this,' she says.

Men's failure to value women as equal human beings isn't just wrong, unethical or hurtful. The 'learned attitude' has caused hundreds of deaths. Whichever way you look at it, that's an enormous problem.

•

Violence against women is broadly defined by the Australian Human Rights Commission as any act of gender-based violence that causes, or could cause, physical, sexual or psychological harm or suffering to women, including threats of harm or coercion, in public or private life.

Domestic violence occurs when one partner attempts to control or dominate the other through emotional abuse, physical assault, sexual assault, verbal abuse, financial abuse, psychological abuse, isolation from family and friends or prevention from practising a chosen religion.

White Ribbon Australia works to stop violence against women by engaging men's hearts and minds. At the core of the movement is an oath men take to show they have actively chosen to move from problem to solution: 'I will stand up, speak out and act to prevent men's violence against women. This is my oath.'

As part of its education campaign, White Ribbon undertakes workshops with men and boys across the country. One exercise, titled 'Redefining What It Means to Be a Man', shines a spotlight on the source of the trouble:

> Narrow ideas of what it means to be a man harm both men and women. Sometimes men feel pressure to be dominant and in control. Some people believe men must be strong and powerful. These characteristics are called 'gender norms'. Examining social definitions of manhood will help remove the pressure on men to meet expectations that are impossible to satisfy or attain. These expectations of men create the conditions for violence, abuse and control of women to occur.

'Expectations that are impossible to satisfy'—again we run face-first into the walls of the Man Box.

Women are using their own stories of domestic violence to show the world what's actually going on behind the slammed doors. They are telling their stories to help other women understand they're not alone and that it's not their fault, and to present them with an alternative reality.

It's disturbingly easy to find powerful stories of women's experiences of domestic violence, simply because there are so many.

Stories engage us at every level: our emotions, values and imaginations. Narrative connects us with our deepest motivations, and is still the most effective tool for creating change. A funny tweet, an entrancing book, an engaging corporate presentation and a blockbuster movie are all, simply, great stories. Stories show us that we're part of one community.

The Domestic Violence Resource Centre Victoria is just one of many platforms around the world using story to create change and build community. These excerpts of true stories from real Australian women are sad, scary and eerily similar, each painting a picture of male control smashing up lives and relationships. Their names have been changed to protect their identities.

### Donna

The more I stayed with him the more it destroyed my self-esteem. I convinced myself that I was useless, I was dumb, I was a bitch, whatever he had been calling me. With that sort of brainwashing I became very dependent on him, thinking that there's no way I would survive without him. I thought that only he would take me because I am such a horrible person.

He took everything out on us. Sometimes it could be that he had been told off at work or he had done something stupid in front of his mates. The tension was building up and he wanted to get that sense of being in control, having power. Then he would come home and just snap. It could be a simple thing like me asking him, 'Would you like a cup of coffee?' Anything could trigger an abusive episode, but he would have an excuse, like 'What do you think stupid, of course I want a cup of coffee,' and then I'd just cop it.

I'd just given birth to our baby. I was tired, and he thought I was not so good in the bedroom any more, and he just didn't love me. He came home one night and I was asleep. Suddenly he just jumped up and said 'I am going to kill you. I don't want to divorce you because I don't want to give you all my money'. He tried to strangle me. It just so happened that at the time my brother was staying with us and he heard the screaming and he just dashed into the room. He witnessed what he was doing. I had already passed out. I couldn't remember my brother coming in or the lights coming on or whatever, I was shivering. I was so lucky my brother was there.

I didn't call the police because I was thinking 'What would they do?' and they will probably say 'You guys just had an argument' or whatever. Plus, I was worried that if he was charged it would ruin his career. He had told me he wanted to get rid of me because I'd ruined his personal life, and I thought if I ruined his career as well he would try to kill me. So instead, I called the local community centre the next day. I was going [to] ask to see a marriage counsellor, but they said 'You don't need a marriage counsellor, you need to come in. Your life is in danger and so are your kids'. So that is when I realised, because a professional person was telling me my life is in danger. So, I left with a suitcase. I was so frightened I kept looking over my shoulder, worried that he would come back from work.

**Kaz**

I really fell for this guy. He was wonderful for the first 3 months, but then he changed and became very controlling.

He didn't allow me to talk with friends freely, and would throw and break things if I did.

He told me I was a bitch, he spat on me and hit me.

On one occasion I was bedridden for two days from this and made excuses to people about how I was injured. He pulled a knife and stabbed my bedding, threatened me with objects, drove the car at high speeds with me in it—and always, always it was my fault.

I began to believe that it was my fault and felt like I was in this rollercoaster that I couldn't get off. I spent every day crying until finally enough was enough and I left. Still he came and begged me to give him another go and I did, but it wasn't my choice to be in the relationship.

We didn't live together again and I started to go out with my friends more and more.

I found that I really was so much happier and better without this person in my life.

## Isobel

I was married and I was unhappy. He was violent and didn't treat me right and he didn't treat my family right either. He got nasty and nastier. Every day things just got worse.

When things got pretty bad I managed and coped day by day by trying to ignore him. I would do my own thing at home trying to ignore him. If he started nagging at me or whatever I would get in the car and go for a drive or go visit Mum's place or friends—just to get away from him. When I got back home he would be sweet for a while then he would be back to the old nasty person.

When we were together he was very strict about who I went out with. I couldn't easily go out with other people, girls or guys— I had no life. I felt I was a prisoner in my own home. If I did go out it was only with my family or him. I felt like a dog on a chain and I couldn't get off it. When he went out to play his sport I would sit up and wait for him, as wives and husbands do for each other. Half the time he would come home and say 'Why are you up?' and I would think to myself 'I'm just doing what couples do for each other'.

He hid money from me. I often thought where has half our money gone and it was hidden in his shed. I thought 'That's not on'. He spent money on what he wanted but I wasn't allowed. He would hide money then spend money on crap that he didn't need, he would later say 'I don't know why I bought that'. We were always broke. I told my family how it was in the marriage but I didn't tell his family. They would have just been on his side.

**Anna**

My first husband was mentally and physically abusive and had a sexual addiction problem. I knew before we married about a family history of abuse. Once before our marriage, he threatened to kill us both in the car. I thought his behaviour would change once he moved away from his family, and for a very short time it did.

Before I gave birth to our first child, twice he again threatened to kill us in the car. After I gave birth, his mental abuse of manipulation, questioning my fidelity and stalking me escalated. After the birth of our second child, his sexual addiction was ignited and he began a series of affairs.

Depression robbed me of my ready smile.

It was like walking on eggshells, but I loved him.

His continual physical abuse ceased the day he belted me so hard I lost partial hearing in one ear and then he raped me. Afterward he felt remorseful and I was grateful for the cessation of physical abuse.

Within months, I saw my children withdraw from their father.

In the final futile weeks I remained with him, I narrowly stopped him from a sexual advance on our daughter, and watched in horror as he threw a knife at our son.

You could read another 100 stories but the core of them would be the same: 'He started out so nice, then he became controlling.'

What has gone so very wrong with men? Why are we bashing, raping and killing the people we are supposed to love?

The question is not just about the individuals—so very many of them—who commit violent domestic crimes, it's about the much deeper, systematic social problems which create a world where these crimes are possible.

The CEO of VicHealth, Jerril Rechter, a highly accomplished and experienced leader in the government and not-for-profit sectors, has no doubt where the problem lies. 'A culture that excuses rape and violence is one that allows it to happen,' she says. 'Violence is a choice, not an instinct, and it's never excusable.'

At the moment, our culture isn't even asking men to have a hard look at what we've done, let alone be held to account for it, to explain it, and ultimately to stop it. Somehow, men are magically missing from the discussion on what is one of society's most serious problems.

The feminist linguist Julia Penelope showed how, even at sentence level, we neatly turn what is clearly a male issue into something more about the woman, the victim.

Start with the sentence 'John beat Mary.' That's pretty clear. But John starts to make his escape from the scene, moving down to the end of the sentence when we phrase it as 'Mary was beaten by John.' Now, the most important information is that Mary was beaten, not who did it. Next we move to 'Mary was beaten', which leaves John out of it completely, and we finish at 'Mary is a battered woman.' And that's the language we typically use about the legions of bruised and bleeding Marys.

Now that we know Mary is a battered woman, we can ask why. What was she wearing? What did she do to annoy him? Why doesn't she just leave?

We're ignoring the most important question, however: 'John, why did you beat Mary?'

Domestic violence isn't a women's issue—it's men's.

•

While researching for her book *Dude, You're a Fag*, the American writer C.J. Pascoe spent eighteen months with teen boys at a suburban US high school. She found that the term *fag*, or *faggot*, is an insult that is intended to police the boundaries of masculinity, and has pretty much nothing to do with being gay. According to Pascoe, the teenage boys saw it as far worse to be an unmasculine man than to be a man who sexually desires other men. If you like to dance, care about your appearance and clothes, seem at all emotional, or show any incompetence, you're a fag.

There were three boys at the school who were openly gay. Two got through relatively unscathed, but the third was tormented so relentlessly that he eventually dropped out. The first two boys were outwardly masculine, physically large and sporty. The third boy, Ricky, had long hair, an effeminate persona and loved dancing and cross-dressing. It was his lack of masculinity, not simply the fact that he was gay, that earned him his years of torture.

The power of such policing is staggering: it's a stern, Orwellian gaze that oversees every word and action, making sure every man's or boy's behaviour is always worthy of the Man Box.

As well as brutally enforcing gender roles, the Man Box does a great job with race, religious bigotry and homophobia. It's everywhere. I remember wearing a pink shirt down Sydney's George Street one day, proudly strutting my creative credentials. 'Bwa-ha, pink shirt,' a bloke said to his mate as they passed me. I had a favourite pair of shorts with flowers that were also loudly mocked by a gang of hi-vis guys. Personally, I couldn't care less about such insults, but they were perfect examples of the Man Box police at work: men I didn't even know reminding me that I had stepped outside the box with my (in their eyes) effeminate clothing.

The Man Box exists because men can identify, target and suppress difference. It grants permission for aggressive behaviour, and sets up a closed loop of emotional suppression, self-policing and the policing of others. When the rules are broken, punishment can be shunning, contempt or sarcasm, but it can also escalate to economic sanctions, physical violence and even murder.

Men have no choice but to put on the performance of manhood, constantly reinforcing their manliness to other men. This accounts for men behaving even more badly in large groups: football teams, gay-bashing gangs, gangs of tradies, gangs of bankers at the bar, gangs of men on company boards.

The constant attempt to prove we are truly manly is extraordinarily destructive in the lives of men and those close to them.

Work is a key part of a man's life, where the dangerous elements of masculinity are seen as core skills. For centuries, men schlepped off to the mines, the office or the damp paddocks of the family farm, and accepted the spirit-crushing boredom and physical toll in a kind of bargain with the devil. They would do the work—but, as the provider for their family, the economic superior, they demanded absolute obedience at home.

But technology has revolutionised the workplace, so that now creativity and communication skills are in far greater demand than mad forklift-driving skills. The automation revolution we're living through right now is seeing traditional male jobs mowed down like chaff, as artificially intelligent algorithms take over even some white-collar jobs, as well as truck driving, shelf-stacking, mining, agriculture, manufac-turing and telecommunications. In short, every industry in which men used to be assured of a decent living for life has been decimated.

My own chosen industry—publishing—was chopped off at the ankles by the rise of digital platforms in the 1990s and 2000s. Why would you buy a weekly gossip magazine when *TMZ* is right there on your phone, with the latest Kardashian shots or leaks from *The Bachelor*? I used to try to explain this to friends, so that I could prove that the implosion of my industry wasn't my fault—so I wasn't showing any weakness, okay?

The only thing someone could do in this situation was adapt their core skills—in my case, writing, design, creativity and storytelling—to the new digital media environment. I, and legion of my colleagues, have done just that. We took our special skills to the marketplace with eagerly launched businesses and freelance 'consultancies'—with varying degrees of success.

This sudden change in how we work has rendered men financially powerless, weak, out of control and failing to find the simple respect their labours bought them, despite their most desperate efforts. It's hard to 'be the man' when you're unemployed. Jobs that were supposed to be for life have disappeared like a ten-second Snapchat.

Worse, men are being asked by the new job market to be creative, empathetic and communicative—the very skills that would once have seen a man thrown onto the sharp rocks where we fling the unmanly.

The deal with the devil once saw men accorded power and privilege because they were the bread-winners in society. When this was overturned, it sparked a backlash against feminism, and an outpouring of entrenched sexism and homophobia. This is why MRAs and other far-right hate groups are so damned angry. And popular. It's a fight for turf, wages and respect.

After decades of conditioning, men are emotionally isolated, without community or connection. Their fears and sorrows are hidden, borne alone. The battle to prove we are real men has left us exhausted, with only one available emotion: anger. It has encouraged them to value women only as sexual objects. It is the combination of these two things—anger, and seeing women as 'lesser'—that has created the conditions for an explosion of domestic violence.

Because men are unable to communicate properly, tiny triggers— like cooking or money or talking to that guy—cause our feelings to erupt, and we take control of our problems with verbal abuse or a slap or a punch.

There it is: the direct line between gender discrimination and the deaths of women at the hands of men through domestic violence.

•

What, if anything, can be done to repair men's attitudes and start saving lives? The good news is that sexism, discrimination and policing are learned behaviours, and that means they can be changed.

It's about leadership. It's time for more men in positions of power and influence to stand up and challenge each other. It's time to change how our boys are socialised. In short, it's time to redefine what it means to be a man.

Steve Biddulph, the Australian psychologist who has been driving the discussion on turning boys into good men for more than twenty years, believes passionately that boys need good men to show them how to be good men. In a 2018 story for the *Sydney Morning Herald*, he wrote:

> Most boys, it is important to remember, grow up to be caring and safe, with clear values about treating others well. They may take risks or show poor judgement at times in their teens, but these lessons are well learned and they grow into decent men.
>
> Toxic masculinity is neither the norm nor the default for Australian males. It's a perversion of what manhood is supposed to be, a contagion that occurs in the absence of proper transmission of healthy manhood. It's what happens when elders are absent and men do not step up, and the peer group becomes the substitute source of life wisdom.

Good manhood, according to Biddulph, does not just happen. It has to be taught.

Any group of young men together is either a safe, regulated environment, usually because of the presence of older men who set the tone and actively stamp out bad behaviour, or it's a mob mentality, with a bully boss and his lieutenants dishing out *Lord of the Flies*–style treatment.

Misogyny, Biddulph says, isn't the core value of such a gang, but power is. Talking trash about girls happens because doing the opposite— being tender, affectionate and empathetic—makes you a target, liable to be called a pussy. So a young man will end up saying terrible things about a girl he actually loves: he will demean and objectify her, because that's the price of membership in the club.

Biddulph despairs at the pointlessness of wagging a finger at boys and telling them not to be bad. In order to become good adults, he says, young men need relationships with men who care about and value them.

In the last few years, especially, as I've researched for this book and written on men's issues, I've come to understand senior men in society have an obligation to our younger brothers.

It is up to us—I put myself in the senior category at the age of 53— to show them by example, and through our direct, loving counsel, that there's value, joy and wonder in a relationship with a woman you love and respect.

We need to help them understand it's way sexier than anything you'll experience when you objectify a woman as a thing. We should chill them to the bone with the news women have great respect-radars. If you don't see a woman as a real human being, you'll end up alone with your laptop, son, saving up for bored prostitutes.

According to Biddulph, this is the message men should have for boys:

> If you want to be loved, and deeply cared about, then you have to see the opposite sex as people, to empathise with them and care about them. That is risky, it makes you vulnerable, it puts your heart on the line but chances are you will find a real joy in life as a result. Women want what men want—fun, closeness, appreciation and companions in the adventure of life.

•

'In the end, what will hurt us most is not the words of our enemies, but the silence of our friends,' Martin Luther King is believed to have said.

We owe it to our sons to help them become better men through leadership by example. More men need to have the courage to speak up and challenge sexist language and behaviour by their peers.

Boys are deeply affected by men's violence. According to Australia's National Research Organisation for Women's Safety (ANROWS), 61 per cent of domestic violence victims had children in their care when the attacks occurred, and 48 per cent stated the children had seen and heard their mother being bashed.

Just like no one laughs openly at a racist joke (we hope) for fear of getting called out, men must start calling out sexist or abusive talk. We need to create an environment where sexism is not okay. Saying nothing makes you complicit.

'Mate, check her out! Hot . . . Hey, babe!'

'Not funny, bro, don't be a dick.'

Men have the tools to create a peer culture in which abusive behaviour is unacceptable. If enough men stand up enough times, men with abusive attitudes to women will start to lose what is most valuable to them: status. No one wants to be the dumb sexist guy.

The crumbling social contracts of the post-#MeToo world leave us with an opportunity to reimagine what it is to be a man. We can create men who are caring, who can connect emotionally, who can enjoy open relationships with men and women, who seek conversation, not control, and who value everyone as equals. We can show boys not to be afraid to love, and the way we can do it is by showing how much joy we get from the love and respect we have in our own lives.

The more of us who stand up, the fewer of us will be killing the ones we love.

# Chapter 5

# WHY ARE WE KILLING OURSELVES?

Today—this very day—six men in Australia will kill themselves. The same thing happened yesterday. The same thing will happen tomorrow. It happens every day. Six men kill themselves.

That might be six fathers who will never be with their children again, six men who will never kiss their partners again. It means six tragic funerals, with six groups of family and friends left asking why.

Every bloody day.

When you add women to the stats, the number rises to eight a day.

The crisis support and suicide prevention service Lifeline reports that male suicide rates are approximately three times that of women. The latest available figures show that, in 2014, 2864 people died by suicide. Of those, 2160 were male.

Suicide is the main cause of death for Australians between 15 and 44. The number of men who die by suicide in Australia every year is almost double the national road toll. We're all justified in asking: what the hell is going on?

Like the figures on domestic violence, suicide statistics are almost too huge for us to comprehend. So we must turn to personal stories in order to understand the pain, the sense of waste and the endless, unanswerable questions.

•

Any family touched by suicide is changed and scarred for generations.

Mine was.

In 1968, when I was three, I spent the weekend with my grandparents—my mum's parents—for the first time. They had a tiny holiday house—a batch, as we called it—in New Zealand's Central Otago, near Queenstown, a couple of hours' drive from the family farm, close to the southern rural service centre of Invercargill.

There are photos of me and my grandfather, Jim, from that weekend, wearing silly hats on a slide and posing with their pug, Sammy. My only memory of that time is of sitting in the car with my grandmother, Olive, listening to an All Blacks rugby test on the radio. Jim, who was a keen amateur photographer, an expert fly-fisherman, and a walker and climber, had gone for a walk up Mount Iron, a fairly decent local hill, saying he'd 'be back before the rugby started'.

I remember the black knobs of the 1960s radio, the wooden dash of the car, and the incomprehensible, crackly yelling and cheering of the rugby test, which started, and finished, as we sat in the car. I remember being very bored.

Jim never walked down Mount Iron. They found his body the next day. Jim was a big personality—loud, brash and bold, with a soft centre. He was never really one for doctors. Somehow, a year or two earlier, he'd managed to have a heart attack, be hospitalised and keep what was wrong with him from his wife and kids.

He was 55 years and one day old. This was not a suicide, but a silly accident.

When he died, the gap he left in Olive's life must have been huge: all that bluster, noise and presence, just gone. For four years she did an amazing job. She learned to drive. She joined the local lawn bowls club and became a champion. She looked after the family finances for the first time in her life.

As was the way with older people in the early 1970s, she had all her teeth out and was diagnosed with what at the time was called 'post-operative depression'. At the time she told my mother she 'felt like she did when you kids were born'—meaning she'd suffered post-natal depression too.

To my mother's surprise, Olive admitted herself to the infamous Ward 12 at the local hospital. (At school, being told you'd end up in Ward 12 was a dire insult.) But when Olive got there, she was horrified.

'They're all mad in here,' she told Mum. 'They won't let me out now, and all my friends will know.'

Four years to the day after Jim died, Olive said she was going up to spend the weekend at the batch. Mum thought it was a bit weird and sad, going away by herself like that. It was also kind of odd how she'd said, 'Don't worry, darling—I wouldn't do anything silly.'

She was due back either Sunday or Monday. Mum called her on Sunday. Nothing. Monday was a nasty, miserable day, as only the deep south of New Zealand can turn on. There were no mobile phones then, of course, so Mum went to Olive's house on Monday evening to wait for her. Her list of things to take was still on the kitchen table: she'd never left for the batch. But Mum couldn't find her.

Mum went to the police station to report her mother missing. She found out Olive was dead by overhearing the 'crackly', as she put it, police radio say an elderly Caucasian woman's body had been found. At Olive's address—the house where Mum grew up.

Olive had put a pile of sacks behind the little powder-blue Triumph Herald in the garage, and left the engine running until it ran out of petrol. Mum identified Olive's body. She still remembers the crusted soot on her mother's face. Mum doesn't really like watching TV crime shows.

My memory of this time is strange. I remember aunts and uncles and friends gathered at our house, but it wasn't the usual party, where the adults were chatty and jovial and happy to watch me do tricks on my bike. I guess it must have been Olive's wake. I did ask what was wrong with everyone, but didn't get a satisfactory answer, as was generally the case for seven-year-olds in 1972.

It was only years later that we finally understood the impact of Olive's suicide on our family.

My mother was just 29 when Olive died. What was supposed to be a beautiful time of life for her never happened. Olive only knew my brother and sister as babies. She never got to proudly drive the fifteen kilometres out to the farm in her little blue car again and have dinner with us. Decades of love, closeness, support, joy, growth, companionship, mother-and-daughter understanding—it never happened.

So suicide is a bit of a dirty word in my family. My mother still worries if she hasn't heard from any of us for a day or two. 'I just wanted to know you're all right,' she says when she calls.

I know that, because of the loss she's experienced, she really means it. She couldn't bear to go through that again. Even though Olive's was just one suicide, and took place decades ago, it still reaches out to us today.

•

Even so, it was quite a surprise when suicide came stalking me not long ago.

I started my career as a journalist in newspapers in New Zealand. I followed a girlfriend to Australia in 1988 and joined Rupert Murdoch's *Daily Telegraph* in Sydney.

News Corporation's culture was wild, larrikin, work-hard-play-hard, and I loved it. Delivering the front page to the editor for his sign-off at his stool at the bar at the paper's local in Surry Hills, the Evening Star, made me feel part of something bigger. Watching in delight as a drunk chief of sport didn't make it across the editorial floor to the bathroom, his bout of explosive diarrhoea bringing the newsroom to a standing ovation, made me feel I had found my people.

Back then, it was hilarious, mad and bad, and I still feel very grateful to have rubbed up against the glory days of print journalism.

Eventually I made the jump to magazines, and went on to edit gossip titles *NW* and *Woman's Day*. In the late 1990s, *Woman's Day* sold more than 500,000 copies a week at $3.95 each, and each issue had up to 60 pages of paid advertising at a rate of around $25,000 a page. You do the maths. It was, and still is, a big business, despite being built on the foolishness of celebrity gossip.

Later, I jumped back to News Corp as publisher, then managing director, of the magazines division.

So there I am, slightly tubby in my suit in my corner office in the late 2000s, in my forties. It was, in many ways, a golden time, but my colleagues and I knew it wouldn't last. Something called the internet was coming to get us, and the general feeling was that there was nothing we could do about it. So in 2008, armed with my experience, contacts and a considerable ego, I charged out into agency land.

At a great little outfit called SoDUS, I learned the agency ropes from a fellow refugee from print, David Hutton, a super-talented creative and one of the nicest blokes you'll ever meet. I owe him a debt of both friendship and intellectual property to this day. He became unexpectedly emotional when I read him that sentence at dinner on my patio one night recently, after two stiff gin and tonics. I said I'd put that in the book too. He laughed and said, 'As if you'll remember.'

After a few more years I launched my own agency, The Artistry. In 2016 it was shortlisted for B&T's Emerging Agency of the Year. As a piece of brand development I conceived and drove, I am still proud of it as the best work I have ever done. In my eyes, my confidence in my own abilities was justified. See, I've launched an agency and it's an award-winner already!

But, as it turns out, as a businessman I'm an awesome creative. I'm also great at talking to people and having lunch. Tax law? Not so much.

Not surrounded by the checks, balances and systems of a major corporation, I still behaved in the same devil-may-care way that had brought me so much success in the past. We did deals, trusting people we shouldn't have; in hindsight, the risks we took are much clearer to me than they were at the time. In the end, two major events collided in the business—one of them our fault, one not. We couldn't trade our way out of it. We had to close up shop.

As I'd been focusing so hard on the business, I hadn't been bothering much with a property separation I was going through, either. I wasn't paying myself much as we grew the business—staff always came first—and had borrowed money personally. The plan was that, once the property separation came through, I would pay off my debts. And by then the business would be rolling again anyway, so life would be sweet.

Everyone knows smart people borrow money to make money, right?

As it turned out, a couple of cards slipped out of the bottom level, and the whole house came tumbling down.

My home was gone. My savings were gone. My business was gone. The best car I've ever had was gone (clearly a first-world problem, but still). In a few short years, I'd gone from being a big swinging dick to an unemployed, middle-aged dickhead.

Given my run of success—for the first 45-odd years of my life—I was kind of shocked by this. For the first time I felt despair and depression. For a while I didn't know what was wrong with me. There were physical symptoms, my memory was terrible and I couldn't focus. My head swirled with increasingly desperate and hopeless plans to fix everything, like I always had.

I didn't say much to anyone. It was my problem, and therefore mine to fix. And I was so deeply embarrassed at my stupidity and failure that I just couldn't think about it sensibly. My whole identity had been built on who I was professionally—my success had been the cornerstone of my personality. I was also very angry at things I'd had no control over.

My mindset at the time was pretty much: 'Fuck you all!' As I saw it, I had tried my best. I wasn't a bad person but things hadn't worked out, despite years of grind. Where was the reward for all the effort I'd made?

So the only solution was, clearly, to kill myself. That would show everyone how much I really cared.

•

For every suicide, there are an estimated 30 attempts. This means that today, in Australia, around 240 people came to the brink, looked over and decided to jump. It just happens that they got lucky and lived.

One of the reasons men outstrip women in the suicide statistics is that we choose to kill ourselves in ways which are more brutal, violent and more certain to bring the death we desire. Women tend to overdose with drugs, or maybe to drift away in a crimson bath. Men use guns, hanging, and high things to jump off.

Here's how my thought process went, and how deep my planning was. I didn't want to jump off anything because I thought I'd chicken out and it might hurt. An overdose seemed sort of gross and uncool. I didn't want to be found in the foetal position in a pool of wee and vomit. I briefly considered death by cop, because if I was going out, it had to be glorious and insane so that everyone would talk about it. But to annoy cops enough to shoot you, you have to do some pretty dramatic stuff involving nudity and knives. I was worried I wouldn't seem nuts enough, and would just get tasered and locked up.

Then one day I saw it, my own special place. There's a road in Sydney's east that curls through some corners before straightening out for a few hundred metres, then another sharp corner. On that last corner is a pole and a stone wall.

I am an avowed car freak and motorsport nut, which means I have a pretty keen understanding of how fast I can get a car to go over any given distance. I reckoned I could get up to about 160 kilometres per hour before that last corner.

If you were to ask my partner or my daughter how I might suicide, they both would have said: 'Fireball.' I'd managed to talk about it enough for it to be out there, although always in a light way that never alerted anyone to the real danger.

I did a few test runs. Screw the cops, I thought, I'm doing suicide practice. I came down that road five times, each time tyres squealing around the corners, then gunning it in the straight. Yep, 160 kilometres per hour, easy. Each time I came to the corner I made the turn, but I could feel how easy it would be just to let the car run straight, and be gone. Knowing that there was a Hogwarts Express Platform 9¾ escape hatch waiting for me there, if I needed it, was somehow relaxing.

I decided to text everyone I thought needed to be texted at the start of my speed run—a digital suicide note. I ran through who I'd have to message in my head. Here's how messed up your thoughts are when you're in this state.

First, family. *Nah, they'll be fine*, I thought. *I'm old, I live overseas, they'll get over it.* I was ignoring, particularly, what it would do to my mother.

Next, my deeply loved partner, Jayde. To my considerable shame, I thought: *She's quite a bit younger than me, beautiful and vivacious. She has time to find someone else, and new happiness. She's better off without a loser like me anyway. And the new guy won't be able to compete with my memory anyway, so it sucks to be him.* There's no doubt suicide can also be a mean, aggressive act.

Now, my daughter. She was just seventeen at the time, and struggling with the pressures of life as a young woman. She'd just finished high school and was starting uni life. Our conversations, over her teenage years, had flowed through areas like ethics, critical thinking, philosophy, psychology, writing, work, life, relationships, spirituality, atheism, what is wrong, what is right, our responsibilities as individuals on the planet. All the big stuff. So how could I do this to her? It would render everything I'd ever said to her as bullshit. It would take her memory of her father and make it about one thing only: when he left.

So strange was my thinking in these moments that I wasn't worried only about the immediate agony and long-term damage it would have caused her. I was also thinking about my long-term legacy.

In the end, obviously, I didn't go through with it.

There have been so many wonderful things happen between then and now, things I would have not experienced if I'd done what I planned. Driving 120 hours with my daughter on her L-plates was a privilege and a joy. That's a lot of time to spend together, getting to know each other as adults.

We have since shifted house, and Jayde runs her communications business out of a wonderful, purpose-built space out the front, while I write from a converted garage out the back. If I had killed myself, I would never have had the joy of writing this book (nor would you have had the questionable pleasure of reading it).

I literally potter in the garden. There must be a gene which kicks in at a certain age and makes you say things like: 'Nice to get some rain on those baby shallots I just put in . . .' If I am ever to reach grandpa-ish age, I will be as Bad Grandpa as I can. The freedoms of being a codger and being able to say what one likes, as loud as one likes, are going to be sweet.

Jayde and I enjoy an exceptionally comfortable, simple, life together, built primarily around a love of cooking, wine and each other. We spend a happy hour or two in the kitchen each evening, simply talking about work, testing out business, creative and life strategies on each other.

My brother and his family came to stay recently, and for a week our house was filled with my nephews and niece. It had been a couple of years since I'd seen the kids, and reconnecting with them has been wonderful.

The obvious point is, of course, that I'd have missed all those moments if I'd decided to go gentle into that good night. And I'd miss all the joy and magic that is still to come. I know it, and I'm profoundly grateful to be here. But, today, six more men are not here.

The big question is: why?

•

Depressingly, as ever we find the answer in the Man Box.

Consider this quote from a US study by Konstantinos Tsirigotis and Marta Tsirigotis-Maniecka and Wojciech Gruszczynski into gender differentiation in methods of suicide:

> Women are twice as likely as men to experience major depression, yet women are one fourth as likely as men to take their own lives. One of the possible explanations to this paradox may be that men highly value independence and decisiveness, and they regard acknowledging a need for help as a weakness and avoid it. Women appreciate interdependence, and they consult friends and readily accept help. They consider decisions in the context of a relationship, take many things into consideration, and they feel freer to change their minds.

One of the key drivers of male suicide is in the 'way we define what it means to be a man in Australia', according to a 2017 article in *HuffPost Australia*. It quotes Dr Michael Flood, a sociologist specialising in men and masculinity:

> It's broken down a little, so it's shifted in some ways in Australia and it's uneven across Australia. But there's still a powerful ideal of what it means to be a man.
>
> It's the idea that to be a man is to be tough, to be strong, to be invulnerable, to be heterosexual, to be in control, to avoid feelings and so on.
>
> If we teach men to always be tough, to be stoic, to not show pain, then we stuff up men's physical and emotional health, we limit men's friendships with other men and women, we limit men's relationships and we limit men's participation in society.

If men don't have the ability or freedom to talk about how they're feeling, they're effectively prevented from being able to seek help if they encounter any mental health problems or feel suicidal.

The statistic is worst in rural Australia. Out back there's a perfect storm of isolation, climate change–driven drought cycles sucking the life from the land, and the strict requirement men of the land are tough, stoic, and get-on-with-it . . . until they die. Suicides in rural areas are 40 per cent higher than in metro areas.

A spokesperson for Sane Australia, Sarah Coker, says high travel times to find someone to help and decreased spending on rural mental health services have contributed to the tragedy in the bush. 'And there is still a stigma around mental illness in many smaller communities,' she says. 'There is plenty of work to be done, particularly in rural and remote areas, in spreading the word about the need to talk about these issues, to talk about your feelings.'

The problem is worst among older men, who are most likely to take their own lives.

The confronting truth that men are killing themselves to be 'real men' is supported by a major 2015 study for Beyond Blue and the Black Dog Institute, called 'What Interrupts Suicide Attempts in Men: A Qualitative Study'.

'All of the men we interviewed, spoke [of] growing up in a culture where the message was implicit that they should not be speaking about their feelings,' Dr Andrea Fogarty, a research fellow at the Black Dog Institute, told the *Huffington Post*

The Beyond Blue website says: 'Men are known for bottling things up. But when you're feeling down, taking action to call in extra support is the responsible thing to do.' It notes that, on average, one in eight men will experience depression, and one in five men will experience anxiety at some stage of their lives.

Everyone's mental health varies across their life, and can move from positive and healthy to negative and unhealthy in response to stresses and experiences. Beyond Blue's website also features a checklist which men can assess their mental health against: a list of signs and symptoms of mental illness, and what action to take.

The Movember Foundation has been raising money for men's health issues since 2003, particularly in the areas of mental health and suicide prevention. Its homepage headline is: 'It's time to have an honest conversation about mental health.' It points out that one in two Australian men have had a mental health problem at some point in their lives, and that three out of four suicides are men. 'What can we do?' it asks in bold.

Then it answers: 'Talk. Ask. Listen. Encourage action. Check in.'

The Movember Foundation makes the point that most of us say we'll be there for our mates if they ever need us. Yet most of us say we're uncomfortable asking mates for help. Those two positions are not compatible. As the Movember Foundation says, 'Something's gotta change.'

The founder of the R U OK? movement, Gavin Larkin, lost his father, Barry, to suicide in 1995. On the R U OK? website there's a video telling the story of the organisation, and it includes some terribly sad audio of Barry speaking on the day he died.

'So I've sort of cut off from everybody,' he says, as the camera lingers on a black and white shot of Barry and his young sons, looking so happy. 'Now, um, in that time, I haven't spoken to anyone—it's only been, you know, someone in a shop to order something or get a paper or some bread or something like that, and, uh, I've decided that tonight's the night that I'll finish my life . . .'

Barry's suicide had a massive impact on Gavin's life, and he launched R U OK? to honour his father and prevent further unnecessary deaths. If someone had asked Barry if he was okay, and they'd had a conversation, the outcome might have been different.

R U OK?'s strapline is 'A conversation could change a life', according to Gavin, 'because it is actually the one thing that all of us can do to make a real difference. Getting connected and staying connected is the best thing we can do for ourselves and anyone at risk . . . we want everyone right across the spectrum in Australia to reach out to those they love and let them know they do care, by asking "are you okay?"'

R U OK?Day falls in September each year, but these conversations aren't for a single day—they're for every day.

Gavin died from cancer in 2011. His legacy is a movement that has pushed a simple, powerful idea into our minds. Start a conversation. Ask your mates and loved ones if they're okay. If they're not, help them.

If there's anyone reading this who is feeling deep despair, or even suicidal, let me reach out through the pages and beg you, please, to talk to someone and get some help. There's a page at the end of this book with phone numbers you can call. Do pick up your phone. Call a friend or loved one. They won't judge you. They won't think you are mad, or weak. They'll listen, and they'll help you get help.

•

Being a man is killing us simply because we're so busy being tough and stoic that we can't bring ourselves to ask for the help that could save our lives.

A few years ago, a friend of mind, as we drove together after a night of music and mates, talked of a tough time in his career in media. He joked that he'd be 'better off under a train'. I asked him if he was serious, and he was weirdly calm and steely in his view that he'd be better off not here.

Later that night, I spoke to a mutual friend of ours, and we both called him to ask him to see someone as soon as he could, to get help. Saying what he'd said, especially with the cool air of intent he displayed, was as clear a communication we were going to get about how he was really feeling.

Our friend did get help, and he got better. His career settled down and he is now loving fatherhood, and his guitars, and posting some startlingly good photography online.

We've never really talked about how close he came that night, but we do know that the nudge we gave him to get help was timely and necessary, and brought about positive change in his life.

If you're feeling down, understand that pretending to be a tough, self-contained man might be standing between you and the help that might eventually save your life.

If you're fine, great. Be the sort of man a friend will feel safe opening up to about how he's feeling. Be the guy he knows won't judge him.

Keep an eye out in your friend group, and with your family and colleagues. Has someone gone through something traumatic, like divorce or job loss? Is someone expressing anger and hopelessness, or even joking about suicide? Don't wait. Make every day an R U OK?Day. Pick up the phone. 'Hey, man, just checking in—how are you going?' That's all you need to do.

The knowledge that behaving like a man is potentially fatally dangerous should be enough to change how we think and what we do.

# Chapter 6

# THE VIEW FROM THE CORNER OFFICE

As Roger Ailes took the lectern, a hush fell over the largely hungover crowd. We were in the presence of greatness. Ailes, looking a bit like Jabba the Hutt, his neck wider than his bald head, gazed around the room. 'Hello,' he said. 'I'm Paris Hilton.' Cue guffaws and wild applause.

The scene is a luxury hotel in Cancun, Mexico. It's 2004. The best and brightest of Rupert Murdoch's loyal lieutenants from the United Kingdom, the United States and Australia had gathered for a week-long conference to discuss how to counter the looming threat of digital content, and to exchange ideas about our markets. And to argue. And to drink until dawn.

The seniority and rarity of the speakers was incredible. A then soon-to-be US secretary of state, Condoleezza Rice, spoke to us at lunch. General Tommy Franks, straight out of *Platoon* or *Full Metal Jacket*, responsible for the 2003 invasion of Iraq and the overthrow of Saddam Hussein, gave us a rousing lecture on leadership. Some guy from the Massachusetts Institute of Technology showed a solar-powered keyboard and screen that rolled up like paper. It worked. Did I mention this was back in 2004?

The intellect and experience we were exposed to that week was truly amazing, and something that could never happen now. It all cost a few bucks, I seem to remember.

Ailes was particularly revered because he embodied, in his considerable body, the entrepreneurial, larrikin, can-do ethos of News Corporation. We used to call it 'the largest small business in the world'.

In the 1980s, whenever Rupert Murdoch visited News's bunker HQ in Sydney's Holt Street, nestled among the rag traders, cafes and bars of Surry Hills, a special square of new carpet was carefully placed in the foyer lifts, covering the usual journo-scuffed, cigarette-burnt one. Afterwards, the pristine carpet was carefully put away for next time Murdoch came.

Company legend has it that, in 1996, Murdoch personally asked Ailes, already a proven TV marketing genius, to launch Fox News as a direct competitor to the sexy CNN. Ailes would have an open chequebook. It took him just months to procure talent, studios and equipment, to develop content and a brand, and to launch what has become one of the most powerful and controversial American news platforms.

Ailes died in 2017. His legacy—apart from being an adviser to Donald Trump during his presidential campaign—is the campaign of systematic, long-term, hardcore sexual harassment he ran against young female staff at Fox. Eventually he resigned from Fox in 2016, with a US$40 million payout and not a word about the storm of allegations from current and former staff.

Fox has settled out of court with at least three women, for their silence. A number of lawsuits were outstanding at the time of Ailes' death. Yet his incredible speech on company culture was the best thing I remember from the 2004 Mexico trip.

In the workplace, power is a weapon and a shield, and bad behaviour is openly rewarded . . . as long as you're making money.

Things were nasty at the top at Fox. Bill O'Reilly, a rich and powerful commentator on the network, agreed to a US$32 million sexual harassment settlement in 2017. He is reported to have paid a total of US$13 million to five other women. Before O'Reilly was forced to resign, Fox extended his US$25 million a year contract, despite being aware of the allegations against him.

The allegations against Ailes and O'Reilly broke around the same time in 2017, as the extraordinarily predatory conduct of Hollywood's most powerful men, particularly film producer Harvey Weinstein, was exposed. It was like lancing a boil, and what squirted out was almost too horrible to look at. Women stood up together and named and shamed their abusers in the extraordinary #MeToo campaign. One woman, actor Rose McGowan, threw open her window and screamed she was mad as hell and not going to take it anymore. Another actor, Alyssa Milano, added weight when she tweeted that women should come out and 'give people a sense of magnitude of the problem'.

They were joined by an army of sisters, and some men, who added their voices until we all had to listen. Celebrities, including Gwyneth Paltrow, Ashley Judd, Jennifer Lawrence and Uma Thurman, added their star power to the campaign. More and more women felt safe and supported enough to come forward and tell their stories.

With allegations now made against a horrifying array of media, entertainment and business stars, the #MeToo movement has driven real change and forced employers to make workplaces safer for women, or risk brand-damaging public shaming at the hands of the embold-ened victims.

All this has forced men to rethink how they behave towards women in work and social environments. What might have been acceptable twenty years ago certainly isn't today.

The magic of #MeToo is that the sheer numbers of complaints—from all over the world, and at all levels of society—has empowered women to speak up. It has raised awareness about sexual abuse as a real issue in the lives of many people. It has given women a new, exciting, powerful voice. There was a heady moment in late 2017 when it felt like a revolution was sweeping the world, driven digitally but with whiffs of flowers, patchouli and a fervour for change not seen since the late 1960s.

The movement has since slowed, but it has contributed to a world-wide shift in perception about what is, and what is not, appropriate conduct between the sexes. The idea of 'enthusiastic consent' is gaining momentum, meaning that unless a partner gives an active, clear, happy, resounding 'yes' to sex, there is no consent.

At the time of writing, the New South Wales government is in the process of reviewing the state's consent laws, after the high-profile case of Luke Lazarus, who was acquitted of anally raping a terrified, frozen virgin in the gravel in the lane behind his father's Kings Cross night-club. Because teenager Saxon Mullins did not say 'no' and consent was deemed unclear, Lazarus was found not guilty.

'I know part of me died that day,' Mullins told the ABC's *Four Corners* program in a powerful interview that sparked national debate on the nature of consent. She felt safe to speak out, and identify herself, because of the supportive, empowered environment of #MeToo. Her brave story has moved the state government to review what it means to give consent.

Former Network Ten newsreader Tracey Spicer has driven the #MeToo agenda in Australia, and has railed, with justified anger, against the blokey culture of Australian media. Fair enough, given the way she was sacked by email two months after having her second child. Her famous 2014 TEDx Talk, in which she wiped off her makeup and removed her glamorous dress, and her memoir, *The Good Girl Stripped Bare*, both savage a media industry that reduces women to the sum of their looks and age.

Motivated by guilt 'for working in the media for 30 years and knowing there was serious sexual harassment and predators within our industry, but not doing stories on it', in October 2017 Spicer tweeted to ask victims in the Australian media industry to come forward. The result was extraordinary.

'I was inundated with 500 messages within the first couple of weeks and that's now reached almost 1500,' she told the *Australian Financial Review* in early 2018.

Don Burke's predatory behaviour was an open media secret for years, finally exposed by Spicer, the ABC and Fairfax Media after a six-week investigation. Spicer maintains there is another high-profile man in the Australian media who should be lifted with tongs from under his rock. Another twenty high-profile figures are being investigated as a result of the information Spicer has collected.

She has no doubt where the line is in male–female relations at work. 'You're never going to stop inter-office affairs,' she says. 'I met my husband at work. So many of us do because we work such long hours but the difference is consent and the context is that power imbalance. It's a very different thing to have an affair with an office member than use your power to indecently assault or harass someone.'

Spicer was made a member of the Order of Australia last year for her service to the media and her work with welfare and charity groups.

'Huge change doesn't come easily. Make no mistake, the grounds are shifting beneath us very quickly,' she says.

•

Years before Weinstein, Burke and #MeToo, it was a different world, where behaviour that would see you sacked in disgrace today was actively encouraged. I know because I lived in it, and the Cancun conference was a perfect example.

There, I was witness to one of the most bizarre and compelling events in Australian media folklore. It was the Chairman's Dinner, where Murdoch would speak and officially welcome everyone to the conference. It was decided that the famous *Sunday Telegraph* editor Roy 'Rocky' Miller should introduce him.

Miller was a fearless, brilliant and sometimes quite terrifying editor. He had the helm of the *Sunday Telegraph* for eight highly successful years from 1990, and was a hardbitten Murdoch newsman for nearly half a century. He came from a time when journos chased ambulances and drank with cops and criminals, when the paper was edited from the pub, and when betting on the dishlickers and ponies was as important as tomorrow's lead.

In his book *Man Bites Murdoch*, the gentlemanly Melbourne editor Bruce Guthrie describes Miller as typifying 'the sort of executive Murdoch prefers: hard-driven, hard-partying, a doer rather than a thinker'.

Although very happy screaming abuse at subeditors, Miller wasn't quite as comfortable introducing Murdoch to an audience that included the cream of his international peers, as well as Michael Howard, the leader of the British Conservative Party, and his novelist wife, Sandra. So he enlisted the help of an equally feared and legendary editor, Col Allan, another senior Murdoch henchman, to get him prepared for the evening.

Allan had made an extraordinary jump from Sydney's *Daily Telegraph* to run the *New York Post*. He was infamous for urinating in the sink in the editor's office at the *Daily Telegraph* during editorial conferences. The sink was behind a little door, and everyone knew there was no toilet in there. We could hear him. Allan was a bully and a tyrant, enabled by his power and the News culture. Once, on winning a Stanley Award, the cartoonist Warren Brown, sick of years of abuse, famously threw the trophy at Col's head, burying it in the wall behind him.

In Cancun on the afternoon before the Chairman's Dinner, I remember returning from the beach and seeing Col and Rocky at the bar, already more than a little worse for wear. Col had clearly been helping Rocky steady his nerves with a supply of drinks for the last few hours.

We dressed and were bussed to another luxury hotel for dinner.

Miller's big moment came. He lurched from his seat towards the stage, wearing an untucked black shirt and black jeans, unusual among the dinner suits and ties. Finally reaching the microphone, and amid a growing murmuring, he started well enough. 'Good evening, ladies and gentlemen. My name is Roy Miller, and I have the great honour of introducing a very great man, Rupert Murdoch.' From there things went downhill. 'I fucking love Rupert,' Miller observed.

All around me, media executives from London and New York sat in stunned disbelief. 'Oh. My. God. This is disgraceful,' someone hissed in a plummy English accent behind me. The Australians in the room were in hysterics. Good old Rocky.

'I fucking love Rupert and I fucking love News,' Miller went on. 'I've been at News for over 40 years. You don't even get that for rape!'

The attempted joke sent a low moan around the room.

Realising he was losing his audience, Miller looped back around to what he knew. 'I fucking love Rupert,' he said again. 'I fucking love News.'

By now the room was pretty much in uproar. Finally Murdoch made it to the stage. Holy shit! Was he going to sack Rocky on the spot?

The chairman put his arm around the swaying newsman. 'Ladies and gentlemen,' he said, 'I give you Rocky Miller, the only editor ever to personally preside over the demise of an opposition newspaper!' Murdoch started a hearty round of applause. Everyone joined in.

The *Daily Mirror* was News's afternoon paper in Sydney. Under Rocky's editorship, it had whipped its Fairfax opposition, the *Sun*, so soundly that it had closed in 1988.

Murdoch hadn't forgotten, and as he held Rocky's arm aloft, he sent a loud, clear message to some of the world's most senior media executives: this is what I value. This is what is important. It doesn't matter how you behave. Do the right thing in business and you will always be protected.

Rupert is reported to have said he was drawn to Rebekah Brooks, the first female editor of the UK *Sun* from 2003 to 2009 because she was 'a larrikin'. Brooks managed to avoid being set to jail for her role in the *News of the World* phone hacking scandals, arguing that even though she was editor at the time, she had no knowledge of the crimes. Later, as CEO of News International in London, she authorised the destruction of millions of potentially damaging internal emails relating to the phone hacking investigations.

In 2015, still part of the News Corp fold, she was named CEO of News UK, the renamed News International. Murdoch hadn't forgotten the sterling service of his favourite larrikin in tough times.

•

It's 2006. My phone rings. It's another senior News executive, older than me, from the hard-drinking, hard-swearing, ex-tabloid old school. He is most famous for the bottle in his top drawer, his temper and the 'flabbit'—the infamous 'flying rabbit', which he ran on the front page when he was editor of the *Daily Mirror* in 1985. With a picture. Apparently, he believed the story.

We have a disagreement on the future paper stock of the *Sunday Telegraph*'s inserted magazine, these days called *Stellar*. What he said to me sent me out of my seat and directly to the office of the CEO, John Hartigan. It was just so weird, so homophobic, so insulting and so incredibly aggressive.

My position was that the executive had overstepped the boundaries of a heated office conversation and, with personal insults, had now opened the door to me 'kicking his arse'. I was just letting John know that. Given that, without the protective cloak of his suit, tie and title, it would have been like pushing over your drunk old uncle at a Christmas barbecue, John was a little concerned.

'I'll have a word, mate,' Hartigan said, clearly wanting to avoid any Tuesday afternoon arse-kickings on Mahogany Row (which is what every newspaper's executive floor is called). I never heard about the matter again.

The same year, a mate lounged at my office door. He'd been overhearing a few things he thought I'd like to know about. Yet another executive had been bad-mouthing me, and even starting a campaign to roll my division into his and take over the whole thing.

Again, I was straight out of my seat, this time heading down the stairs to my nemesis's office. I walked straight past his EA and into his sanctum.

'Mate, I know what you've been saying and what you're trying to do. Stop it.'

He actually leaned back in his seat, paused and smirked slightly. 'Hmm . . . so?' he said.

I had rehearsed this. 'Mate,'—for some reason you even called people you hated mate—'if you don't leave me and my shit alone, I'll kick your arse,' I said.

'What?' he spluttered. 'What do you mean?'

'If I hear one more word about this, I'll kick the shit out of you in the car park,' I said. 'I mean it. I will.'

By the time I sat down at my desk, my phone had started ringing, with other executives congratulating me on my very manly stand.

Looking back now, I'm not proud. What a dick. But back then, I couldn't have been more pleased with myself.

Doing the tough thing, the manly thing, the aggressive thing, was loudly and soundly applauded. And this included embracing a culture of booze, cocaine and sex, where women were valued most for their sexual attractiveness.

During the 2000 Olympics and 2003 Rugby Union World Cup, both hosted in Australia, the level of corporate schmoozing reached insanity, with hotel rooms booked in constant readiness for execs to take girls upstairs for sex, during and after functions. These weren't prostitutes but young women working in PR, marketing and the media who, at the time, seemed more than happy to party hard and trade sex for the career opportunities it might bring. They seemed willing to join in the raucous 'fun'. I never gave it a thought, beyond 'Boy, someone's going to be in trouble if their wife finds out!'

I wonder how many of those girls, now senior women, have had their own #MeToo moment, like so very many women are reporting now.

I've thought long and hard about if there's someone, somewhere in my corporate past, who might have felt harassed or abused by me. I was once contacted by email by a former staffer who now lives overseas. She wrote to me that she was still angry that I'd asked her to walk the streets of Sydney to see if she'd receive any catcalls or harassment; we were doing a story about sexual harassment.

I answered that I was a 32-year-old journo thrown into the deep end of management with no experience or help whatsoever, and that I had indeed made some questionable decisions. I agreed that I'd said and done a lot of dumb things that may have upset people. I apologised profusely, saying I wasn't trying to harass her—I just wanted the story. She thanked me for my response, and its content, and seemed happy that she'd said what she needed to say.

I was sorry. Even so, I basically gave the 'that's how it was back in the day' excuse, which has been rolled out by every high-profile sleaze caught out.

I have personally yelled 'Two-button rule!' at female salespeople before they met with important clients—which, everyone knew, meant they should undo at least two shirt buttons. The client likes cleavage. I am deeply ashamed about that now, but it wasn't unusual at the time, and, as far as I know, no one batted an eyelash. That doesn't make a bad thing right.

Of course, I have to acknowledge that just because no one said anything doesn't mean everyone was happy about what was going on. I didn't know then, and I don't know now, and I have to feel shame for any discomfort, or worse, that may have come from my behaviour as a gregarious, overexcited young media executive.

•

There are a couple of incidents in my life that I now look back on and think, *Holy crap, that could have gone badly*. In the early 1980s I was still at uni but becoming increasingly ambitious for a career in media.

So, in the holidays, I popped into a local station for a voice test. I figured I might want to be a broadcaster. I was eighteen. A veteran radio and TV star, who once briefly even had his own chat show in New Zealand, was the senior broadcaster. He was the man who could get you on air.

I ended up going for multiple tests over the period of a year. Each time I'd get back from uni for holidays, I'd call him to see if there were any openings. 'No,' he'd say, 'not yet—but why not come back in for one more test?'

This was very confusing. The voice tests only took about five minutes, but then we'd spend an hour chatting in the darkened studio. One time the broadcaster seemed very concerned that I'd put on weight since the last holidays. My jeans were very tight, he observed. My bum looked fat. It slowly dawned on me that this man didn't really think I had the makings of a radio man, but he really did like our little chats.

I was naive, though, and didn't actually get what was going on. I was aware of a vague sexual frisson in the air—but we were both blokes, so what did he think was going to happen? And how would going for a drink at his place help my career? Surely, he could tell me how to make my next voice test better right here, at the radio station?

In the end, nothing physical happened, although he did draw me back to the station again and again for over a year. I suppose the power relationship wasn't unbalanced enough. I didn't want a radio job badly enough to make myself more available, and there was no way he could have physically compelled me. I had a good twenty kilograms on him, to his annoyance. (He once commented to me I was a 'big boy', and that 'big men don't know themselves'—whatever that meant.)

But I did experience being in an environment where, if things had been a little different, I might have found myself trading sex for a job in entertainment. I understand how it's happened to men and women, countless times, the world over. And I can see how, in the moment, especially if the power is tipped the abuser's way, there's very little you could do about it.

A radio show about his career positioned him as a kind of edgy, controversial, figure with a naughty humour. Indeed.

That same year, when I was eighteen, I worked during the holidays driving a front-end loader, making up huge orders of peat moss for people to put on their gardens. The manager of the 'Peat Factory', as I called it, seemed to employ only casual students and blokes straight out of jail.

One of the jail guys, who had a self-administered tear tattoo on his cheek for each time he'd been inside, seemed to think it was very, very important I have a broom handle shoved up my bum. He had four tears. So, each smoko and lunchtime I'd end up in the corner of a shed, waving a four-by-two at a couple of ex-cons, who were armed with a broom or a shovel.

It wasn't that they were just threatening me—they were really trying to do it. I was held down, with a couple of blokes on my arms, and Four Tears giggling excitedly and trying to get my pants down.

Again, I was so naive that I didn't see this as sexual assault or attempted rape. I just saw it as the jail guys being dickheads. I was a raw-boned farm boy, straight out of the woolshed and off the hay paddock, who had already played years of rugby union against fully grown men. I didn't mind getting in fights. Having spent five years in a New Zealand boys' school in the 1970s and '80s, I had defended myself with my fists many times.

Sometimes they'd get my pants down, but were frustrated by my ability to struggle violently and clench everything up, and they never achieved any insertion. We'd often start the next shift covered in bruises and bleeding cuts.

A few times, you might even have seen me chasing Four Tears with the broom, yelling 'Bend over, Rangi, it's your turn with the broom, bro!' I actually quite liked the bloke.

Here's how it stopped. One day, I was just sick to death of it. They were coming for me again. This time, I singled out Four Tears. 'Mate, you're fuckin' gay. Blokes don't like other blokes' arses this much,' I screamed, enraged.

A couple of the other jail guys thought this was very funny, and very true. They laughed at Four Tears. To be laughed at and labelled 'gay' was too much for him, so he gave up.

This was not just blokes messing about. Flip the situation and make me an aspiring Hollywood actress. Imagine the horror of her story of physically fighting to avoid anal rape with a broom at work. Every day! And being held down and bashed by multiple people.

I didn't even tell my boss, or my parents.

The reality is that I haven't thought about this matter for years, and I'm not scarred by it. Again, this is likely because the power relationships were pretty even. We were all 90-kilogram-plus men. I wasn't scared. I was just annoyed. That's obviously a key difference to the experience of the Hollywood actress. But if I'd been a little less confident of myself physically, a little less physically capable of defending myself, I'd absolutely have been repeatedly raped.

I'm not for a second holding these experiences up as my #MeToo. Because of my low awareness and big body, while I was still a victim, I was unscarred by it. My mind is not haunted by the horrific memory of sexual assault. I don't pretend to understand what it is like to be a real, powerless victim. But my stories do show how often, and how powerfully, sexual abuse and harassment can become real in our lives. I'm simply very lucky my own experiences weren't worse.

•

I don't for a second want to give the impression that because I consider myself unscarred, it's not possible, or even easy, for a man to become a victim of sexual assault.

The actor Brendan Fraser was once a big star of films such as *The Mummy* trilogy, *Encino Man* and *George of the Jungle*. Now middle-aged and living with the legacy of a litany of painful on-set injuries, Fraser has made a few, intense appearances in *Texas Rising* and Showcase's *The Affair*.

Fraser has publicly alleged that Philip Berk, a one-time president of the powerful Hollywood Foreign Press Association (HFPA), grabbed his buttocks, in plain view in a crowded area in the Beverly Hills Hotel, and wiggled his finger around Fraser's perineum—or his 'taint', as Fraser put it.

Fraser, in his first interview for years, told American *GQ* magazine, he was overcome with 'panic and fear'. Berk, in his memoir, agrees the grab happened but left out the invading finger. An investigation by the HFPA concluded that 'Mr Berk inappropriately touched Mr Fraser [but] the evidence supports that it was intended to be taken as a joke, and not as a sexual advance.

Somehow, because Fraser is a man and the incident happened in a public place, it's seen as so trivial as almost to not be sexual assault at all.

Actor Anthony Rapp was fourteen when then 26-year-old Kevin Spacey picked him up 'like a groom picks up the bride over the threshold' and tried to hold him down on a bed. Spacey's response was not to deny the incident but to reluctantly come out as gay. This instantly made the attack on Rapp about sex, not power—about drunken sexual revelry, not attempted rape.

Sexual assault is something the more powerful does to the weaker, and sometimes men are on the receiving end. Overwhelmingly, the offender is still another man.

•

Both the corporate and blue-collar worlds absolutely adore the manly attributes of aggression, sexual dominance, leadership, toughness and bravery. I have no doubt that if I'd been senior at a big bank or advertising firm, the attitudes I witnessed in the media world would have been the same. What behaviour was acceptable, and what was not, was as clear as if it had been emailed to us in an executive memo.

All these were frowned upon: being a 'wimp'; not standing up for yourself; not being able to hold your own at the bar; not being 'one of the boys' and stick with your group; and not swearing for your country.

One old exec on Mahogany Row once took me aside to give me some advice. 'Sorry, love,' he said to his female assistant, 'I'm just gonna shut the door. The language might get a bit fuckin' blue.' He told me not to worry about most of my fellow executives, who were just normal News 'cunts'. What I had to worry about was the 'real cunty cunts', he said, gesticulating wildly down the hallway, at whose office I did not know.

What all this meant was that I, and a thousand other men like me, went home each night a ball of rage and stress, in full-blown fight-or-flight mode. All I wanted to do was slump on the couch with a vat of wine and unwind. Helping with homework seemed a difficult distraction, and my appetite for playing ball in the back lane was low. My desire to talk to my wife about my day was even lower.

When I think back to the time I threatened my colleague, I am surprised at myself. I'm not actually one for issuing arse-kickings at all. How on earth did I get myself into a situation where threatening to bash a co-worker seemed like the right response, and was admired by others? How did I end up pretending to be a man I was not, playing a role in the most manly of worlds?

The answer is: it's hard to stop. The rewards, though considerable, were pretty much completely financial. Earning a lot of money might seem like a dream, but all that happens is your lifestyle and spending grows like a baby demon too, demanding more and more to sustain itself. Soon holidays and houses and cars and schools are all bought and booked, and there's no way you can step off the corporate treadmill, even if you wanted to. So you crank it up and start running faster.

As it turns out, though, men don't love being in a suit, or fighting pitched battles with other blokes in suits, for ten hours a day. Men struggle with their work/life balance just as much as women. We just don't talk about it, because . . . men just don't.

Researchers at the University of Georgia, in the United States, spent several years collating the findings of more than 350 studies, with more than 250,000 participants, from all over the world. The results, according to Assistant Professor Kristen Shockley, were surprising:

We essentially found very little evidence of differences between men and women as far as the level of work-family conflict they report . . . Women hear that other women are struggling with this issue, so they expect they will experience greater work-family conflict. There is also some socialization for it being OK for women to talk about it more than men . . . I do think it's harming men, who are silently struggling and are experiencing the same amount of work-family conflict, but no one is acknowledging it.

Previous research shows men feel uncomfortable discussing work and family problems, because they're afraid of being stigmatised, their masculinity being called out or even feeling vulnerable and judged by their employer.

So women are talking to their friends, while most men, as usual, aren't talking to anyone.

•

More and more of us are looking at our lives and asking: 'Is this all there is?' We are now more motivated than ever to make personal changes before it's too late.

One American dad, who happened to be the CEO of a US$2 trillion global investment fund, PIMCO, earning a tasty US$100 million a year, learned a hard lesson from his ten-year-old daughter. Mohamed El-Erian shocked the finance world when he quit his role in 2014, after his daughter presented him with a list of 22 milestones he had missed so far that year—things like the first day of school, and the first soccer game of the season. 'I felt awful and got defensive,' he said.

I had a good excuse for each missed event! Travel, important meetings and urgent phone calls, sudden to-do[s].

But it dawned on me that I was missing an infinitely more important point. As much as I could rationalize it—as I had rationalized it—my work-life balance had gotten way out of whack, and the imbalance was hurting my very special relationship with my daughter. I was not making nearly enough time for her.

El-Erian was struggling to balance his work and his private life. 'Work-life balance was an initiative that we had been devoting more time to at PIMCO. But that knowledge did very little to dampen this very personal wake-up call,' he said.

Also in the United States, Max Schireson, CEO of MongoDB, a data analytics and management company, found himself with three children and flying half a million kilometres a year. 'I was not with my kids when our puppy was hit by a car, or when my son had minor emergency surgery,' he said.

In Australia, we're following the same trend. When Cameron Clyne, CEO of NAB, pulled the pin on his job, he said: 'This is what it looks like when you prioritise your family over your career.' He also noted that he'd like to be married longer than he was a CEO.

When Labor senator Stephen Conroy retired from the federal parliament in 2016, he said: 'When you resent being in Canberra because you're missing your daughter's soccer training, it's time to retire.'

In May 2018, a Western Australian MP, Tim Hammond, also retired to spend more time with his children. In his announcement, he pointed to long periods of time away from home as his reason for leaving politics. 'It just wasn't working,' he said. 'I just cannot reconcile the father that I want and need to be to three little kids, while serving as a federal parliamentarian from Western Australia.'

It's still the case, for men and for women, that you can have work or a life, but it's very hard to have both. It may be a bit easier to quit and spend time with the kids when you've got a few million stashed away from your years at the top. It's more difficult if you're, say, a plumber with a young family who has to work seven days a week to keep a struggling business with two staff afloat.

But over the past few years, the number of men working part-time has grown six times faster than the number of men working full-time. This may say as much about the digital workplace as it does about men's desire to reconnect with their homes and children, but it does show that many men are actively looking for a better work/life balance.

I left News Corp in 2008, funded by a quite spectacular redundancy payout, and slowly ventured out into the weird and wonderful world of creative and communications agencies. I also took a few months off. I was able to spend time with my daughter, who was in her early teens. We would drive to Sydney's Clovelly Beach on weekday afternoons when almost no one was around, and bump and sway in the cool, crystal water above a garden of sea life and flocks of fish flying below. It's something we still do to this day, so strong is the memory for us both.

I cooked, gardened, shopped and kind of bumbled around the world, blinking in awe. It was as if I was seeing all the nice things in life for the first time. I lost more than ten kilograms. I swear the period changed my life and set me on a new path, pursuing things that are fun and creative, that fit my limited skill set and that have some meaning or purpose.

I was one of the few daddies at school drop-off and pick-up. Until they get to know your wife, the schoolyard mummy mafia generally view you as some sort of unemployed gigolo and/or paedophile, in my experience.

Child care is a joke. For the almost 5 million people in Sydney, there are an estimated just over 90,000 childcare places. Barely a third of those are available outside standard business hours. Now try to find one near where you work. But who can walk out of a board presentation at 5.15 pm to go and pick up their kid? The board might want to stay until 7 pm, then have some drinks. There's no way around it: someone has to look after the kids.

I've seen many a file dropped on a colleague's desk at 5.05 pm, with the following exchange:

'Can you look at this for tomorrow's meeting, please? Just a topline would be great.'

'Sorry—I've got to leave on time to pick up my child.'

'We all have our obligations, but we don't drop our colleagues in it just because we made a decision to have a child. The rest of us are staying to get this done.'

'I guess I could call my sister . . .'

'Great! That's the attitude!'

There are a thousand studies, and my experience backs them up, which say that if you show your employees freedom and respect, they will give it straight back. The moment someone asks to work four days a week or to leave at 3 pm on a Thursday, say yes. Your employee will then push hard to prove they can stay on top of their work and preserve their hard-won privilege. And they'll have a sense of gratitude that's a wonderful attribute in an employee.

In 1998 Daniel Petre was running Microsoft in Australia, a big deal at the time. He wrote a book called *Father Time*, which was quietly revolutionary. Petre worked with Microsoft founder, Bill Gates, who was once famous for being a 'six-hour man'—taking only six hours between leaving the office and returning to work. But Petre argued against striving for a 60-hour work week, plus client functions, as you'd rarely have a moment with your children, even on weekends.

I remember scoffing and thinking, *Yeah, well, he's a former vice-president at Microsoft—he's loaded so he can take his foot off the pedal now.* I had a mortgage and a kid on the way. There was no way I was stepping back, or someone would have jumped directly into my footprints.

When his book went into a third edition in 2016, Petre said there was still a long way to go to make the working culture in Australia a little more 'father-friendly'. 'I think it's more acceptable to raise the issue now and to talk about going to spend time with your kids in general,' he told the *Record*'s book review.

The big problem is when young men join the workforce and they want to improve their job prospects, and then feel under pressure from older bosses to work longer hours. Unless CEOs understand the importance of fathers spending time with their kids, the problem will still be there. We need to reach out to these men and remind them that younger men shouldn't need permission to be better fathers.

Good communication between couples, and a willingness to break out of traditional patterns of housework and parenting roles, helps a lot, Petre says. 'I think women have for so long now been expected to take on the burden of childcare and domestic duties, so the first thing we need to do is split domestic duties fifty-fifty.'

You can image more than a few blokes having a whinge about that.

'It's also true that we've alienated stay-at-home dads: the community generally doesn't accept them, but perceives them as career incompetents or weird.'

Once, when I worked at ACP, the magazine monolith owned by Kerry Packer, my 'Batphone' rang. The Batphone was the internal phone system—evil yellow things that never carried good news. We each had our own number. I think, as editor-in-chief of *Woman's Day*, I was 142. Number 1 was Packer—and that was the number blinking on my phone now.

I picked it up, hands trembling. 'Hello?' I squeaked.

'Are you going to fuck up my perfectly good magazine?' boomed a familiar voice. It was like God, only more powerful, scary and likely to unleash punishments from above. 'Circulation's down. Get it up. Your job depends on it,' he yelled, then he hung up.

Rumour has it there was a prankster at work in the building, so I'll never really know—but the call definitely came from KP's Batphone.

The point is that it was more than a little stressful. And it's a very good thing that this type of old-school aggression, as well as the bullying, sexism and even sexual harassment, is increasingly a thing of the past. We're all better off for it.

What's the point of fighting tooth and nail to get up the ladder, grabbing at fatter and fatter pay cheques, when you'll probably die sooner than later, fat, bald, alcoholic and lonely?

•

American comic Marc Maron, around the same age as me, often does a set about not wanting to go to boring places and do tedious things, because he 'doesn't want to die doing that'.

This absolutely speaks to me. I don't know how long I have on the planet and time does seem to be getting short, so why would I waste it on pointless things?

Imagine feeling the sudden tightness in the chest at the world's most boring barbecue. 'At least I don't have to hear about gifted young Tarquin learning Mandarin at the age of three anymore,' you'll observe, as you flop gently into the potato salad.

Much as I have tried 'I don't want to die during that', is not seen as a good enough reason to avoid various gatherings and functions I don't want to go to.

Too many wonderful people I have known are dead already. The lesson here is simply: life is short, make the best of it.

Jeremy Bowdler was a big, loud, smart and funny man, passionate about two things: motorbikes and his daughters. His eldest was in the same primary school class as my daughter. Jeremy was the editor of bike mag *Two Wheels*. I had known him for years through mutual friends, and in 2007 became his boss when News Corp acquired his title.

We used to chat on his front porch when I picked my daughter up from his place after play dates, glad to be away from the office. He had the names of his daughters embroidered on the collar of his leathers, to remind him why he should make sure he made the next corner the safest possible, not the fastest. This was a man who could sling a superbike around Phillip Island not much slower than Casey Stoner.

In 2012, after a trip to the Middle East, where he rode bikes in desert storms, he felt a bit crook for a few weeks with a chest infection. It moved to his heart and he was put into a coma. He died at the age of 52.

Iain Shedden was a music writer for *The Australian*, and one of the most respected scribes around. You could write authoritatively about music if you'd toured on drums with the influential Australian punk pioneers The Saints. I'd ask him to tell me cool muso stories at the pub, and he'd oblige, laid-back, leather cool, always dressed in black, like a missing Ramone brother. He died in 2017, aged 60.

Caroline Roessler was one of my closest friends, and a godmother to my daughter. She was a hilarious, foul-mouthed, gold-hearted, hard-drinking, loving and loyal companion. She was also a brilliant editor, holding the *Australian Women's Weekly* together for years as associate editor. She was never able to take the spotlight, though; she was a lesbian, and that wasn't really very *Women's Weekly* at the time. Still isn't.

I poached her to edit the now-defunct *Notebook* magazine, and she did an amazing job attempting to keep it afloat, despite some unfortunate financial weights around its neck. It was the third time we'd worked together.

Once, my daughter, who was about five years old, asked 'Aunty Caroline' not to swear so much, because she might repeat a bad word at school. In response, sweet Aunty Caroline boomed: 'What are ya, a fuckin' parrot?'

She died of aggressive leukaemia in 2014, at 52, leaving behind her devastated partner, Donna, a dear friend to whom I owe so much.

Thankfully, Caroline, Jeremy and Iain did what they loved. None of them was what you'd call a corporate climber. But the simple horror of them being whisked away, so very suddenly, is a blunt lesson that we'd better make our lives and relationships valuable, deep and rich now, because we don't know when we'll be gone. And when we're on our own deathbeds, we can all be sure that it won't be our bank balance or the title on our business card we'll be thinking about.

•

The workplace has significant impact on mental health. Prolonged or excessive job stress is a significant risk factor for mental health problems. Beyond Blue reports that work stress accounts for 13 per cent of depression in working men.

And the factors that contribute to work stress read like a list of all the worst aspects of corporate life:

- high demands;
- low job control;
- work overload or pressure;
- lack of control and participation in decision-making;
- unclear work role;
- job insecurity;
- long working hours;
- bullying;
- poor communication; and
- inadequate resources.

Men's mental health has a massive impact on their family, friends and workmates. It also has a direct impact on the bottom-line performance of businesses and the economy more broadly, through absenteeism, reduced productivity and increased costs.

Stress is simply adrenaline and cortisol rushing through our bodies, which was necessary back in the day when we had to, say, rush to save Harold the village pig from the blaze engulfing our Neanderthal shack, but it's generally harmful to us now. Over time, being in a constant state of hormonal fight-or-flight alertness can:

- damage our immune system and heart;
- increase our chances of other serious health problems;
- reduce our life expectancy; and, horrifyingly . . .
- damage our sex lives.

The workplace of the future will require empathy and creativity. In fact, there's a very good chance your workplace will be your family home, and you'll spend your day working on projects, connected to your colleagues through digital technologies. You will not only have to interact with your workmates as equals, but be a loved and loving father and partner to those around you. You're going to be with them all day. The two-button rule certainly won't be required anymore. Well, not for a sales call, anyway.

As the enclaves of boys' clubs and brutal, aggressive sexist workplaces shrink, fertile areas are opening up for good men to stand up against the behavioural rules policing the still male-dominated boardrooms of Australia. Some of us are turning our backs on the office completely and starting our own businesses, using our creative skills to make meaning and income for ourselves.

We can help create the cooperative workplaces of the future, where every human being is equally valued and respected. And when we embrace the anti–Man Box values of empathy, creativity, compassion, communication and care, in both our lives and our work, we'll be happier and the world will be a better place.

That's not too much to ask, is it?

# Chapter 7

# THE VIEW FROM THE FUTURE

There once was a time when men were men and sheep were nervous, according to a lovely interspecies rape joke told freely to kiddies in 1970s New Zealand. In the near future, however, men will be truly able to be whoever they want to be. Sheep, and everyone else, will remain unmolested.

To be a man will simply mean you identify as a male person. It will no longer mean you have to spend your life in a ludicrous, agonising charade of pretend manhood. What emotions you choose to show won't matter. You can be loving, sad, scared, silly, chatty, caring and emotional, without anyone, male or female, stepping in and warning you that's not how a man talks, or what a man does.

In the future some people will be male and some people will be female, and some people will choose not to identify with either gender. Some people will be transgender. It won't matter. Your genitals and your personality traits will no longer be linked. The only judgement other people may make is: are you a good person or not?

No person may touch another person's body unless they are given enthusiastic consent. It will be a deeply entrenched, highly socialised rule. No one is allowed to make another person uncomfortable through sexual talk or touch. It will just be taboo. Sexual assault will be an even worse crime than it is now, and viewed as such right across society.

I'm not guessing. This is where we're going. The science is in. Get ready for a bizarre, unimaginable and hopefully wonderful future—and it's coming so fast that many of us are going to live to see it.

The only constant now, and in the future, is change. It's happening at an exponential rate. As technology springs ahead, society struggles to keep up, leaping into a digital world that is changing us before our very eyes, and in the process giving us opportunities we never imagined.

It's going to be a world where nanotechnology—tiny ($10^{-9}$ of a metre) self-replicating robots—is so yesterday. Picotech, apparently, is way too big at $10^{-12}$ of a metre small, but femotech—$10^{-15}$ of a metre small—is where it's at right now, I was reassured by Twitter the other day. Impossibly small and incredibly smart robots replicating at some subatomic level is scary.

Robots can open doors, dance, drive cars, jump over things, talk and have sex on our social media feeds. They can be snakes, bees, dogs, birds and fleas. Some are balls that can make other balls out of them-selves and roll around doing . . . whatever they can think of. They're blindingly fast. Already.

Rockets routinely fly into space and land again, right now, and no one's surprised. Personally, I'm delighted every time Elon Musk's Twitter feed shows me another extraordinary, fiery landing of dancing rockets. Human life seeding on another planet is a firming reality that may well be a choice for the younger of our generation.

Artificial intelligence, as we will see, is busy chewing up the working lives of men and women—and changing what a 'job' is, forever.

Social media has connected us like never before, allowing discussion and calling for societal change like never before. In the future, our digital connections with each other will deepen. Our searches and chats will happen in the blink of an eye—even by the blink of an eye. A head-up display will overlay and augment the real world we're walking through, beamed onto our retinas. A personalised Google will whisper gently and play music through the bones of our skulls in response to our requests by thought. The line between perceived and digital reality won't exist, and no one will care. Well, they may blink an eye.

Ideas will fan the flames of change higher and higher. Huge, like-minded communities, previously silenced by the centralised control of media, can now join hands and shout: 'No more!'

The murder in June 2018 of the beloved 22-year-old comedian Eurydice Dixon in a Melbourne park sparked first grief, then rage, then an open discussion, driven by social media, but which engaged main-stream media. Women, especially, are right to demand: 'What the fuck is wrong with men, that they keep killing everyone?' Why should women have to worry about where they walk, about what they're wearing, about calling a girlfriend when they get home? It's not as if there are packs of wolves out there, yet women are behaving as if there are. But the danger is their fellow human beings, men. Remember, more than one woman a week is killed in Australia by a man—men are dangerous.

The debate following Dixon's murder shone a light on the link between how men are socialised to behave and their violence. Society is seeing men for what they are, for what they have become, and we're turning away in disgust. A number of passionate pieces of journal-ism demanded that governments and institutions do more to help young men understand, and break away from, the shackles of enforced male behaviour.

Every death of a woman at the hands of a man should cause the question to be asked, louder and louder: what is wrong with men?

Last year, for my Fairfax Media column, 'Life on Mars', I inter-viewed the wonderful Rebecca Swift, Global Director of Creative Insights at Getty Images. Her eyes twinkled with delight as she told me how her twenty years of work in Getty's Insights division has gifted her a snapshot of what we're becoming as a society, before we know we're going there ourselves. It's like magic—and the magic is science.

This picture of our future is created by the images we search for online—it's that simple. Getty Images, and its fellow photo bank iStock, were searched more than a billion times in 2017. The idea is that what we're looking for online—for our websites and creative, our ads and EDMs—shows what we're looking for in our hearts.

Swift told me that in the last year there had been a 53 per cent increase in searches for 'gay dads', a 126 per cent increase in images of 'man meditation', and a 60 per cent increase in 'single father' searches.

'We've also seen an increase in searches for "men crying", which shows people are using words to try to get to the more emotional side of imagery,' Swift said. 'There's also been an increase in searches for quieter moments, men contemplating, thinking, meditating, not necessarily "doing".'

This is powerfully indicative of a growing trend away from traditional masculinity, and of a desire to portray men as being soft, caring, loving and emotional.

Swift is scientific in her approach. If she and her team are to be advising some of the world's largest companies, like Unilever, with brands such as Lynx and Gillette, on the future face of masculinity, which they do, they'd better be able to back up their claims.

'Our role is to look at the content and meaning of the imagery choices over time, beyond simply filling space on a page,' she said. 'The data gives you a rationale and an argument in a commercial environment. I can't talk about things I'm seeing in a "fluffy, fashion-y" way. The data gives me a foundation to build these strategies and ideas.'

And big business is listening.

'We came to the point of view that masculinity needs to be less stereotypical, through looking at men's mental health,' Swift told me. 'Men need to be able to show their emotions and discuss their feelings. So, understanding that, global brands are taking on male mental health and gender stereotypes as their mission.'

The beauty of Swift's work is that the pictures we choose to represent ourselves today are showing us a picture of who we will be tomorrow.

The legendary futurist Faith Popcorn—she's been doing it since 1974—founder and CEO of trend prediction shop BrainReserve, kicked off the Cannes Lions Festival of Creativity with a bold declaration: masculinity, as we know it, is changing. You can see the direction of her thought on the cover of the cool zine *The Future of Masculinity*, which features a colourful array of erect penises dressed up as lipsticks, flowers and ice-cream cones.

'We're going to be asking why men are in such pain, why they account for 70 percent of suicides, what the definition of new masculinity is, how we raise kids, where does gender fluidity come in,' she told *AdWeek*.

Popcorn sees a rejection of traditional male behaviour among younger men:

> They are finding their roles more equal, the division of labour more fluid. You'll see some indicators, like how street fashion is almost unisex. How men's cosmetics are on the rise. How men's facelifts are going up. I think men are realising subconsciously they have to work on their attractiveness. Men are more active in raising their children. Men are more active in preparing food for the household. Men, if they are living with a female partner, are working more in collaboration with them. This is just the beginning and advertisers should be paying attention.

Brands, she says, are already becoming unisex. Why is there men's deodorant and female deodorant? Men's and women's shampoos? A lot of these splits are artificial and created simply for marketing purposes. 'We're not saying that men are going to become women, either,' she noted. 'The truth is that we're at the very beginning of this work.'

Popcorn agrees on the impact of tech on gender roles. 'By the time we have figured [gender roles] out we're going to have crossed with robots and all of this will just be meaningless. I'm not kidding. I think the robotisation of the human body will happen.'

Brands of the future are going to understand that the marketplace is rejecting traditional gender roles. They're not going to be making his or hers products, but products for either and all shades in between.

It is the job of a successful advertiser to lead, not follow, the evolution of masculinity. Successful, purposeful, meaningful brands will 'futurise' their language and imagery, presenting men in a new light, as complex, nuanced, thoughtful and loving. Here, Popcorn's thinking neatly aligns with that of Rebecca Swift.

Brands should celebrate men as caregivers and for doing work at home. Give them the benefit of the doubt and accept that they want to be good partners and parents. They should support the 'left behinds', the men who are feeling scared, powerless or angry. Help men accept and resolve their own sense of vulnerability, confusion and fury. If brands are to express a point of view on social change—such as Qantas's support for marriage equality, and its focus on gender-equal language—they also have the same responsibility as formal media outlets to evoke only positive change.

Popcorn's last statement on the matter is this: 'Understand this is just the beginning of the revolution.'

·

When New Yorkers Bobby McCullough and Lesley Fleishman had a baby last year, they were uncomfortable with the idea of a doctor waving the baby in the air, shouting 'It's a boy' or 'It's a girl'. From that moment, they felt, the baby's identity would be prescribed, like a Hollywood script, by its sex.

'It would have just fucked us up,' says Bobby.

Ahead of their baby's birth, hospital staff were told: 'At minimum, do not describe the anatomy, or what you think the anatomy means, when this baby's born.'

'We definitely wanted to prevent them being gendered in any intense moment. And everybody was aware of that.'

Bobby and Lesley are not extremist nuts. They came to their position carefully and thoughtfully, and had their baby's best interests at heart.

At first, while not reinforcing gender was on their radar, the research they did during their pregnancy revealed small, hardcore groups of people raising 'theybies'.

A 'theyby' is a baby whose parents have decided to not reveal their sex. The parents use they/them pronouns for their children, with the lofty and—when you come to think about it, given how dangerous gender roles clearly are—admirable goal of creating a childhood free of pre-packed ideas about how a child should dress, act, play and be.

They knew their decision would be difficult and confusing and uncomfortable. What the hell do you tell Grandma? They had shared the baby's sex with family but wrote an email asking them to disregard that, saying 'the greatest gift you could give me would be practicing the pronouns'.

Bobby and Lesley spoke with their parents, trying to help them understand. It became a clear decision for the couple. 'We wouldn't tell anyone else how they should identify or who they should be or what they are,' says Bobby. 'I've definitely had thoughts, like, "why isn't everybody doing this?"'

Some nineteen years after I had my only child—who most definitely identified as female, loving pink tutus, Barbies, fairy parties and magic ponies, with the enthusiastic help of her parents—my views have shifted. If I had another child now, I'd consider the issue of gender very deeply. Even a couple of years ago I'd have thought the idea nuts. Now, not so much.

Just as I have no right to decide my child's religious beliefs (although if she ever decides to become a born-again Christian or a nun, there'll be some uncomfortable chats in the kitchen), I also have no right to assign them a gender identity before they've decided for themselves.

Grandparents really struggle with the idea of not knowing their grandchild's sex. I consider for a moment attempting to explain to my own parents: 'They're not a little boy or a girl . . . well, they are . . . but they aren't.' Not being able to bath or toilet a grandchild and not knowing their medical sex until some vague future moment would be more than a little confronting for many giddily excited grandparents-to-be.

Kyl Myers is the parent of a two-year-old theyby, Zoomer. She strongly agrees that when you choose to raise a theyby, you're becoming a change agent and sending a counter-mainstream message to the world. She told *The Cut*:

> I'm very tired of the heteronormative and cisnormative model. I'm very tired of the patriarchy. A part of why we are parenting like this is because intersex people exist, and transgender people exist, and queer people exist, and sex and gender appear on a spectrum, yet our culture loves to think people, all 7 billion of them, can and should be reduced to either/or.

That's not to say the fast-growing theyby movement has broad acceptance. One woman's sister had a meltdown at the baby shower over her decision to have a theyby.

> I think it was very disturbing for her on a very deep level, and she told me all of the ways she found it disturbing . . . how we're forcing our beliefs on other people. We could be damaging our child. She likened it to me having joined an extreme cult and trying to proselytize my religious beliefs.

When people ask a baby's sex, it can be argued, they might as well be asking if it is more likely to develop an eating disorder or die in a car crash. (Guess which goes with boy or girl . . .)

So many of the root causes of future health issues in people is not sex but gender. One of the most important determinants of a child's future, besides family wealth, is gender, given the way society is currently constructed.

There comes a moment in a theyby's life when they identify as having a gender. 'Around 3, our kid was just like, "I'm a girl," and we said, "Oh, yay, we've always wanted a girl. You're amazing. Welcome,'" says one anonymous theyby parent online.

She wasn't pushed there—she got there herself. The residue was not damage. Now thirteen, the girl shares her expanded view of gender with her peers. 'She thinks critically,' her parent laughs. 'Every queer and trans kid somehow manages to invite theirself over to our house.'

•

While we're still debating nature over nurture, and it cannot be denied that our hormones and genitals play a role in our sexual identity, there's a spreading understanding in the world that the act of being a man is a dangerous thing that strangles our emotions until we're dead-eyed killers.

And if we think we can run off to work and not have to think about what it is to be a man in the future, we'll have to think again. Because work—the thing that once defined us as men, our suits and high-vis uniforms announcing to the world that we were real blokes who did important stuff for money—will fail us in the future. We will no longer be able to justify a spreadsheet of bad behaviour just because we're the 'provider'.

If you were a man 10,000 years ago, the job market and career management wasn't particularly difficult to negotiate. There were three jobs to choose from. Hunting, gathering and procreation.

Personally, I would have put my hand up for procreation. The hunting seems more than a little dangerous, and the gathering . . . well, filling a leaf with berries all day seems like it would grow tiresome.

We'd all gather around the campfire in the evening and discuss our day.

'How was the hunting, Og?' I'd ask, hopefully.

'Oh, bit rough today,' he'd say. 'Three of our party got crushed by a woolly mammoth and one more was eaten by a thing with a lot of teeth. But we caught this yummy rat. How was the, uh, procreating?'

'You know, same old, just hanging around here all day with the women. It never gets any easier.'

'I feel your pain,' he'd nod sagely, staring into the flames.

Unfortunately, apart from a few rare exceptions, procreating just isn't a job these days. Not only have a huge chunk of the jobs that kept people in cosy lifelong employment gone, but millions more are about to disappear into a black hole created by technology. We have no idea how to replace them.

CEDA, the Committee for Economic Development of Australia, reports that 'almost 40 per cent of Australian jobs that exist today have a moderate to high likelihood of disappearing in the next 10 to 15 years'.

Once, in return for providing for a woman and their children, a man expected subservience from a woman. It was an unwritten contract. She cooked the meals, did the housework and looked after the kids. She kept herself attractive and submitted to regular sex with stoicism and no regard for her own pleasure. He looked after the finances, put the bins out on garbage night, and, if she was very lucky, sometimes might 'babysit' his own children.

But with the automation revolution removing the need for men to spend eight hours a day in a factory slinging crates on a diesel forklift, the traditional power, relevance and status of men is eroding. An automated system can do it much faster, at lower cost, 24 hours a day. Driverless trucks will plough the outside lanes, and delivery drones will fill the skies. Hyper-realistic avatars will replace actors in our films, TV and online content. You will order your coffee from a chatbot. When you shop, you'll just walk out of a store with your purchase and the amount will be automatically deducted from your account.

A US company called X.ai raised US$23 million in 2017 for 'Amy' and 'Andrew', bots that can operate as virtual personal assistants, helping you organise your professional life. If you email someone who works at X.ai today, they'll have the word 'human' in their email address, so you know you're talking to a real person, and not to their Amy or Andrew. That's pretty much the only way you can tell, however.

Technology, manufacturing, retail, fast food, construction, media, marketing, medicine, law, entertainment and a myriad of other major industries face unprecedented change with the automation revolution in the next fifteen years.

Consider medicine. IBM's artificially intelligent supercomputer Watson, famous for winning an exhibition match of the TV quiz *Jeopardy!* against legendary champion Ken Jennings, may now be the world's best doctor. 'Watson basically went to med school after it won *Jeopardy!*,' says Andrew McAfee, co-author of *The Second Machine Age*. 'I'm convinced that if it's not already the world's best diagnostician, it will be soon.'

Watson has all our medical knowledge at its digital fingertips, having analysed 605,000 pieces of medical evidence, 2 million pages of text and 25,000 training cases. It has also experienced 14,700 clinician hours. It's accurate, using the same intuitive algorithms that won it a game show—for which it learned 'all the world's general knowledge'— making it excellent at diagnosis. It's also consistent: it will return the same result for the same inputs every time. Inconsistency is a common flaw even among experienced doctors. Once up and running, built and trained, Watson costs virtually nothing to run. He is always available. He's everywhere. If you have a mobile phone or a computer, you can call on Dr Watson. Elementary.

So even a medical degree no longer guarantees a lifelong income.

Now consider the media. Not only has online allowed people to aggregate their own news feeds on social media from multiple free sources, they can now self-publish and become citizen reporters themselves. Phone footage appears in most TV news stories these days.

Even what seems the most very human of creative pursuits, writing a news story, is under threat. After an assistant business editor at Associated Press, Philana Patterson, taught a piece of software called Wordsmith to write finance stories, it had written more stories by the end of the year than she had produced across her twenty-year career. Most major news-gathering organisations now run some sort of software to help them report business, sport, education, finance, rural, political and lifestyle stories.

Translating even the simplest data means converting the loose guidelines a human reporter might follow into hard rules for an AI. 'To come up with a system to trigger the right type of story, we as reporters and editors and programmers have to figure out this stuff ahead of time,' Patterson told the *Nieman Report*.

Wordsmith can't make a reporter's instinctive, intuitive leaps, based on experience, to, say, investigate a company if its earnings don't seem to make sense, compared to that of its competitors. To work, the system requires a head-spinning set of parameters in data and metrics.

One side effect of such software, however, is that it can free reporters up to do what they do best: tell the big stories that matter, the stories behind the stories. With sharp new digital tools to dig meaning out of unprecedentedly massive amounts of data, journos are able to find nuggets of authenticity and emotion buried in the numbers. Sure, pork bellies are up, but why?

•

This requirement for human input, creativity and instinct is a clue to the shape of our future careers.

Consider fast food. An American company called Momentum Machines has built a burger-flipping robot that can produce 360 hamburgers an hour, one every ten seconds. It slices the toppings, such as tomatoes and pickles, immediately before assembling the burger, making it fresher than food assembled by humans. The robot can even create a unique blend of pork and beef in the patties, in response to a customer's wishes.

There are currently 150,000 fast-food workers in Australia.

Momentum Machines is aware that its machine will put people out of work. Indeed, Momentum's co-founder, Alexandros Vardakostas, has said: 'Our device isn't meant to make employees more efficient, it's meant to completely obviate them.' Momentum's marketing claims that its machine 'can do everything employees can do, except better'.

Momentum also issued a statement about the impact of machines on blue-collar jobs, attempting to make the argument that theirs will create more jobs than it destroys:

> The issue of machines and job displacement has been around for centuries and economists generally accept that technology like ours actually causes an increase in employment. The three factors that contribute to this are 1. the company that makes the robots must hire new employees, 2. the restaurant that uses our robots can expand their frontiers of production which requires hiring more people, and 3. the general public saves money on the reduced cost of our burgers. This saved money can then be spent on the rest of the economy.

•

Men are disillusioned and deeply suspicious of governments they see as having left them out to dry. The rise of right-wing politics can in large part be attributed to furious men sticking their middle fingers up at the system that promised them a dream, and then took it away.

Cult author Chuck Palahniuk lived life in a blue collar—he was a diesel mechanic—before he encountered the concept of 'dangerous writing'. A brand of minimalism taught by creative guru Tom Spanbauer, 'dangerous writing' means exploring what personally scares or embarrasses the author, in order to artistically and creatively express those fears more authentically and honestly. For Palahniuk, the result has been a fabulous body of work, including the novel *Fight Club*, which was made into a hit film starring Brad Pitt and Ed Norton in 1999.

Personally, I adored the film, and the book even more. When I finished reading it, I felt a moment of despair that I had no talent with the written word, compared to Chuck's intense, unique and unhinged prose, I flung my copy from a moving car. I soon bought another one.

When I was in my twenties I studied a Chinese martial art called Wing Chun Kung Fu for seven years. I learned in Sydney's grimy Surry Hills, on a wooden floor in a second-floor warehouse that wouldn't have been out of place in a Bruce Lee film. I have three terrifying full-contact bouts in the ring under my belt. This was part of my personal quest to prove my personal manhood and ensure my physical capabilities were at least the equal of every other man I encountered.

The core premise of *Fight Club* is that men meet in car parks and abandoned buildings and fight, shirtless and with bare knuckles, until one is beaten into submission. The anarchy and physicality of this idea appealed to me deeply when I first read the book. I loved the primal appeal of men fighting to prove themselves in the only way that really matters . . . to men. Who's the best, toughest, manliest man in the room, able to endure pain and enforce his will over another by the sheer power of his physicality? *Fight Club* lets you know.

Brad Pitt plays Tyler Durden. In a key scene in the film, after having beaten another man unconscious with his bare fists, he walks among his fellow fight clubbers, all blood, sweat, muscle and swagger, and delivers a menacing soliloquy, straight from Palahniuk's machine-gun pen, that perfectly describes the rage and hopelessness burning in men's hearts.

It's a rant about 'working jobs we hate so we can buy shit we don't need,' about how we've been duped into believing we'll all be rich and famous, and we're starting to understand we'll never be. 'And we're very, very pissed off.'

Palahniuk himself has noted that, at the time he was writing *Fight Club*, 'bookstores were full of books like *The Joy Luck Club* and *The Divine Secrets of the Ya-Ya Sisterhood* and *How to Make an American Quilt*. These were all novels that presented a social model for women to be together. But there was no novel that presented a new social model for men to share their lives.'

Most commentators believe *Fight Club* is about men fighting back against consumer society, which has repressed a core element of their masculinity: individual freedom. Palahniuk says his books are all essentially about one thing: 'a lonely person looking for some way to connect with other people'.

That's men.

•

The Industrial Revolution started around 1760. It was driven by the change from making things by hand to making things with machines. It's characterised by the production of iron and the use of steam power, and by the development of machine tools and steam-belching factories. Steamships and trains transported products to new markets. Textiles and trade cranked the world economy.

There was an explosion in both average income and population. Standards of living and health improved dramatically. Communications jumped forward with the electric telegraph in the 1850s. By 1870 a second wave of innovations, sometimes called the Second Industrial Revolution, sprang from large-scale steel manufacturing and advances in machinery in factories.

After steam power came the internal combustion engine, rail networks, electricity, medicine, plentiful food, flush toilets, cars and aircraft. Our modern lifestyles are built on more than 250 years of extraordinary change and evolution.

Now, we're at the start of the Automation Revolution, and it's only going to take fifteen years. Already it's becoming clear this is the first generation of men who will not be better off than their fathers.

And the jobs aren't coming back anytime soon. As AI grows in strength and machines continue to learn at an exponential rate, and as AI starts creating more AI, it will assume new roles and find new applications in almost every field of human endeavour.

But as the use of technology grows, so does the need for experts on that technology. For a marketing professional, for example, understanding how and when to use automation tools, and managing these, will be a big part of the industry in the future.

'These things don't destroy jobs, they just change what jobs are needed,' says Larry Kotch, co-founder of Brainbroker, a start-up business helping clients navigate technology and talent. Instead, he says it 'pushes people into the managerial, consultative and search function rather than the implementation function'. He means the thinking, not the doing.

There are really only two core human enterprises: coming up with ideas, and then bringing them to life in the real world. Take this book, for example. First, it was conceived as an idea, then it was written, edited, designed, printed and distributed.

The good news is that while machines will outstrip us in logic, they are absolutely hopeless at creativity and empathy. They can do bread, but they most certainly can't do circuses.

A man who knows all about circuses—Yaron Lifschitz, CEO of the Brisbane-based circus Circa—expresses the value of creativity beautifully. 'Art lifts our species, puts us in touch with our gods, encodes our memories and harnesses the collective imagination in service of our possibilities. The act of making art is inherently hopeful,' he said in an extraordinary speech on creativity at Currency House. No machine could have written that sentence.

How wonderful is it that creativity, empathy, humour, communication, storytelling—the things that make us human—are going to become the most sought after skills in the future job market?

Imagine a world where one of the most revered and highly paid jobs was caring for children with special needs. How extraordinary would it be if someone with the skills, empathy and patience to spend time with people in aged care—talking to them, listening, making friends with them and simply making them happy—enjoyed the same status as a CEO in 2018?

But if everything goes to plan, we'll all be free to explore every aspect of our uniquely human creativity anyway. In the future, the very notion of what it means to be a man will have changed dramatically. Our present discussion of the role of gender in our lives may well show that we're at the start of a profound change in society.

The concept of a 'universal basic income [UBI]', where everyone receives a decent, liveable income whether they work or not, could be the answer to the Automation Revolution's jobs massacre.

Stephen Hawking, who died in 2018, was not a fan, however. According to him, it all depends on whether the owners of the machines hold on to the wealth generated by the machines or not. Our response to the rise of the machines is going to be as critical to our future as the machines themselves. In 2015 he told a Reddit AMA ('ask me anything'):

> The outcome will depend on how things are distributed. Everyone can enjoy a life of luxurious leisure if the machine-produced wealth is shared, or most people can end up miserably poor as the machine-owners successfully lobby against wealth distribution.

And how would we fund a UBI? Perhaps by higher taxes of the super-rich, especially those whose money comes from capital, not labour, like Elon Musk.

The founder of SpaceX, Tesla electric cars, the Hyperloop high-speed transportation system and SolarCity says his vision is to change the world by reducing global warming through sustainable energy production and 'making life multi-planetary'. He's also a big fan of the UBI—even though, as the world's 54th wealthiest person, according to *Forbes*, he'd be paying for a good chunk of it.

'I think we will have to have some kind of basic income,' Musk told a forum in Dubai in 2017. 'I don't think we're going to have a choice.'

•

Should a UBI become a reality, the challenge for men obviously won't be about supporting a family or being a 'breadwinner'. It's going to be about finding a purpose, adding value and experiencing relevance. It's going to be about finding something interesting and worthwhile to do with your time. When your identity as a man doesn't come from your career or from your role as provider, where can it come from?

The concept of the technological singularity, in the AI world, is the moment when super-intelligent machines outstrip human beings in cognitive ability, and technology advances beyond our ability to foresee or control its outcomes. Imagine a super-intelligent computer, using all the world's data, at super speed, that is programmed to create an even better computer. And it never takes a break. It's very easy to imagine things getting out of control very quickly.

Revolutions in AI, genetics, nanotechnology and robotics will all contribute to the super-intelligent machines of the near future. And the singularity theory says self-creating computers will increase in intelligence exponentially, not incrementally.

Our fear of future machines has been a topic of entertainment for years. In director James Cameron's 1984 sci-fi classic, *The Terminator*, a global missile defence system called Skynet achieves singularity, becomes self-aware and instantly decides to wipe humanity off the face of the planet.

Futurists such as Ray Kurzweil, author of *The Singularity Is Near*, believe singularity will occur around 2045. If that happens, it may not be the end of the world—2045 could be the year we all become immortal.

The idea is that we will be able to download our full consciousness into a virtual reality, where we never get sick or die, where there's no poverty or war, and where we're free to indulge ourselves for digital eternity, doing whatever the hell it is we like in fully immersive, hyper-realistic fantasy worlds we may never want to leave.

In the more immediate, realistic, understandable near future, virtual reality as entertainment will become a huge industry, like film and gaming before it. It will create millions of jobs that don't exist right now. Someone will have to code and design the virtual worlds, and to create characters and storylines. Someone is responsible for the amazing sunset you're enjoying on your virtual beach. Someone gave your pina colada its amazing taste. (It's your fantasy and you'll drink what you like, right?)

In the service industries, a smiling, analogue human person is still going to be necessary for the social element of a transaction. People will become 'ambassadors' for the AI, helping their customers understand, and get the best possible service.

In a coffee shop, machines might make the coffee, take your order, charge you and clean up after you, but a person will guide you through the process. It might go like this . . .

'Good morning, Mr Barker, and welcome back to Robobaristas. We've got your usual ready, but we were wondering if you'd like to try our new Robovanillachocafrappamocchachino? It's very popular. Here's a taster . . . Oh, I see you spat that on the floor. No problem. We're cleaning that now . . . Well, here's your triple espresso. Have a wonderful day. We hope to see you tomorrow!'

The person in the room can devote all their time to making the experience warm, human and fun—maybe even better than when they had to do all the distracting coffee grinding and milk steaming.

Machine training is another field where there will be a jobs boom. Machines need to be shown the best way to do things, given parameters and so on. People will still need to service and calibrate the machines, and ensure the programs that run them are up-to-date and glitch-free.

Entrepreneurs will be free to concentrate on their creative ideas, without having to worry about manufacturing, supply chains, marketing and sales. The AI systems can do all that. One person will be able to create, build, test and sell a product where once it took an entire corporation.

Professor Ross Harley, dean of the University of New South Wales Art and Design program, says a 'creative mindset' is needed 'to respond in productive ways to the decline in many familiar 20th century blue and white-collar jobs'.

With phenomenal advances in the digital technologies that enable us to create, collaborate and communicate across a room or across the world, the creative industries are thriving. In NSW, the creative industries now directly employ more than five per cent of the workforce, they pay 18 per cent more than the average wage, and they are growing twice as fast as other sectors.

. . .

The idea that we are limited by access to local factories and their conventional production lines is increasingly redundant. In our highly mobile, highly networked, globalised economy new jobs, roles and services are being created everyday [sic] by innovative, imaginative people who are asking just the same question we continuously pose in art and design schools: 'What if things were different?'

Australia is in the box seat for creativity-led success. A study by the Australia Council found that 85 per cent of Australians think the arts make life more meaningful; 66 per cent think the arts have a big impact on the development of children; and almost half of all Australians, 48 per cent, participate in creating art themselves.

With this rise in public interest in the arts and creativity, Professor Harley says, governments are seeking to foster Australia's creative engagement with a globally connected and disruptive world, and are recognising the role creativity can play in rethinking the way things are done.

We do need to step back from the kind of blinkered economic rationalism that has long linked technical skills to specific jobs that may not endure. Instead, we need to infuse creativity and 'design thinking' into curricula from our primary schools up.

In a rapidly changing world, it will be those hard-to-define attributes like creativity, originality, critical insight, empathy and foresight that best enable us to protect our prosperity by fostering new industries as traditional ones decline.

Creativity. Originality. Critical insight. Empathy. Foresight. Unfortunately, you won't find any of these traits in the Man Box. You never hear: 'Wow, dude, you're just so creative and empathetic. You're the man!'

The future is telling us that it's time to reimagine what it means to be a man. Toughness, stoicism, bravery, not showing any feelings and not communicating won't cut it in the future job market. So men will be shut out from the key career currency—creativity—simply because they are men being men, as they were taught.

Of course, there are many exceptions—there are a lot of smart, creative, open, caring, empathetic men out there. It's just that we need a lot more.

Worldwide employment figures and the careful brilliance of the futurologists leave us in no doubt that traditional male jobs are disappearing forever. What it means to be a man is changing forever. The rise of Donald Trump, Pauline Hanson and others of the far right is a window into the thinking of angry men: *The system screwed me—so screw the system.*

To cope with the future, and to get reward, joy and relevance from our work, men have to change the way they think about job-robbing technology. The Automation Revolution is not a disaster, it's an opportunity.

We will be unfettered from the social rules that govern our behaviour. We will no longer have to pretend to 'be men'. We'll suddenly be free to be who we really are. So if future tech forces us into being creative, open, empathetic and communicative, then let's recognise that that's a good thing.

Don't get angry—get creative.

# Part Three

# BEING A BETTER MAN

# Chapter 8

# FOOD IS LOVE

If we were to visit a camp of our simian forebears, around 400,000 years ago, they would not be huddled around a fire because they had not discovered it yet. Our friends Og the Hunter and Phil the Procreator lived only 10,000 years ago, but they lived in comparative luxury, being able to burn things before they ate them.

The scientists are still proving and disproving each other's theories (i.e. arguing) about when humankind mastered fire, but between 300,000 and 400,000 years ago seems a decent stab. It probably went something like this . . .

Our ancestors were friendly folk and let their pigs wander through the basic structures they used to shelter from the rain, as well as from enraged woolly mammoths and starving sabre-toothed tigers. (Even woolly mammoths weren't immune to the influence of proving they were tough men, by the way. A great majority of fossils are young males, which means they were the idiots showing off and doing stupid stuff like jumping in tarpits.)

One day there was a thunderstorm and a prehistoric shack got hit by lightning and burnt down. The unfortunate family pig was trapped inside and ended up baking in the embers for some hours.

Taking our ancestors' tiny frontal lobe, oversized jaw and total lack of language skills into account, the spirit of their conversation was probably something like this:

'Good grief, Barry. I think Harold the pig got caught in the fire. I can't believe he's gone.'

'I loved him too. Um . . . Simon, what's that unbelievably delicious aroma?'

'I don't know . . . but it's like nothing I've ever smelled before!'

Some hours later . . .

'*Burp!* That was incredible! Who knew if you burnt things they tasted better! Let's do it again! From now on this delicious stuff shall be known as Harold!'

'Hmm . . . not sure about that. What about bacon?'

'Brilliant! We invented bacon!'

Together: 'Yay, bacon! Let's use that fire stuff to make some more!'

This moment changed the path of human history, and turned us from plant-eating apes into omnivorous *Homo sapiens*, proudly taking our place at the top of the planet's food chain.

Before the advent of fire, cooking and bacon, we simply ate raw vegetable matter, like the great apes still do. Because there weren't many kilojoules in the nuts, berries and leaves, we had to eat a lot of them to stay alive. We were eating all day, putting away as much as possible, and very probably had a large, hard distended gut, like a cow's.

All the foraging, chewing and wandering around with a huge belly took a lot of energy, as did digesting roots and leaves. We were about as neurologically developed as our diets would allow us to be. But when everyone started burning their dead cows and making burgers, something incredible happened.

Cooking food, especially meat, makes it much easier to chew and digest. It releases more kilojoules than raw food. Tasty energy bombs of meat supercharged our brains. And the brain is a total energy hog, using 20 per cent of the energy we consume, despite being only 2 per cent of our body mass. If a gorilla were to grow a brain as big as ours he would have a really huge head, and would have to eat for another two hours a day—on top of the nine he already spends eating.

And because we didn't have to spend all day foraging, we spent more time socialising around the newfangled campfire. We lived longer, and more of us lived. And instead of chewing our food with our huge jaws, we used our bigger brains to make tools to cut our food. We came down from the branches, abandoned the morphology that allows apes to swing through the trees, and started sleeping on the ground, our beloved fires keeping the things that might snack on us away.

Our faces changed shape, and speech and language developed. It is safe to say that cooking literally made us human.

If our ancestors had remained vegans, we'd all be gym-lean but, ironically, way too stupid to work out how to make tofu.

A leading proponent of the theory is the Professor of Biological Anthropology at Harvard University, Richard Wrangham. 'When our ancestors first learned to cook, the initial impact of the extra energy would have been they would have had more babies than they did before,' he says. 'The babies were able to survive better, and the adults had more regular menstrual cycles and put more energy into their immune systems.'

Food is still the foundation of our families, communities and cultures. Food creates warmth, nourishment and conversation. Food, love and sex are all wrapped around each other, in both our prehistoric brains and in every element of our popular culture.

•

Being able to cook is an essential skill for men. Not only do you lose weight, save money and eat much better food than UberEats delivers, you're using your creativity, empathy and communication skills, you're being nurturing and unselfish, you're being vulnerable, and you're showing love—all the opposite of what's in the Man Box.

There's no doubt an angry incel would be much more successful with the opposite sex if he turned off the computer and started
chopping an onion.

Women love a man who can cook. They love watching a man cook.
They find it sexy. There's no doubt it's hot in the kitchen. 'Men look sexy
when they cook, regardless of what they're making,' says Dr Maryanne
Fisher in *Psychology Today*.

> There is a very close relationship between love, sex, and food. It's
> hard to feel romantic if you're starving, On the other hand, when
> you first meet someone and are completely infatuated, often you
> lose your sense of hunger, our bodies produce a chemical stimulant,
> phenylethylamine (PEA) and norepinephrine. They make our bodies
> feel alert, alive, giddy, excited and many of us lose our appetite. The
> human need for food and sex are basic, part of the foundation of
> our nature.

I'm going to focus on cooking now because it's the domestic task I find
most pleasurable. Apart from that, it's a wonderful skill that makes all
men better men. I don't know one man who has learned to cook who
doesn't adore the process and the joy it brings, to him and to others. All
human beings love praise, and most men are suckers for it. We are easily
delighted when women tell us we've done a good job.

There may well be an element of 'look at me' about men stirring
a risotto with determined concentration. It's in our genes. When
our primate relatives, chimpanzees, are campaigning for the coveted
position of alpha male in the family group (I believe the collective noun
for chimps is a 'whoop', but I can't bring myself to use it seriously), they
play with babies and hold them aloft, like human politicians. They're
sending a signal to the females: 'Look, I didn't kill the baby!'

They're also very attentive and domestic, making sure the females
know what nice guys they are. Because the alpha male gets the pick of
the females and all the sex he wants. That's a big reward for being the

alpha. He gets all the girls and his strong genetic material is passed on to the next generation. There's a link not only between sex and food, but between sex and other domestic work as well.

We may be well into the 21st century already, but men are just not pulling their weight at home. We're not doing it because we don't have to. We get away with it when we can. The reason men talk of 'baby-sitting' our own children is simply because we do it so rarely. We ignore washing and cleaning until someone else does it—a woman. Somehow, work around the house—doing what is necessary to keep us comfort-able, fed, clean and clothed—is still seen as women's work.

Data from the 2016 Census shows that the typical Australian woman spends between five and fourteen hours a week doing unpaid housework. Men are doing less than five. The time and mental stresses of housework have real-world and long-term economic consequences for women's employment. Two children can knock a woman out of the workforce for a decade, reducing the total of her lifetime earnings. One in three Australian women retires without any superannuation at all.

When we are single, housework is divided most equally by gender. But when a woman starts living with a man, her housework time goes up, and his . . . well, we're busy on the couch.

The issue is just not the unequal division of labour but also the way caring for children means women somehow have to do almost every-thing else as well. Even women who work full-time remain responsible for arranging child care, checking homework and lunches, wiping vomit, feeding puppies and listening to emotional anecdotes about a mean girl at ballet practice.

The key to the shackles that tie women to the washing machine is in the hands of men. We must simply do our share. Then our partners might be less stressed. They might be able to earn more. Even more importantly, they might realise their potential, which can only make them happier people.

This is why women think that a man who can cook, and who pulls his weight around the house and with the kids, makes an attractive partner. It speaks to his values as a human being. The level of a man's domesticity can be seen by women as a demonstration of his 'goodness'.

There's no doubt that a man who's great around the house is also going to have a great time in bed. She's less tired, for a start. But, at its extreme, the idea of rewarding men with sex for work around the house is more than a little icky.

Feel relieved if you've been fortunate enough to avoid the idea of 'choreplay' so far in your life. The idea took root after an opinion piece in the *New York Times*, in 2015, by Facebook COO and founder of leanin.org, Sheryl Sandberg, encouragingly entitled 'How Men Can Succeed in the Boardroom and the Bedroom':

> Research shows that when men do their share of chores, their partners are happier and less depressed, conflicts are fewer and divorce rates are lower. They live longer, too; studies demonstrate there's a longevity boost for men and women who provide care and emotional support to their partners in later life.

Then came the zinger: 'Couples who share chores equally have more sex.' Sandberg cited a study by researchers Constance T. Gager and Scott T. Yabiku, called 'Who Has the Time? The Relationship Between Household Labor Time and Sexual Frequency'. Sandberg suggested that instead of buying flowers, a man pick up a load of laundry. 'Choreplay,' she said, 'is real.'

This idea flew around the internet and somehow became flipped on its head. It was suddenly about making the man do more housework by rewarding him with treats—sex—instead of the idea that sharing the load could be the catalyst for a better relationship.

I abhor the idea of choreplay. I want to be wanted for me, like every sane person on the planet, not because I took the bins out. Also, the idea that women are more interested in a clean house than in hot sex is clearly utter rubbish. But only a slight step back from that is the truth that balanced relationships, where both work and play are shared, are more rewarding, great for our mental health and memories, great for kids and . . . more sexy.

There is no doubt food is where the love is. (But not 'made with love'. I prefer my food cooked with good produce as well as a loving attitude, sure, but nowhere have I read a recipe where love is an actual ingredient.) Our brains give us pleasure rewards for doing things which keep the species alive and, wonderfully, eating is one of them. Life and pleasure come from sex, and life and pleasure come from food. When you cook for someone, you're offering the gift of another day of life, through sustenance. And by making that food as delicious as possible, you're giving another human a gift of the pleasure of eating.

(To be clear, before you hit the kitchen, make sure you're pulling your weight with child care, laundry, cleaning, bed making and shopping. Only then can you put on your private cooking show.)

The very act of cooking, thinking in advance about what you're going to make, being sure the people you're cooking for will like it, the purchasing, the prep, the execution and the eating—they're all profound acts of love.

The kitchen is the heart of every home. There's simply nothing more convivial than sharing a glass of wine (come to think of it, we can have one each) with someone you truly love, as things simmer on the stove and roast in the oven. Smells fill the warm air and you know the next few hours are going to be devoted to the deep and simple pleasures of eating and talking.

The act of cooking makes time for conversation. And conversation is a key ingredient in your family's successful relationships which is a key to mental health and happiness.

The number of words that fill a house can make the difference between a child's success and failure in life. Two intrepid education researchers, Dr Betty Hart and Todd Risley, conceived an amazing study. They recorded every word spoken in the homes of 42 families, professional, working-class or welfare-dependent, for an hour a month, for three and a half years following babies from before they could talk.

As the researchers painstakingly transcribed and tallied every word, they came to an extraordinary realisation. By the age of three, the 'professional' children had heard 45 million words. The 'working-class' kiddies had heard 26 million words, and the poor welfare kids just 13 million.

The 30-million-word advantage the richest children had over the poorest meant they were able to learn more, increase their language skills and build neural pathways on their own. The more words a child hears, the more their brains grow.

And the words the professional children heard were a lot nicer, too. They got six positive 'affirmations' an hour, and one negative 'prohibition'. Working-class children got two positives to one negative, while the welfare children were slammed, hearing two negative comments for every one positive.

Children mimic their parents' language, so by the time they started school, the affluent children, with their big, shiny vocabularies, had learned all the language skills and traits that made their parents rich. And the poor kids, short on verbal ability and encouragement, were doomed to repeat their mums' and dads' failure.

So talking in the kitchen, and everywhere else, is critical. If, like me, you're not in the 'rich' category, you can still give your kids a rich-kid advantage simply by talking to them.

But there's no point in learning to cook just to attract women, like some pick-up artist. You can't fake the love, care, thought, practice and effort involved. That's why it's attractive to women. It's the authentic you at work.

Here's what being a man who cooks says about you:

1. You're sensitive. You are showing you care with your work, time and thought. You want to make your partner happy and spend time with her.

2. You're creative. Artistic people are great at expressing themselves, and you can show you're an exceptional human being with a creative soul through your food.

3. You understand success. Cooking is about completing a project successfully, planning, coordinating, using multiple skills and bringing an attractive dish together on time.

4. You're a grown-up. If you exist on chocolate milk and cheeseburgers, she's going to work out you're not a sophisticated, worldly person, open to other ideas, cultures and experiences.

5. You're interesting. Being able to cook makes her wonder how you learned to make such wonderful food, when and who for. She'll want to get to know you better and become part of your food life story.

6. You're skilled. Great chef skills are amazing to watch. She'll love seeing you reduce an onion to dice with a flash of steel, or deglaze a pan in a drama of hiss and flame.

7. You're sensual. As you touch and taste with fingers and mouth, she's going to innately understand you're good with your hands and comfortably connected to your sensual self.

Our guitar face may be the same as our sex face, but you could argue that the grimaces and moans of pleasure that come from eating are also very close.

Lipstick shouts attraction simply because the flash of red is supposed to mimic the flush of female sexual arousal in our male brains. Both eating and sex involve all our senses. They both involve taking things into spaces in our wet, warm bodies. They both involve hunger, savouring, joy and, ultimately, satisfaction.

So if cooking is so wonderful, why aren't more men popping on an apron and whipping up a pineapple upside-down cake?

There are lots of things barring us from the joys of the kitchen, just because we're men.

We don't like taking direction. Men like to pretend we know how to do things, because not knowing is a sign of weakness. That's why we don't like asking for directions. Recipes are directions.

We also don't like the unfamiliar. If we're not good at something, men don't like to do it. And we're terrified of being judged incompetent if we do have a go. Closely related is a fear of failure. This is why I never play golf.

We're often reluctant to commit the time. Or the effort.

And even though, at the top of the rock 'n' roll world of celebrity chefs, it's a sausage party, with Gordon Ramsay and Heston Blumenthal and Jamie Oliver and Rick Stein and a thousand other men running the world's leading commercial kitchens, somehow cooking is still seen by some men as a little too . . . feminine.

In fact, the world of professional food is a pretty standard man's world. Many chefs are ravaged by drug and alcohol abuse. Commercial kitchens are bubbling with anger, aggression, violence and sexual assault. The brutal hours and stress routinely ruin minds and lives. But it doesn't have to be like that at home.

•

Cooking is basically an exercise in good project management. It involves procuring the best tools and produce, utilising the best techniques and consulting experts, and the aim is delivering a quality product, on budget and on deadline. These are things in which even the most 'manly' of men consider themselves expert.

There are basically two phases in learning to cook. Like learning a martial art or high-performance driving, there's a boring bit at the start where you have to hit the heavy bag for ages, or walk the track putting out cones. There's no avoiding that learning to cook requires a bit of time and effort. But you can make it rewarding and fun, and you're upskilling yourself for life.

Try books like *How to Cook Everything* by Mark Bittman, or *I'm Just Here for the Food* by Alton Brown, for basic recipes and pointers.

First, you need to get your equipment sorted. This is a fun part.

Great cooking equipment is wonderful precision technology, just like the best in watches, racing bikes, cars, audio and computer tech. It's a specialist field, but once you're into it, the equipment is as sexy and drool-worthy as what you'd see through the window of a Porsche dealership.

Like everything in life, get the best quality you can afford, and you'll be rewarded for years after you've forgotten the price.

Get a big, heavy, double-sided wooden chopping board, the bigger the better. Google how to look after it. Look after it. Don't ever put a wooden chopping board in the dishwasher. Only use one side for garlic and onions.

Cooking is one of the only areas in life where you're actively encouraged to play with knives. Get a knife made for chopping, so you can learn good knife technique. Knife skills are critical because speed and precision are critical to a successful, scrumptious spread. To do that super-fast chopping thing chefs do, flashing the blade along the back of their fingers as a bunch of parsley becomes . . . chopped parsley, the knife needs to be curved to rock on the board. Get a slicing knife, for carving and frenching cutlets, and slicing chicken. Maybe you'll need a fruit knife and a paring blade. And anything else you like the look of. Most good knives come in a block with everything you need, or with a magnetic strip that attaches to your kitchen wall and looks cheffy cool.

When I started cooking, some twenty years ago, I got a set of Global knives, which look brilliant. They're crafted in one piece and have steel handles. The brand's website says encouraging things about samurai swords; a thousand years of Japanese sword-making history are going into a weapon for you to chop spuds.

Pots and pans are the same. The heavier the better. Weight means there's a big chunk of metal on the bottom, which will distribute heat more evenly. Understanding the dynamics and properties of heat is also critical to cooking. It's also better to cook with gas because you can change the heat more quickly. It's a saying for a reason.

My personal choice was the French brand Le Creuset (for which you are fully excused in muttering 'Wanker'). They're a bit rough on the wallet, no doubt, but chunky enough to be a decent weapon in the event of a home invasion. They're also forged in one piece and come in an array of funky colours—blue, pink, green, yellow, red, cream: an ice-cream parlour of culinary chic.

I am thoroughly ashamed to say that, at a time in my life when I earned more than a struggling writer, I had a full set of cream Le Creuset and—in matching cream, darling—a toaster, jug, espresso machine and cake mixer by the old-school American brand KitchenAid.

'There is no object you own that is anything like your kitchen knife,' says British food writer Tim Haywood. 'Think about it—eight inches of lethally sharp, weapons grade metal lying on your kitchen table, possessing the same potential for mayhem as a loaded handgun—yet it is predominantly used to express your love for your family by making their tea.'

The winner of *MasterChef Australia* in 2010, Adam Liaw, owns a $1500 Japanese yanagiba, but his favourite knife, for its balance and fit, cost only $400.

Former *Sydney Morning Herald* food critic, former host of the *Gourmet Farmer* TV show and now the owner of the Fat Pig Farm in Tasmania, Matthew Evans, loves a knife made from an old saw blade with a handle from a deer antler. 'The maker decides on who the knife suits only after it's forged,' he says. 'The whole thing is a work of art,' he told the ABC. 'Holding it, you can feel the energy of the blacksmith pounding on the steel.'

•

Find a few recipes you like and learn them. Try Jamie Oliver or Curtis Stone. I had the pleasure of working professionally with food publisher

Donna Hay, a very smart, dynamic, canny and driven business woman, She is also a brilliant marketer and peerless food stylist and cook. Her recipes offer a lot of bang for your time and buck. We used to talk about 'special made simple' as a core element of the brand.

As you practise, you'll learn how much oil to glug into a pan, how hot that pan should be, how you like your onions chopped, how lots of tasty things start with a base of onion, garlic, vegetables and herbs sautéed in a pan, how to tell when a steak is cooked by feel, when the pasta is ready, how to steam rice. All the basic stuff.

You reach the second level when you've spent enough time in the kitchen to know how much a tablespoon of something is by looking, how much of any given seasoning you like, what goes with what. You taste constantly, adjusting as you go, your palate telling you what to adjust for perfect balance. You can upgrade or dumb down recipes to your personal taste. It's kind of a magical moment, like when you realise you can ski properly, or have mastered barre chords on the guitar.

Great cooking isn't about complicated technique, it's about letting wonderful produce be its best on the plate, and treating it with respect and simplicity. Fresh-caught fish needs only oil, lemon juice and salt. Lamb loves rosemary. Chocolate loves chilli. Duck loves orange.

There are few things more satisfying—and, I would suggest, more attractive—for a woman than telling her, on a weekend morning, what you're cooking her for dinner. Take her on a leisurely walk or drive to a local market and buy the freshest produce you can, stuff with dirt on it that's straight from the farm. Try to buy things that have had a happy life. Have lunch. Pick up dessert and wine. Meet in the kitchen, freshly showered, and talk as you cook. Guaranteed best date ever.

Like most men, I have a childlike fascination with fire. I once shoved aside a maître d' at a restaurant who was fiddling ineffectually with a huge blazing fire. I just had to stoke it and lay the wood in the correct manner.

A kettle barbecue can be a wonderful addition to a man's quiver of food tricks. My partner bought me my second kettle barbecue for

Christmas a few years ago, and jokes that it's 'the gift that keeps on giving'. And they work by fire.

A kettle barbecue uses indirect heat, meaning the coals are in piles at each side, not directly under the food. With the lid on, they heat the air as hot as a kitchen oven. The unique and delicious barbecue flavour comes from the meat juices squirting on the coals as it cooks, making smoke and steam that flavours the food and keeps it moist.

The other great thing about the kettle is that, as you cook, the aromas blast out the top of the barbecue; by the time you're ready to serve, your rosemary lamb or lemon garlic chicken is pretty much all your guests can think about.

If you really want to push the boundaries when you get expert, consider a slow-cooking smoker. These require what can be days of planning—and you have to wake at 3 am to light the fire on game day—but the effort is well worth the praise you'll get for your twelve-hour pork belly.

Australia boasts a food culture influenced by the cuisines of migrants from all over the world, and a cornucopia of fresh produce from the sea and land, which is the envy of the world.

It wasn't always so. 'No other country on earth offers more of every-thing needed to make a good meal, or offers it more cheaply than Australia; but there is no other country either where the cuisine is more elementary, not to say abominable,' said the clearly judgy Edmond Marin la Meslée, founder of the Geographical Society of Australasia, in 1883.

Mind you, the early explorers weren't the sharpest of chaps. On arriving in Australia and meeting Aborigines, English seafarer William Dampier observed, massively incorrectly, that 'the Earth affords them no food at all. There is neither herb, root, pulse nor any sort of grain for them to eat that we saw.'

After World War II, factories started making refrigerators, not bombs. By 1955, around 73 per cent of metropolitan homes had a fridge. In the 1950s and '60s, Australians were travelling to Europe by boat and tasting contemporary, sophisticated cooking for the first time.

TV delivered ads for processed food brands, snack and fast foods. And the Greeks and Italians arrived with their zucchinis, capsicums, eggplants, olives, anchovies, artichokes, garlic and chilli. They could only find olive oil on the chemist's shelves. They began the slow and painful process of convincing white-bread Australia that there was a better way to eat than meat and three boiled veg. No wonder generations of kids hated vegetables.

McDonald's, Pizza Hut and Kentucky Fried Chicken arrived in the 1960s and '70s.

Slowly, after a generation, 'contemporary Australian' cooking emerged, a joyous fresh fusion of Thai, Chinese, Japanese, Malaysian, Vietnamese, Indian, French, Greek, Italian, African, Lebanese, Mediterranean, Middle Eastern and Portuguese food, to name but a few. Our young, smart, colourful, multicultural food perfectly matches our brilliant, diverse, unique society.

Today, thankfully, people are understanding the value of sustainable, organic artisanal produce, for better health, taste and environmental impact. The suburbs are bristling with bearded bros who make beer, cider and whisky. You can find handmade cheeses and breads, cured meats and organic vegetables in farmers' markets and community gardens everywhere. The reaction against processed food and factory farming has seen us growing our own food on balconies and backyards once again. We're understanding the pleasures of picking our own herbs and fresh tomatoes. Bees buzz in our hives and chickens croon in backyard coops.

Those of us still eating meat want the animals that lay down their lives to become our dinner to have lived the best lives possible, in sunshine and fresh air, gambolling in wide open spaces, before the inevitable unfortunate moment.

It's a great time to start cooking.

•

It makes sense to work smarter, not harder, so great cooks make the best use of their time and effort.

Here's a favourite recipe of mine that originally came from Jamie Oliver, but this is my interpretation. It delivers amazing flavour bang, it looks incredible and you only need basic kitchen skills to pull it off. The sauce is the hero—sweet, zingy, sour, caramel, fishy, aromatic, thick and sticky.

It's so good I've had people refuse to believe I cooked it.

# Crispy-skin Salmon with Caramel Tamarind Sauce

## Ingredients
vegetable oil
1 knob fresh ginger
soy or tamari (in the Asian section at your supermarket)
tamarind paste (in the Asian section at your supermarket)
fish sauce (in the Asian section at your supermarket)
brown sugar
cucumber
baby salad greens
vietnamese mint
olive oil
one salmon fillet per person, skin on
lime

## Method
### The Sauce
Make the sauce first. Heat a blob of oil in a pan—it's hot when it looks like it's rippling. Skin and grate a knob of ginger the size of your thumb, and cook it off in the hot oil.

When the ginger is just turning golden and you can smell it in the air, add half a cup or so of soy, which will sizzle and deglaze the pan (get all the good sticky bits off the bottom). Then add a tablespoon of tamarind paste, and a tablespoon of fish sauce. Dissolve half a cup of brown sugar in the hot liquid and let it simmer. Now taste it. Is it too sweet? Salty? Sour? Balance it by adding more sugar or tamarind or soy until it tastes just how you want it. You won't believe the complexity of flavour just five ingredients can generate.

As the sauce simmers down, it will become thicker and stickier. Turn it off when it's the consistency of bottled barbecue sauce.

### The Salad
Pre-prepare your salad once you've done your sauce. Simply slice the cucumber thinly on the bias to make some elegant strips. Who needs their good knife and some skills now? Tear up the greens and mint leaves and have everything ready to hit the plate.

### The Salmon
Rub your salmon with olive oil, salt and pepper. Do it with your hands. Heat a non-stick pan until it's scarily hot. Put the fish in with the skin side down, and keep it moving with some tongs. After just a couple of minutes you'll notice a line of pink-white cooked flesh creeping up into the fillet. When it's a third of the way up, flip the fish and sear the top for a minute. Let it sit for five minutes out of the pan. It'll keep cooking, and when you fork it you should be able to flake off delicate petals of pink flesh that melt in your mouth.

### The Plating
Arrange the salad: cucumber strips at the bottom, greens on top. Be careful and delicate. Put the fish on the side and, with a teaspoon, drizzle the dark, pungent sauce over it. Squirt with lime juice to cut the sauce.

•

This is how food should be—simple, healthy, delicious, fresh, easy. It is guaranteed to blow your friends and family away. (If it doesn't, tweet me.)

To be able to cook connects you directly with the human joys of nurturing, caring for and loving other people. It requires empathy and creativity. If you're having fun in the kitchen with the people you love, domestic violence is probably a long way away. Cooking is an antidote to what's in the Man Box, banishing toughness, stoicism, control and aggression. It's difficult to sexually objectify a woman you're making a risotto for. This is completely different from thinking your partner is hot, and wanting to be romantic and sexy with her. That's actively encouraged. Food will always play a central role in our sex lives.

You'll be healthier when you're eating less processed food. And you cook to your own taste point, so your food is always the best. You save money on home delivery and restaurants. You give your friends and lovers the gifts of pleasure and nourishment. What's not to love?

Gentlemen, you're a better man with a better life if you can cook.

Your time starts . . . now!

# Chapter 9

# SUPER MAN

'With great power comes great responsibility,' said Voltaire—and also Peter Parker's Uncle Ben, in the 2002 movie *Spider-Man*. Winston Churchill, Lord Melbourne, and both Teddy and Franklin D. Roosevelt are also claimed to have said it. In French it's *noblesse oblige*, the unwritten obligation of people from a noble ancestry to act honourably and generously to others.

As hardly any of us in modern Australia are, thankfully, from noble ancestry, perhaps a more apt modern translation might be: 'Don't be a dick.'

Men are blessed with amazing, beautiful, powerful bodies. At our best, we have explosive strength and amazing stamina. We were built to chase things for lunch across the grassy plains, fight the beasties that wished to lunch on us and our families, climb trees to see how far away the water is, and lift the rock that fell on our unfortunate eighth child. (She was never as good at cave painting again but will still pick berries if pointed at a bush. Good result.)

There is no doubt men can run the fastest, for the longest distance, lift the most, jump the highest, throw the heaviest thing, compared to women. We won the genetic lottery, and nature gifted us the power to be at the top of the food chain on the planet—and among our own species.

But when you're the strongest, you must also be the softest. When you can batter, bruise, break and kill, you must also be gentle. With great power, there is indeed great responsibility.

Here's another homily. Absolute power corrupts absolutely. Every act of domestic violence, every time a man puts his hands on a woman, unwanted, every time she flinches, he's abusing his power—because he can.

The pathetic conga line of losers outed in the extraordinary revelations of the #MeToo movement wouldn't have been so keen to ask so many young women to watch them have sex with themselves if they were garbos or baristas. If regular people did that to random people on the train, or to their co-workers at lunch, the victims would likely just call the cops. Dick out, when the lady says no dick out, generally means jail to Joe Suburbs.

But when a man feels he has so much power over his victims that they won't complain, or will even willingly comply, he releases his inner pig.

Is that impulse in all of us? Perhaps that's a question for a bigger and smarter book.

It's self-evident that if, beyond what most of the time lies asleep in our undies, men and women had equal physical strength, the world would be a different place. A man would find it more difficult to smash his partner's face in with a hammer (from a particularly vile New South Wales case in 2017) if she had equal ability to do the same.

Imagine if it were equally possible for either a man or a woman to win the World Strongperson Competition. Domestic violence would be a different thing. Let's think it through a little further. As human beings we're flawed, and we seem to want to bash, rape, grope, abuse and start wars with pretty much everyone else, every chance we get. All that would happen is society would still divide into strongest and weakest, just not along sex lines.

Sure, there are big, strong women who can bash six types of snot out of your average man. And there are tiny little weak men. MRAs are obsessed with every case where a female teacher abuses a male student and the headlines read 'Teacher's Sex Romp with Teen Boy'. Just google 'teacher sex romp' and you'll find a disturbing array of stories of adult female teachers having sex with teen boys. They're right when they say the headlines would read 'Rape' if it was a man having sex with a fourteen-year-old girl.

But, on average across the population, men are physically dominant. It's easy to get caught up arguing about exceptions that don't do anything to change the broad statistical situation, like female-on-male rape or sexual violence.

In one scene in the highly questionable *Entourage* movie (I loved the TV series—I am a weak person), Turtle challenges the real-life arse-kicking female Mixed Martial Arts fighter Rhonda Rousey to a fight. If he can last 30 seconds in the ring with her, she will go on a date with him. Sixty seconds? 'You can "ding" me.' In the film, the 'ding' was the ring bell masking, I'm fairly sure, the word 'fuck'. She smashes him, of course.

All that would happen is big strong women and big strong men would prey on weaker men and women. The strong would hold the power, the money, be over-represented on boards, government and at the senior levels of business. Just like white men now. The weak would earn less, hold lower status in society, and be frequently sexually objectified—'I love the weak; they're sweet little things'—and sexually assaulted. The weak would frequently get bashed to death by their strong partners. Just like women now.

So it's a mess either way, because those with the power can't help but abuse it. We really are a bunch of bastards.

The fact is that men and women live with bodies that are almost exactly the same, with ever-so-subtle differences supplied by our differing chromosomes. We are wired up to love those differences, simply to ensure that the species continues. If we all suddenly lost interest in each other's glossy hair, broad shoulders, soft skin, strong jaws, warm breasts, broad chests, wet, warm clefts and curves, muscles, bones and boners, we'd be gone in a century.

Differences that are not environmental—nurture—and that can be attributed to our DNA from the moment of conception—nature—are many, and mostly meaningless. Here are a few:

- The average man is taller and heavier than the average woman.
- Men have more body hair than women, on the chest and extremities.
- Women are more sensitive to sound.
- Men are approximately 30 per cent stronger than women, especially in the upper body.
- Girls begin puberty around two years before boys.
- Men have larger hearts and lungs, and our higher testosterone levels give us more red blood cells.
- Due to differences in our ability to take in oxygen and convert that to energy and movement, a woman needs to exert herself at 70 per cent to keep up with a man running at 50 per cent.
- Female fertility decreases after 35, but men can father children pretty much for their whole lives, our primal desire to mate fading only with our last breath.
- We have different levels of hormones. Men have more of androgens such as testosterone, while women have more oestrogens.
- As is already clear to most men, we have 4 per cent more brain cells and a massive 100 grams more brain tissue. As is clear to women, there is no correlation between this and intelligence. Both men's and women's brains are equal in proportion to their bodies.
- Men have better distance vision and depth perception, and usually better vision in lighted environments. Women have better night vision, see better at the red end of the light spectrum, and have a better visual memory.

•

In other weird male body news, we have little erections in the womb, before we're born. Science says the periodic movements help the growing penis tissue stay oxygenated. Either that, or our little brains, just clumps of cells, are already vibrating with lust. Maybe it's our restless, formless yearning for our future sex lives that gives us a baby boner.

As the proud owner of a penis, I believe the latter. I know sexuality is all in the brain, and the penis is only responding to stimuli, but the startling effect is that it's really like 'He' has a mind of his own.

In your teens and early twenties, He keeps leaping out at the worst times, at the least provocation. Just lingering over one delightful mental snapshot—perhaps a glimpse of lacy bra captured on the school bus that morning—would see you sporting a diamond-hard erection in your woolly shorts as you deliver a killer speech in the Year 12 inter-school debates. Not that I would know . . .

Then, when your penis is finally confronted by a real-life girl, with all her hands and kisses and silky warmth, he promptly has a fit of nerves, throws up and goes to sleep.

And this is after years of Him attempting to leap from your pants at girls in shampoo and Fanta commercials, at girls in the street, at girls in shops, at girls in movies, at pictures of girls, and, of course, at your massive harem of wild and willing imaginary girls.

He is annoyingly unpredictable and unreliable. And we're attached to the sick little bastards for life.

In trying to explain to my partner, Jayde, what it's like to try to be in charge of a penis, I have talked her through the unspoken dialogue that goes on in your head when you own one.

For instance, in the car she often puts her hand on my thigh as we drive. It's nice, loving and sweet. She is not offering me a handjob. Yet up He pops, straining to be heard under my pants.

**Him:** 'Why is her hand there? Is she gonna do something to us?'
**Me:** 'No, of course not, you idiot—we're driving.'

155

**Him:** 'Might be nice, though . . . Go on, ask her. Bet she would, she's a good chick.'

**Me:** 'Will you fuck off, you (literally) silly little prick! Now I have to adjust.'

**Him:** 'Take me out! Take me out!'

**Me:** 'No! Now I'm going to think of Pauline Hanson to make you go away.'

**Him:** 'Okay . . . Well, can you see if she wants to do some sexy stuff with us tonight?'

**Me:** 'Well, maybe . . .'

In the kitchen this week, Jayde patted me on the butt and said something sweet and hot about what she'd like to do later that evening. (Women, please note: men really like that sort of thing.) I greatly appreciated both the attention and sentiment. And there He was, straight away.

**Him:** 'What was that? What did she say? What'd I miss?'

**Me:** 'Nothing, bro. Go away, but keep in touch—I might need you later.'

**Him:** 'No way! Go get her now and let's do it!'

**Me:** 'Absolutely not, you sick little pig. Now fuck off and go back to sleep.'

**Him (shouting):** 'Boobies! Butts! Sexy wooooommmmaaaannnnn!'

**Me:** 'Oh my god . . . Die, you little freak!'

Or something like that.

Men are surging with testosterone, right? We have floods of the stuff, raging through our veins like superhero juice, like spinach to Popeye.

Err, no, actually. The average amount of testosterone in a healthy man under the age of 40 is between 350 and 1000 nanograms per deci-litre of blood. That does indeed sound like bugger-all. If you were to pour all the testosterone in your body into a shot glass, it would barely fog the bottom.

And, you'll be disturbed to learn, there's going to be even less of it around. Men today simply have less testosterone, when compared to men of the same age a generation ago. No one knows why. The reason is hidden in a tangle of factors, social, environmental and behavioural.

A 2007 study in the *Journal of Clinical Endocrinology and Metabolism* showed that levels have been declining by about 1 per cent a year. So a 60-year-old man in 2004 had levels that were 17 per cent lower than those of a man the same age in 1987.

Other international studies have confirmed the findings. And apparently musculoskeletal decline in men is matching the drop in our t-juice—our grip strength is down about 15 per cent since 1985.

There are a lot of factors, including how fat we are, environmental toxins and even how we live. We're not digging ditches by hand anymore, so as a species we just don't need to be as strong. Could the drop in our testosterone levels be nature saying, 'Well, if you're going to sit around doing bugger-all, I'm going to let your bodies wilt like steamed spinach?'

Air conditioning, lack of exercise and even tight undies have also been blamed. Somehow, our bodies are evolving to follow our swift socialisation by YouTube and UberEats.

•

Men's feet are longer and wider than women's, but there's no correlation between a man's shoe size and the length of his penis. It is a persistent urban myth, perpetuated, no doubt, by blokes with big feet.

The average erect Australian penis is 15.71 centimetres long, according to a website I am delighted to announce exists, www.aussiepenis. com. That's considerably chunkier than the world average of 13.12 centimetres, according to a study by the *British Journal of Urology International* of 15,521 men. To help you visualise, a standard school ruler is 30.40 centimetres long. The average Australian penis is about half that.

A monster 16-centimetre-plus porno penis falls in the 95th percentile—meaning only five men in 100 will sport one. And only five men in 100 have an erect penis smaller than 10 centimetres.

A 'micropenis' is only 6 centimetres or less when erect, and I for one would not like to be the owner of one. It would be a tough life. If mainstream and social media puts pressure on women to look and be a certain way, imagine you're a tall, good-looking, successful man with a penis like a raisin on a button mushroom.

The Man Box demands that you be big, hard and ready at all times. If you're motivated by those demands, and it's very hard not to be, then having a tiny penis would most definitely make you feel less of a man.

I have a colleague and close mate who has a story of her own encounter with a micropenis. As a beautiful young single woman 'in charge of her own sexuality', as she puts it, she sometimes indulged in casual sex, if she ran into a man she liked the look of. In a Melbourne hotel bar after a media function she saw him: 'So good looking, sitting there by himself in a pea coat.'

Some hours later, in a room above, she discovered, to her considerable disappointment, that Mr Handsome Pea Coat was packing something she illustrated by wiggling the end of her little finger. She did not enjoy the encounter at all and was 'mortified'. Whenever she tells the story to female colleagues and friends, they laugh and squeal, cover their mouths and say 'Eww! Oh my god, what a let-down!' Every time.

Imagine being a man with a micropenis and hearing that. You'd be pretty clear on what women want in the bedroom—and it wouldn't be you.

A writer going by the name of JF penned an agonising essay headlined 'I'm Tired of Being Ashamed of My Micropenis'. You could cry for the man. 'The average flaccid penis is longer than mine when I am erect,' he writes.

The number of times I have heard women making fun of men for the size of their manhood is staggering. At one time I overheard three or

158

four of my work colleagues all agreeing that 'men with small dicks should be made to wear a sign warning women.'

JF is 35 and has had only one sexual experience with a woman—a 'very attractive' university student twelve years earlier.

> When I stripped she stared at my micropenis, giggled, put her hand to her mouth and muttered 'OK' in a tone that suggested she was taken aback . . . Even when I was inside her, she kept asking me, 'Is it in?' Every time she asked me that, I wanted to die . . . [After a while] she suddenly huffed in an annoyed way and got up, saying she needed a glass of water. That was it.

He reports watching a dating show in his native United Kingdom, where the female presenter asked a female contestant if penis size was important to her. 'Yes, I've been in a situation before where a guy treated me like an absolute princess and then when it came down to it, he had the tiniest penis,' she replied.

> As a guy with a micropenis, watching what looked like such an amazing woman say that sliced through my soul. It made me feel totally worthless . . . She was only being honest, but the message was clear: We are not good enough for you.

The poor guy actually wrote the words 'sliced through my soul' . . . Good grief. He finishes with a painful entreaty:

> Guys with micropenises know they are not well-endowed, they don't need reminding of it. If I'm attracted to a woman, then what she has in her pants doesn't matter to me; I care more about what she has in her heart. My deep shame about my body makes me feel like everyone's opinion *must* be right, that there *is* something wrong with my size. I wish people could look past it, so I could too.

You're judged as less of a man if you have a little dick. And that can be a horrible, life-ruining experience.

It is of interest to note oral sex draws more blood into the penis, making it a good percentage longer and thicker.

In further penis news, the heads of our penises have a ridge for a very good reason, and it's not only (to quote the Durex box) for 'her pleasure'. Again, it goes back to our ancestors. We're programmed to want it to be our semen that makes a woman pregnant, not the semen of the last bloke she had sex with. (Our ancestors clearly weren't big on monogamy.)

In the simple action of penile/vaginal sex, the hood of the penis acts as a scoop, busily clearing out any semen not put there by you, before you ejaculate.

Then some other guy comes along and scoops out your semen a few hours later—goddammit!

•

Another sex-based difference—one which is extremely annoying to women—is that men age better. We lose collagen density more slowly than women, which means our skin doesn't wrinkle and sag as we age. We also have more collagen to start with. Collagen loss accelerates when women hit menopause.

Having worked in the media industry in Australia for nearly 30 years, I find it interesting to see the physical changes in my female colleagues. I'll see a media maven who was once an attractive young freelancer setting the room alight with her presence, and be genuinely shocked by the extent of the wear and tear done by the years. Harsh, but true.

It must drive women nuts. To go from being someone who based a good amount of her game on her 'hotness' (in the pre #MeToo world, this did happen), to being rendered invisible by a cloak of years must indeed be a bitter pill. And don't the Botox, fashion, beauty and cosmetic surgery industries know it.

In some cases, men's breasts can make milk—but not very much, and only if we've got pituitary problems, are on certain medication or are in a state of extreme starvation, so don't break out the expressing pumps just yet. Our nipples, however, are as sensitive as a woman's.

The shape of a woman's breast is an evolutionary trick to get men to notice her. Boobs are mostly made out of fat, which has nothing to do with milk production. But if a woman's nice and healthy, she'll have enough fat on her body to get through childbirth and breastfeeding. Big boobs are nature's sign that she's healthy and fertile. That's why we like them.

A man's Adam's apple is larger than a woman's because we have bigger voice boxes and the protective cartilage protrudes more. Interestingly, the pitch of a man's voice correlates to the amount of testosterone he has, which is in turn an indicator of his genetic quality and sexual fitness. So women like men with lower-pitched voices because they're more likely to produce healthy strong offspring.

More testosterone means a stronger brow, cheekbone and jawline, which is why women are attracted to angular faces in men. Women judge men with more angular features as likely to be dominant over men with rounder, more effeminate faces. Conversely, the more oestrogen a woman has, the wider her face, the fuller her lips and the higher her eyebrows.

Pretty much every physical attribute that says a man will have strong, healthy DNA and be a good protector translates into hotness. Broad shoulders, big hands, muscular forearms—he can carry me to safety. Facial scar? Delicious, he can fight and win. Guys with slim hips and long legs make the fastest runners.

It's not rocket science. In fact, it's just normal science.

•

There are a million and one studies into what body type women around the world find most attractive. And the cultural differences they reveal are actually more interesting than the final results. Women in Pakistan and Egypt, for example, seem to like a 'dad bod'—a bit of muscle and a bit of comfort. In Russia, he's a little bit Putin. Spanish women like their men surprisingly chubby. In the west, he's Brad Pitt. Not *Ocean's Eleven* Brad Pitt, or *Seven* Brad Pitt, but *Fight Club* Brad Pitt!

I am delighted by this! Just as I've loved the book and film of *Fight Club* for years, I'm also in love with Brad Pitt's *Fight Club* body. If you don't have it in your head, take a quick google.

If I had my choice of fantasy bodies, that would be it. That's what my brain feels it should occupy, not this 53-year-old sack of steak, pinot noir and a number of other things I can't mention . . . like in Rufus Wainwright's creamy song 'Cigarettes and Chocolate Milk'.

It's up to us to look after the magnificent, ridiculous temples in which we are housed. It's quite the responsibility.

Exercise, as we know, has multiple upsides and no downside, so we should all be doing it. The benefits are clear. It is proven that women are more attracted to fit, strong-looking men. Your self-esteem rises when you're fit, and your mental health is better. Depression is related to low levels of certain neurotransmitters, like serotonin and norepinephrine, which exercise increases. It also stimulates the release of endorphins, the feel-good neurotransmitter that blocks pain like an opiate. Leading research is also discovering that exercise causes neurogenesis, or the creation of new neurons. So exercise could prevent mental disorders like Alzheimer's or Parkinson's. *Lancet Neurology* reports that regular leisure-time activity greatly decreases the risk of dementia in later life.

Exercise battles high blood pressure, one of the biggest killers in the Western world, and diabetes, one of the most widespread diseases on the planet. It may also help in both the prevention of, and recovery from, cancer.

And—the last word—exercise improves erectile function.

Of late, I've had a rather interesting experience with exercise and all things body.

Jayde, battling her own hormone levels after a life-saving hysterectomy at 32, has a personal trainer as part of her recovery and ongoing strength and wellness program. The awesome thing for me? She runs her own communications business, so is constantly on Skype calls to clients overseas, often when she is supposed to be training with her PT. So I go instead.

It's been a year now, a few sessions a month with the trainer, and the rest me training myself. And so, as I sit here writing at 6 pm on a winter Friday, in the garage I laughingly call a studio, I think I am probably in the best shape in my life. And that includes the seven-year period I studied martial arts, and when I played senior rugby union.

(A quick aside—right now, unshaven in trackpants, with the Cruel Sea on the speakers and a beer on my desk, I can't quite see the moment when someone else will hold this book in their hand and read it. It's a weird idea. That being said, someone had better, or else this has been a shocking waste of quite a few months. And personally I'm interested to see if the editing process leaves this paragraph in. Or any of it, quite frankly. Anyway, on with the book. Ed—leave this bit in!)

Simultaneously, journalist, former Wallaby, columnist, author, broadcaster, chair of the Australian Republican Movement and genuinely good bloke Peter FitzSimons has been rediscovering the joys of fitness well into his fifties. The increasingly gaunt FitzSimons has been preaching the delights of ditching sugar and booze for quite a while now.

He was lean, but thought 'anything along the lines of seriously competitive sport was destined to be no more than a distant memory', as he wrote in a column in the *Sydney Morning Herald* under the headline 'Stopping Sport Was Easy, It's Getting Started Again that's the Hard Part'.

I've met FitzSimons a few times, the first being on his family farm at Peats Ridge, north of Sydney, in the late 1980s. He was already working at the *Sydney Morning Herald* back then; I was kind of dating

*SMH* journo Sigrid Kirk and tagged along to what I think was a work barbecue thing.

She's now a leader in digital publishing, data and strategy, as well as being a fantastic, happy, open person, and still a friend of mine. Anyone who knows her finds it quite amusing we ever dated . . .

Anyway, Peter and his parents were warm hosts. It was like being with the Waltons, only the huge Waltons. Peter definitely got his international rugby lock size from Mum and Dad.

The second time we met, he interviewed me for his 2002 book on the magazine queen Nene King. I think he referred to me as a 'nice bloke', for which I am grateful.

In his column, FitzSimons wrote delightedly about how he went back to the gym a couple of years ago, and got 'hooked':

> That drive for intense physical activity was there, as was—and this is what really amazed me—a fair chunk of my one-time physical strength. Yup, even after all those chips, all those durries, all those bottles of wine, somewhere inside me—just as I suspect a lot of it is still inside hundreds of thousands of blokes, and women, my age—it was still substantially intact. To my amazement, it was even possible to get involved in intense competition again.

For me it was exactly the same. Right now, I feel like I could pull the roof off a VW Beetle.

I'm not, by any means, saying I think I'm awesome. Like FitzSimons, I'm simply reeling in shock, and delight, at the resilience a heavily abused body that is well over 50 can show after a few months of training.

Admittedly, it's been hard work. At the gym last week, I vomited quietly into my towel after a PT session, as I sat quietly in the corner, unable to walk. I whined to our trainer, Loki, that I was old and might have a heart attack.

He fixed me with a level stare and said, 'That's what we're trying to avoid.'

Loki subjects us to metabolic training. Here's how an enthusiastic metabolic training fan describes it on a muscle forum:

> Its no-holds-barred, haul-ass, maximum effort, build-muscle, heave-weight, torch-fat, absolutely insane huff-n-puff training. It'll spike your metabolism, crush calories like beer cans, lift your lactate threshold, boost your ability to make muscle and maximize your body's capacity for change.

Metabolic training is simply exercise that requires the maximum amount of energy because multiple joints and muscle groups are involved. It is also done at very high intensity: usually there are three groups of three exercises, repeated three times, over 45 minutes.

It's always different and always agonising. Chucking a 30-kilogram ball over your shoulder twenty times, doing some assisted chin-ups, and then doing about 30 metres of walking lunges while holding a 20-kilogram weight over your head seems hard. And that's just one round. A full session can be up to 27 rounds.

The idea is to lift as much as possible, with as little rest time as possible between sets. It sucks. Back to back, the nature of these 'structural and compound' exercises is to put you into severe oxygen deprivation, like you've being doing sprints. Personally, I've never felt anything like it. You haven't taken a running step and you're gasping like it's the end of a marathon.

But I've always been of the 'no pain, no gain' school, and the quick, impressive results of metabolic training confirm my beliefs in the value of hard work.

I can add it to the list of exercise fads that have, at various times, been important in my life: rugby union, Wing Chun Kung Fu, aerobics, boxing, yoga, Pilates, weight training, running, cycling and CrossFit.

Of course, everyone should find what works for them, but what's not in dispute are the benefits of exercise for men and women, mentally and physically. My 78-year-old father, a retired farmer, still drives tour buses up to New Zealand's ski fields, and is miffed that he's going to have to apply for his licence annually once he turns 80. He cycles up to 40 kilometres a day, walks 3 kilometres to work and reports that he's 'as fit as a buck rat'. Buck rats should be so lucky.

The by-product of this is that he gets to enjoy every day with my equally fit mother, camping, kayaking, pootling about in their little caravan and having more sex than their children should know about. Mum's and Dad's physical fitness has extended their joyful time together by years, possibly decades. So we all have a responsibility not only to ourselves but also to those who love us to look after our bodies.

•

Of course, the major and most noticeable physical difference between men and women is indeed what lies sleeping in our underwear.

Men are so bad at understanding how the different bits of a woman's body work that there's a real gap between the amount of orgasms women are having compared to men.

Guess what? It's because we're crap in bed. Such was my outrage at the discovery last year that I was forced to pen this breathless protest in a column for Fairfax Media.

### New Study Suggests that Men Are Failing When It Comes to Performance in the Bedroom

Men, we should hang our heads in shame. Given that we spend a good deal of our waking time thinking about sex, talking about sex and trying to get people to do sex with us, it's pretty embarrassing how bad we actually are at it.

You could be forgiven for thinking that in the hook-up age, where we're all bumbling around Tinder and only have to swipe right for some casual no-strings nookie, we'd be getting a bit better at it.

But no, it seems we have about the same level of sexual skills as a 14-year-old off to boarding school on the train in 1923. 'Good grief,

Simpkins, everyone knows a lady will faint and have a baby if you look at her bottom. Nanny told me!'

See, there's an orgasm gap out there in love land, and it's all our fault.

A huge study of American adults shows that in heterosexual encounters, a woman will only have one orgasm for every three a man enjoys, and unfortunately, we're not talking about just one night. A slew of other studies concur.

The problem appears to be the clitoris—we don't know where it is, what it's for or how it works.

Now, to be clear, the clitoris isn't just the little nub at the top of her lady parts. It's an extraordinary organ that runs deep into her body and has only one purpose—her pleasure. It has around 8000 nerve endings to communicate sensation. Your penis has only 4000. A 3D image of the clitoris looks like something elegant designed by Philippe Starck.

Women who sleep with women orgasm pretty much on par with men and women who don't orgasm from penetrative sex [and] have no trouble coming when they masturbate. (And it takes her about the same time as you—four minutes). So, there's nothing inherently wrong with women and their finickity bits . . . The problem is us and our shocking lack of knowledge and technique. Knowledge and technique is something smart men apply to every area of their lives, so why not the boudoir?

Poor old casual sex guy is the worst in bed. The orgasm gap shrinks as a woman gets to know her partner better and, for a woman in a relationship, the orgasm gap allegedly shrinks by half.

There's a number of factors working together to create the gap. Freud is partly responsible. His thinking was that orgasm through penetrative sex was the best and most 'mature', and it eventually slipped into science as fact. It's not. Add to that we still value men's sexual pleasure over women's. He is 'sexual', she is 'sexy'. Women still don't seem to feel comfortable asking for equal sexual pleasure. 'I think I felt kind of guilty, almost, like I was kind of subjecting guys to something they didn't want to do and I felt bad about that,' said one survey subject.

'The guy kind of expects to get off,' said another, 'while the girl doesn't expect anything.'

The main contributing factor is we see penetrative sex as 'real' sex, the end-game. Clitoral stimulation is relegated to the murky territory of 'foreplay'.

What's ridiculous is men all want to be seen as sex gods. And there's a little button we can push that will magically turn us into one but instead we just go 'yeah . . . nah.'

If I had a son, we'd totally have clitoris lessons. I'd say 'Mate, it's not confusing or difficult or weird. If it came with instructions, it would simply say, "Rub This." That's it.'

I'd advise him to make sure she was liking what he was doing by . . . asking her (crazy, hey?). If she has any suggestions, feel free to follow them.

Perhaps the same-sex marriage plebiscite money would have been better spent issuing every young man in Australia a delightful, life-sized rubber clitoris with a short fact sheet, like a useful fidget spinner.

'Mu-ummm! I can't find my clitoris and I want to take it to school!'

We follow our American cousins in many things but surely this is one area where Australian men need to stand up and be counted. Do we really want our delightful female partners to be missing out? Do we really want to miss out on the opportunity of being the hottest man she's ever met?

In my sadly very limited experience, the sexiest thing a man will ever encounter in his life is a highly aroused woman begging him to keep doing what he's doing. There should be more of it.

No longer should we put up with this outrageous inequity. We should take to the streets in our thousands, campaigning for the rights of women everywhere to have as many orgasms as possible. I'm sure no-one would have a problem with that and it would also make the news more interesting.

It's time to do a better job. It's time to learn a little more about our partners. It's time to stop being lazy. It's time to #attackthatgap.

In the end, we have to live together with the physical differences nature has bestowed on us. Men have not so much a 'noblesse oblige' as a 'brawn oblige', a clear moral and ethical responsibility to not abuse our physical advantages over others.

It's beautiful being a man. I love being strong. There's nothing more wonderful than the woman you love sinking into your arms, head on your chest, warm and protected. Our bulk should make women feel safe, and sometimes sexy, but never scared.

A smart man can have the best of both worlds. He can strut around in his big man body, all tough and strong, and at the same time enjoy the delights of being close to every woman in his life—mother, daughters, partner, colleagues—because they know he'd never hurt them.

•

The other responsibility we have to our magnificent bodies is to keep them alive. There's no point having three kids with the love of your life if you end up dead because you're an idiot man. You're not providing, protecting or comforting then.

Men make up 96 per cent of workplace fatalities, according to a 2015 Safe Work Australia Report, and 61 per cent of workplace injuries or illness.

Men's health and gender politics website *XYOnline*, citing a 2015 study by Stergiou-Kita, Mansfield et al., says it's the performance of being a man that's killing us at work.

We are socialised to accept risk, danger and injury, and to endure pain without complaint. We are stoic, the breadwinner. We don't want to be seen as weak. And in the modern labour market, of course, profit will beat real occupational health and safety every time.

Even when we do the same work as women, we are at increased risk of 'occupational fatalities'. We are less likely to report injuries or take time off—and if we do take a break, we often come back to work too soon.

Basically, we need to be a lot more careful around the place, and stop showing off. We're not supermen. Our loved ones want us to be with them for as long as possible. We have a responsibility to control ourselves well enough to stay alive. And that doesn't seem a big ask for a grown-up human being, does it?

Our attitude to our mental health is equally appalling. One in eight men will experience depression, and one in five will feel anxiety at some stage of their lives. We know already that six men kill themselves every day in Australia. That's more than double the national road toll. Yet we're not asking for help.

You won't have a heart attack if you quit smoking, become more physically active, eat more fibre and less fat, lower your cholesterol and your blood pressure, lose weight—oh, and manage your stress. It's a wonder I made it beyond that sentence, frankly.

Around 60 per cent of men don't go to the doctor. Nineteen per cent of us go only because our partners make us. We're more likely to die from excessive drinking and smoking, and from not going to the doctor. The top two reasons men offer are the same two reasons I don't go to the doctor: I'm too busy and I'm afraid of finding out something might be wrong.

If I feel fine, why tempt fate? All the sick people I know go to the doctor all the time, my twisted man-logic tells me, so I had better not go or I too might get told something terrible.

We men are particularly afraid of the rectal exam. I am 53 and, shameful as it is, I have yet to have a prostate check. I will have by the time you read this—I have promised both my partner and daughter. I may or may not have waited until a blood test has finally replaced the rectal exam. As a man with a partner who is regularly rendered unconscious by the medical fraternity and probed in every private area, I really have no way to argue my way out of this.

Men are dying because of this silly attitude.

The prostate gland makes semen, which carries our sperm. As we get older, it can start to have problems. Each year, 3300 of us die of prostate cancer, and more than 21,000 new cases are diagnosed. So the problem's going to get worse as the population ages.

With some men, it's a slow thing. Old age will kill you before the cancer does, so it's a position of 'watchful waiting'. For other men, it'll eat you alive, bum first. No one ever really 'battles' cancer, which implies some sort of will, or level of control involved. Cancer does to you what it bloody well wants.

Men are avoiding asking for help. We're afraid of being seen as weak at work. We fear the doctor. We're mental health messes, killing ourselves and others every day. Our bodies are amazing things, yet we can't even look after them, let alone control them.

Men, our bodies are a gift. We must use them well and look after them. You need your body to last you well, so that you can enjoy a long life full of love and joy.

# Chapter 10

# THE FATHER HOOD

My phone rang at about 11.30 am on a Saturday. It's my daughter, Lulu, who's just eighteen. She's supposed to be at work, at a little cafe in a local park, making coffees and toasted sandwiches. When I answer, my heart drops to my stomach and the world stops. She's sobbing, hysterical, and can't even get a word out, but it is obvious she desperately needs me. Has she been attacked, kidnapped? Is she calling from a car boot?

'Where are you?' I yell. 'Can you hear anything?'

There's a pause in the sobbing and out-of-control breathing. 'What?' she replies, confused. 'What do you mean, can I hear anything?'

'Are you hurt? What can you see?'

'I'm at work, Dad. But a man just shouted at me about his sandwich. He said it was no good. But he was wrong, Dad! There was nothing wrong with it. He just went mental!'

Lulu was in the toilet, having become so overwhelmed at a moment of fairly serious aggression towards her that she couldn't get her breathing and crying under control. Mercifully, she had not been abducted by a gang of people traffickers.

Now she was upset about being upset. 'It's so unprofessional and embarrassing,' she howled.

I sped the short drive to her cafe. I texted and she came out to the car, and slowly got herself under control.

First, we got her breathing sorted out. Then, we looked at the situation and saw that it was her first encounter with the nasty, demanding, bad-tempered, entitled, rude, selfish and irrational public. If you work in a public-facing job, sooner or later this will probably happen to you.

Then we developed a mental strategy for the next time—basically along the lines of 'they can't kill you'. The angry man was no doubt angry because he was actually sad, we agreed. Now we feel sorry for him and the sting is gone.

If someone else had told me that story, I'd probably have privately thought, 'You can't teach someone to be an adult by turning up to save them every time it turns to custard. Let the kid learn about life!'

Well, I disagree with me. Sure, I can't go to Lulu's workplace every time there's a problem. I can't go to uni and take an exam for her. (Probably a good thing.) I can't make sure her boyfriend never hurts her. (Well, maybe I can. Just remember, I know where you live, young fella.) I can't keep an eye on her in clubs and bars until 2 am. That would be creepy, and if she caught me she would make me go home.

'Dad, what are you doing here?'

'Er, hi, just popped out for a drink. Fancy seeing you here!'

'Dad, it's 1.30 am and this is World Bar in Kings Cross!'

'Yep, my favourite!'

But this one time, I was so very grateful to be able to help. It was an experience she'd never had before; now, it's one she knows how to deal with when it inevitably happens again.

In that moment, she knew what she needed. Her father. She said later she knew I wouldn't 'coddle' her, and a little 'tough love' would snap her back.

Together, we have a quick chat to her boss, who is also more than a little rattled by the ferocity of the bloke's attack. 'It was a fairly full-on event,' he agrees. 'There's the lesson, Lulu,' he says. 'There will always be arseholes.'

How happy was I that my performance as a father had produced a positive outcome? Delighted. I had fixed the thing.

And that's a problem. Because fixing the thing sometimes gets in the way of being a great father.

•

What is a great father? It certainly is a massive responsibility, shaping the personality of a little person who loves you unconditionally, simply by being the man you are. A man who is happy, open and calm, who can communicate and show love, will be a wonderful father and receive indescribable joy from the process. A man who is angry, closed, aggressive and emotionally or physically violent can leave a weeping wound on the psyches of his children, one that never heals.

The role we have in raising boys is more important than ever in a world where we are actively questioning, and debating, what it means to be a man.

The writer Tim Winton has become a voice in the conversation on the state of men. Men 'need to provide better modelling', he says, whether it's for our own sons or for any other young men we love and have influence over. 'But the first step is to notice them. To find them worthy of our interest. As subjects, not objects. How else can we hope to take responsibility for them? And it's men who need to step up and finally take their full share of that responsibility.'

In his seminal 1998 book *Raising Boys*, the eminent Australian psychologist Steve Biddulph began a campaign for people to recognise that boys' emotional needs were being neglected, especially at school. 'We know a lot more about the way young minds develop,' he told *The Australian* recently. 'We better understand gender differences. Fathers tend to be more hands-on. With all the work over the past 20 years, there has never been a better time to be a boy, at least for many centuries.'

According to Biddulph, there are specific things to know about raising boys. There's a sort of mini-puberty at four, which accounts for a rise in boisterousness. The preparatory phase for puberty, adrenarche, is likely to be more emotional for boys than girls, so Biddulph advises understanding the tears.

'There's still a widespread suppression of emotion in boys,' he says. 'Crying protects mental health and heals the brain after a loss. If boys don't cry it will come out in other ways, often as violence and anger.'

Violence and anger. Suppressing sadness. Not crying. How very early we start socialising our boys. Great male role models—fathers, uncles and friends—have a significant role in developing a generation of young men who are capable of a range of emotions, from which come good relationships and a happier world all round. Doesn't seem too much to ask.

There's more and more research suggesting that a woman's sense of self-worth has its roots in her experience with her father. How you father your daughter affects her career success and financial wellbeing, and her ability to have good and fulfilling relationships with men, and better emotional and mental health generally.

As a girl tries to figure out what men are like, she watches her father. It's your job to show her what a good, respectful, emotionally healthy man sounds and feels like.

Mark Trahan, an American clinical social worker, therapist and specialist in all things fatherhood, quotes some terrifying statistics about the children of absent fathers. Clearly, a father's behaviour can have a massive positive or negative impact on his child's future happiness. These are his numbers, but I have no reason to dispute him, given his background and the respect he has among his peers.

Children with absent fathers are:

- five times more likely to suicide
- seven times more likely to drop out of school
- fifteen times more likely to commit rape
- seven times more likely to become a teenage mum
- twenty-four times more likely to run away from home
- fifteen times more likely to end up in teen prison.

Children with active, engaged fathers are more likely to have a good education, make a higher income, adjust well to situations and form stable relationships. Holy crap! No pressure, then.

Trahan researched what makes an active, engaged father via a nationwide survey in the United States. One factor that rose to the top was a man's confidence in his ability to be a parent.

According to Trahan, as a man you are socialised to solve problems. To fix the thing. Absolutely. Outcomes in our manly lives are largely based on performance. We are rewarded for effort with things like the best job and car, the most money and the smartest, sexiest and most beautiful partner. But we can be socialised away from loving our child because we are too busy trying to fix everything for her. Fathering, Trahan says, isn't about high performance, but it is about wholeheartedly loving your child even in the most difficult moments. It's not an easy thing to do.

To fine-tune our fatherhood, he recommends that we first reflect on our relationship with our own fathers. We should also reinforce to the mothers of our children that they have great power over fathering— we must ask women to remember that we take our cues from them. Trahan's advice for mothers is to notice men doing the right things right, not the wrong things. To men, he says: consider your role. And consider expanding it to include more love and affection.

Trahan believes these are the questions a child with an absent father asks: 'Do you want me? Do you approve of me? Why did you hurt me? Do you love me? Do I have your blessing?' Leaving these questions unanswered, he argues, leads to addiction or depression.

This is a topic close to my heart. Lulu was just twelve when I separated from her mother.

These days, Lulu lives with her mother for most of the week, and in her room at my place for a couple of days. We're only a five-minute walk apart, so there's also random popping in, coffee dates at our local cafe, walks along the Cooks River after work and uni, and of course daily phone calls, emails and texts.

I am very grateful to her mother for providing Lulu with a stable, warm, loving home base. Lulu's mother loves her ferociously and has worked incredibly hard to make Lulu's life rich and wonderful. She has succeeded.

Our separation did mean I was an absent dad at times during Lulu's teen years, though, compared to how it was before. Separation and divorce are a bitch, and to be avoided if at all possible. I am forced to wonder how much my decision to leave, which was more about myself than about my child, contributed to the anxiety Lulu experienced during her teen years.

I said to young Lulu that one day, when she was older, she would have some very hard questions for me. And if she had anything to say to me, I would suck it up, listen and answer as honestly as I could.

That moment came when she was eighteen. She expressed anger and sadness as a daughter over the split in her family. She showed compassion, love and understanding for me as an adult.

I am so very grateful that through all my personal blunders, self-absorption, flakiness, general stupidity and career dramas, Lulu has shown me unwavering love.

When she was suffering anxiety in her mid-teens, actually getting to school was sometimes almost impossible. I remember heartbreaking moments as I gently persuaded her to walk out the door to the bus, knowing each step was agony. She'd look back, eyes filled with tears, silently pleading with me not to make her do it. I did.

Over the years, I tried to fix the thing. I talked and talked and talked. What slowly became clear was the talking didn't make a lot of difference, but just being there when she needed me did.

I didn't do a very good job of that at times.

Yet somehow we've got to a point where she is as much my friend as my daughter. We might not see each other for a few days, but we talk every single day, and relish the time we spend together like the old mates we are.

Once, we were having dinner in Bondi, and a large, clearly mentally unstable man lurched towards us in the street, making a beeline for Lulu. I stood between Lulu and him, and as he got really close just said, 'No, mate.' He took a moment to consider a different course of action and attacked a rubbish bin.

'I love your air of menace,' said Lulu, disturbingly. 'I know that you'd never let anything happen to me.' And she took my hand.

I look forward to our future together. The other day I even got a tiny tickle of what I can only describe as 'grandfather feelings'. I thought about Lulu having a baby and came over all emotional and funny. In a good way. I look forward to that moment, although I hope it takes about ten years to arrive.

Or not. Whatever Lulu decides to do in her life, I'll support her as long as she is happy.

Once you stop trying to fix the thing and just be there, you'll have fixed the thing.

•

There's a foundation in the United States called The Father Effect, which has the primary purpose of 'creating an awareness in fathers about the significant impact their words and actions have on their children and help them become better fathers'. Its website features a powerful video of men talking about the devastation caused by their own absent fathers.

Meg Meeker, MD, author of the wonderful *Strong Fathers, Strong Daughters: 10 Secrets Every Father Should Know*, and a frequent expert commentator on fatherhood, is blunt: 'If a daughter knows she has dad's love, life makes sense. If she doesn't know she has dad's love, life doesn't make sense. It's that simple.'

She says there's a 'dad hole' in every daughter's heart that needs to be filled with a father's love. If it's not filled, a girl will turn to boys for male touch, to feel loved by a man in a moment. 'A dad's love is so fundamental to a girl's emotional, psychological, intellectual, and mental health that if she doesn't have it . . . her mental health is fractured,' she says. 'It's a primal drive. That's how much it throws them off if they don't have Dad.'

One of the most amazing scientific studies on human behaviour ever conducted, the Harvard Study of Adult Development, thoroughly agrees. The study is so very extraordinary because it has spanned almost 80 years, and is now into its second generation of participants. It has followed two groups of participants 'to identify the psychosocial predictors of healthy ageing'.

The two groups were the Grant Study, 268 Harvard graduates from the classes of 1939 to 1944, and the Glueck Study, a group of 456 men who grew up in the tough, underprivileged suburbs of Boston. The study's website says:

> We are particularly interested in what psychosocial variables and biological processes from earlier in life predict health and well-being in late life (80s and 90s), what aspects of childhood and adult experience predict the quality of intimate relationships in late life, and how late-life marriage is linked with health and well-being. We are now beginning to study the children of our original participants in our G2 (Second generation) study.

The study is incredible for two reasons. Usually a longitudinal study over time eventually falls over before it can gather any meaningful data— because the participants pull out, funding disappears or researchers lose interest or die. This study made it, through a lot of good luck and a great deal of dedication by generations of researchers, according to its fourth director, Dr Robert Waldinger.

What the project has discovered, he says, is actual snapshots of life choices, not memories. And hindsight is most definitely not 20/20. '[W]hat if we could watch entire lives unfold through time to see what really keeps people happy and healthy?' he asks. 'We can. It's exceedingly rare.'

All the teen participants were interviewed and underwent medical exams, and their parents were interviewed. Every two years from then on, the Harvard team sent them questionnaires on their lives, interviewed them again, made meticulous copies of their medical records, took blood samples and brain scans, and interviewed their children. The subjects were recorded talking to their wives about deeply personal moments in their lives. When the wives were eventually asked to join the study too, the researchers report the women said 'about time'.

So what's the secret? What is it that keeps us healthier and happier?

The answer is good relationships.

That's it.

The study revealed that people who are more socially connected to family, friends and their community are happier, healthier and live longer. Unequivocally, it showed that loneliness kills. We are less happy on our own, our health declines earlier, our brain function declines and we live shorter lives. One in five Australians reports being lonely at stages in their lives.

Having friends, family and a marriage is not necessarily enough, though. It's the quality of those close relationships that makes us healthy and happy. A high-conflict marriage with no affection can be worse for health than a divorce. What we need is the protective cloak of warm relationships characterised by deep trust.

The people most satisfied with their relationships at 50 were by far the happiest and healthiest at 80. Good relationships protect both our bodies and our brains.

The memories of people who are in relationships in which they really feel they can genuinely count on another person in a time of need stay sharper for longer. And if you feel you can't really count on your partner, your memory declines.

Relationships are hard work but bring great reward. The happiest in retirement in the study were those who had made the effort to replace their old workmates with new playmates.

When men in the study were young adults, they believed fame, wealth and high achievement were what they needed to have a good life. But over 75 years, the study has shown that the people who fared the best were those who leaned into relationships with family, friends and community. People who reached out, who made the effort, and who valued other human beings.

Dr Waldinger offers a quote by Mark Twain as capturing the essence of the study's message: 'There isn't time, so brief is life, for bickerings, apologies, heartburnings, callings to account. There is only time for loving, and but an instant, so to speak, for that.'

That's science telling you how to have a happy life.

The study has yielded more than 100 discrete papers so far, and has enough raw data for scores more. It's a psychosocial goldmine. Isn't science beautiful?

One of the key take-outs has been that a happy childhood has deep, long-lasting positive effects. A good relationship with your parents is a good predictor that you'll have warmer and more secure relationships with those closest to you as an adult.

Happy childhoods extended their effect across the decades into old age, bringing significantly more secure relationships and better physical health.

So being a father is a massive responsibility, and also one of life's deepest joys.

•

Your personal notions of fatherhood, of course, start with your own experience. So let's take a voyage around my father.

Alan Barker was born in 1944 and grew up on the same farm I did, in the deepest south of New Zealand. He did a great job of making sure I knew that, no matter what, even during the unfortunate perm-and-earrings period (mine, not his), he loved me unconditionally. I knew that, and know that, for sure.

For a man of his age and background to have opened himself up so much over the years is a remarkable thing, and I thank him for it. In a lot of ways, Dad's Christianity is a powerful Man Box antidote.

As a kid, I wished Dad smoked and drank longnecks of DB and Speights like the other dads I knew. I wished that, like them, he would swear with terrifying invention and passion. Now, I'm so glad he didn't. Because of his belief, who he is as a person (and my mother's influence) has gifted him an undeniably soft centre, which a little boy knew he could touch if he ever really needed to. Any hardness Dad had as a young man was simply because he was born in rural New Zealand in 1944. How he held true to himself in that environment was admirable, and deserves deep respect.

There'll be no desperate deathbed confessions of love, or burying of feuds, or confessions of secrets. Dad and I have done all that already. Given that he's almost 80, it's a thought. But the way the old bugger's going, he may well outlive me, so I guess I have to thank him for both the love and the genes.

Only a small hill on the southern tip of the South Island stood between us and the freezing winds that blast directly up from the Antarctic, over the furious grey seas of the Southern Ocean. Once, to our delight, an iceberg was visible from Invercargill's Oreti Beach as it floated by. We used to swim there on the three days of the year it was warm enough.

Dad was just eighteen when his father, Sidney, a grandfather I never knew, died of a stroke. Dad took over the farm. He was, and is, a brilliant engineer. He should have been an architect or in computer systems design or construction, but he never got the chance. As a teen boy/man, there he was standing alone on his hundreds of acres of sheep farm, facing down a future of solitude as bleak as the blast from the South Pole.

I'm not exaggerating that Dad is a great engineer. With his welder in his workshop he made me my first car, a motorised go-kart I got for Christmas when I was five. I was a car-obsessed kid (still am). A family friend had a go-kart, and when we visited I'd whine until I was given a go. I'd go around and around their backyard until the thing ran out of petrol and I had to be pulled off it, screaming and crying bitter tears as they prised my fat little fingers from the steering wheel. Now, Dad had made me my own. Winning the lottery as an adult wouldn't come close to my joy at that moment.

Dad also made a huge, four-bay shed, to house all the motorbikes, tractors and farm equipment. One of the bays was his workshop.

You know those things that go on the front of tractors, front-end loaders, that have buckets and other machines at the front? Dad made ours, with hydraulic rams that could pick up thirteen stacked haybales at a time. Neighbours from all over would bring their broken machines for Dad to fix with his magic welder. He'd sometimes pop into town for a part, but only if he couldn't make it himself, which was rare.

Although he got to be a brilliant self-taught engineer, Dad was still a farmer. And running a farm is a lonely business. You get up early, go outside and work by yourself until lunch, come back to the farmhouse for a bite, then go back outside until dark.

I remember standing in a paddock down the back of the farm as a teenager. The house was obscured by trees. I couldn't see any other buildings. The wind moaned over the flat planes of green, dotted by sheep, a miserable sky bearing down. I could have been the only person on the planet. I felt utterly isolated and alone. I had to get out. Although I was only about thirteen, I knew this wasn't the life for me.

I wasn't mature enough to understand that this was Dad's experience as well. He's a gregarious guy. These days, having retired from the farm fifteen years ago, he has the best job of his life, driving tourists around the snowy mountains in luxury coaches. People from all over the world chat to him, and sometimes, to his delight and amazement, tip him enough to buy lunch. He points out interesting farmy Kiwi stuff as he drives by, sometimes with a popstar headset. He absolutely loves it.

How much did he love being out in the freezing winds, alone, day after day, every lamb saved from death by exposure more money in the family account? Not that much.

For me, life on the farm had its moments, of course. Making hay in long, warm southern summer twilights; owning a dirt bike at fourteen, the farm my motocross park; the days after the lamb season, when the big lambs dance off their mothers' backs on meadows of impossibly green and lush grass. The farm could be achingly beautiful.

Dad did a great job, turning an old-fashioned, run-down holding into a neat, productive, modern unit with great sheds, fencing and drainage.

A farm is a small business, so labour you don't have to pay for—your kids—is a valuable commodity. By the time I was twelve I was driving the tractor and doing 'topping', which meant mowing the paddocks to get rid of thistles and weeds that could ruin quality wool. The mower stuck out about three metres on one side of the tractor, four huge blades whirling, as you went around and around in ever-decreasing circles, until you triumphantly cut down the last tiny strip in the middle of the paddock. Then you'd start another one.

Health and safety wasn't much of a thing back then, but Dad did advise me to get out of the tractor on the opposite side to the mower. That made sense. I once purposely mowed up a dead ram to see what would happen—you made your own fun on the farm—and there was a *thunk* and a shower of pink and wool out the back. The mower didn't miss a beat. There'd be nothing to bury if you fell into that thing.

These days, you'd need a special hat, an eighteen-week certification course, a yellow light on top, a safety barrier and a danger sign just to turn the murderous thing on. And the authorities may well now frown on twelve-year-olds operating heavy machinery with exposed whirling blades. But I didn't die. A few kids in my area did. (One family, I remember, all lost their limbs when some dodgy gelignite went off as they were gathered around. They were dangerous times.)

I got my full licence the day I turned fifteen—there were no L- or P-plates back in the day—but I'd been driving trucks, utes and tractors for years already. As I drove the local cop around the block, he asked wearily how long I'd been driving for. 'Ten years,' I told him. He sighed and suggested it would be a good idea to not have one arm resting out the window for the rest of the test. 'Bloody farm kids,' he said.

I was not a nice teenager. I saw myself as some sort of witty, urbane sophisticate. Why, oh why, was I born to this miserable life of sheep poo when I should have been in, say, a New York publishing family? Why weren't Mum and Dad boutique winemakers on Waiheke Island, for goodness sake?

What a little prick.

At the same time, Dad was seeing me turn into someone who might have been really helpful around the farm. He would make me come out most days after school for a couple of hours to help, and then work all Saturday. But I hated it. Sunday, mercifully, genuinely was a day of rest.

Dad and I would butt heads constantly. He'd be, say, laying tiles in drainage ditches, and ask me to help. I'd slink out, surly and distracted, and do the worst job possible, until we came home angry and I could watch TV.

Now I see that, sure, he'd have liked a hand, but what he really wanted was company. He wanted his oldest son to spend some time with him, just be there to break up the monotony and chat occasionally. He was lonely out there. It makes me sick with guilt to write this, even so many years later.

•

By the time I was seventeen, I was gone. University, then newspapers, then Australia. Dad was just 41 when I left home. He was 24 when I was born.

Dad could be a bit of a bastard but he was way less of a bastard than all the other dads. Most farm kitchens had a belt hanging somewhere, so discipline could be dished out quickly and efficiently. When I'd do something dumb and annoying, like I did often, Dad would lose it and punch me in the arm a few times. We might have spent all morning carefully separating one mob of sheep from another, and then I'd leave the gate open and they'd all mix again. I'd have punched me in the arm.

But he never punched me in the head, like lots of other blokes' dads. I know that sounds terrible, but in the late 1970s random corporal punishment was a parenting go-to. It wasn't seen as brutality.

Schools also normalised beatings. In my second year of high school I received more than 30 strokes of the cane on twelve separate occasions. I remember this odd statistic because I kept careful count all year. We called it 'getting the cuts' at my very old-school boys' school, Southland Boys' High School, and for good reason.

A typical caning would happen like this. I'd be in maths class.

'Name this function, Barker.'

'Er, Barry, sir?'

'Are you some kind of idiot, boy?'

'I think that has been fairly well established, sir.'

'Barker, you're going to need maths for your tragic, miserable life after school.'

'Sir, I don't believe so. I firmly feel my future will require no use for algebra, sir. If I need future algebra I shall employ a mathematician, sir.'

'Outside, Barker.'

'Thank you, sir.'

The average cane was about 1.5 metres long. A good one would have some tape around the end, where it was fraying from overuse.

Sir, fully enraged by this time, and no doubt employing the caning for revenge, not discipline, would take a decent run-up and swing. You'd have assumed the position some metres down the hallway, bent over, holding your socks, as sir took aim at your quivering buttocks.

You'd hear the swish, just before the blast of pain. Two or three was usually enough; six was kind of nasty. If sir was particularly angry, he could cut through your shorts and draw a good amount of blood. Mum would get so annoyed—about the shorts, not the blood.

The thing was, it didn't work. Cane strokes became a sort of badge of honour. Once you knew how it felt, you knew it couldn't get any worse and you could endure it. So you had won. If you were experienced and cool, you'd take the cuts, then casually stand up when sir was done, panting, and look him in the eye. Making no facial expression, save maybe a small smile, was important.

'Done so soon, sir?'

'Would you like some more, Barker?'

'If sir would like to give me some more, sir.'

'Bend over, Barker.'

'Well done, sir. I see sir is very enthusiastic and energetic today.'

Even I'd have caned me. Swish-thwack! Still just boys in shorts, we were eager to test our baby man-powers of toughness and resilience against our very frustrated, grown-up male teachers. We were already trying our fresh manhoods on for size.

I remember a particularly disgraceful moment in my last year of school, at camp. One guy had annoyed a notoriously evil teacher so much that they had a complete blow-up. The teacher was not a big guy but was possessed of a temper that made Charles Manson seem calm and reasonable. He had a mean, angular face and an aggressive little moustache.

'If you were a guy out on the street, I'd beat the shit out of you,' said the teacher.

'Bring it on, sir,' said his tormenter, the size of a full-grown man himself.

'You're too chickenshit. You'd cry to mummy.'

'Sir had better call his mummy, sir.'

So, rather than a caning, the teacher and student agreed to a long, brutal, bare-knuckle fight outside, with about twenty kids gathered around to watch the action. We were hooting and yelling for the student, a guy whose last name was actually Smellie, but was so tough and big that no one ever said his name was funny.

It really was like a scene out of *Fight Club*. There was a lot of blood. I suspect sir had some boxing experience, looking back, but our hero had youth, size, rage and pride on his side. And the rest of us. There was no clear winner. Exhaustion and mild concussion eventually halted the bizarre display.

This was a bridge too far. A mum—clearly some sort of left-wing whingeing, liberal champagne socialist—had the temerity to complain to the school. There was even some sort of vague questioning from the deputy principal—but 'no one saw anything, sir'.

So if your dad only whacked you on the arm every few months for being a dickhead, happy days.

•

The other thing that informs Dad's life is his Christianity. His parents were Open Brethren, a bunch of miserable social controllers that make the Amish seem like crazy party guys. I am still angry at them to this day, and the experience fuelled my scepticism, my avowed atheism—not agnosticism, but hardcore atheism, just to be clear—my humanism and my passion for objective science. Critical thinking is my religion, Bertrand Russell my saint. I memorise things Christopher Hitchens said.

By the time I was around twelve, I was kicking off weird philosophical conversations. My parents didn't know what the hell was going on. Where did this devil's spawn come from?

'If God made my brain, how come the one he gave me is wondering if there is a god?'

'If the planet is only 4000 years old, why did God put fossils in the ground to trick us?'

'If God can exist outside time, why can't the origin of the universe also be outside time?'

'How big was Noah's Ark? About 10,000 square kilometres? Because, you know, there are a lot of animal species, and all their food . . .'

'It rained for forty days and forty nights last winter, and there was no flood.'

'Who had sex with the Virgin Mary? God, Jesus or the Holy Spirit?'

'Why is Jesus white in paintings when he was Middle Eastern?'

'Who decides which words are swear words? It doesn't say, "Don't say fucking bastard wanker cunt" in the Bible. That's not taking the Lord's name in vain . . . unless his second name is Wanker.' That one didn't go down well at all.

A big one for me, as I got older, was premarital sex. I was terrible at sex. No doubt still am. (I'm very sorry, you-all-know-who-you-are. I hope you went on to find out that it can last longer than seven seconds.) But I was practising enthusiastically at every opportunity. I was pretty sure something this awesome was no sin. So I'd ask:

'Which definition of marriage across all societies on the planet is the Bible referring to? The American slave "Jumpin' de Broom" ceremony? The Catholic ceremony? Hindu? Muslim? Baha'i?'

And then there was this ripper: 'The thousands of religions in the world all have unshakable faith and belief that their gods are the true gods. How can you be sure you're backing the right horse?'

What a little prick.

Dad and I weren't really that close when I left home. My gaze was on the horizon. But I did know I was loved so unconditionally and deeply that I could always fall back into Mummy's and Daddy's arms. I still do. My brother, sister and I were parented brilliantly, and our life was rich with books, music, laughter, holidays with the boat and caravan, and an array of weird little family dogs, which we all loved desperately.

Dad scoffed at the tiny fluffball Pomeranian puppy we finally persuaded him to let us have when we were young teens. No way was that thing allowed out with him on the farm. It was a dog better suited to a Kardashian handbag than to life on the land.

Mum, a tiny, funny, energetic, wildly gregarious, warm-hearted, opera-singing whirlwind of good deeds and baked goods, named him Dusseldorf Liebe Otto Von Barker—or Dussie for short. Mum's a wonderful woman with a personality as large as she is small, well under five feet in the old money.

(Given my experience with Mum's eccentric pet-naming protocols, I was pretty comfortable and not the least bit surprised when Jayde named our hilarious exotic short-hair cat Princess Clementine Kitty Cat Custard—or Clemmie for short.)

After just a few weeks, Dussie was eagerly accompanying 'Daddy' and the big dogs out onto the farm. He'd sit proudly in the front basket of the three-wheeled motorbike, wind blowing through his fluffy mane, flapping his long pink tongue as they rode off. He was convinced he was top dog.

That's who Dad was, and is: a massive softie. Dussie became his loyal sidekick (and also Mum's fluffy boy), mud having to be brushed from his chest fluff at the end of the day. Tied to the ute, he'd bark madly all day; if allowed off, he'd run in hysterical circles behind mobs of confused sheep, delightedly showing off his completely non-existent herding skills. Perhaps he was trying to prove his toughness in the canine Man Box, the Dog Box?

Over the past few years, I think our whole family has become closer. My experience of losing a business, and a marriage, a good few years ago now (careless, I know) have changed me a lot—for the better. We managed to spend time together at my sister's birthday this year, everyone in the room at the same time for the first time in years, and I love being an uncle when I can.

My family has gathered around me in an extraordinary way, with love, understanding and unrelenting, gracious generosity in many ways. For that I am humbled and very grateful.

When I was checking the facts of my grandmother's suicide, I had a long, deep phone call with Mum, in which she honestly and bravely addressed the past. She credits her faith in her god for her ability to cope with the horrors life threw at her, and live with such lightness, joy and grace. I have no doubt this is true. Christians aren't supposed to 'hide their light under a bushel', which means their lives should illustrate their faith. With Mum's light, you need sunglasses and factor 50.

That's the problem with the Bible. What the hell is a bushel, and why would you put a light under it anyway?

Mum and Dad now believe they were in a 'cult' as young adults with young children. So do I.

In the last few years, we have discussed our early days, the farm, my childhood, Dad's life journey and our deep love for each other. Their faith has become an open, understanding, accepting and loving spirituality. We all swear now (fuckin' yay!). Dad even has the odd beer. How things have changed.

I love and deeply respect my smart, simple, calm, funny, practical, generous, insanely youthful, fit and lean father. One of his lessons to me in later life has been that you keep growing over time, and it is your choice to keep changing for the better.

Recently, one of many financial dogs from the past bit me on the wallet. My dad came up with an elegant and fair solution to help me out. (I hope, Dad, that you're okay with everything you're reading here. I think we understand each other way better than we did back when I left for Australia in 1988.) Anyway, the point is: I was 52 and my dad stepped in and helped me out when I was too dumb to help myself.

Daddy fixed the thing.

•

Like all parents, I am extraordinarily proud of my daughter. I have experienced the truth of parenthood: that we are hardwired to love our children so deeply that we'd gladly put their lives before ours. Before you have a kid, you just can't understand this. Afterwards, you get what everyone was going on about.

There's a theory that the human brain obsessively runs through awful scenarios involving the death of your child, in order to keep you from going insane with grief, if they were to somehow die. You go through it now so you're at least a little bit prepared—just in case.

I believe the theory's correct. I have lain awake at night, especially when Lulu was a toddler, imagining her death under rogue cars, falling from ships and slipping down flooded drains, watching her disappear into the torrential murk. In my fevered brain Lulu has been lost in the bush forever, fallen down open mines, and been in school bus crashes and crossing collisions. Of course, she has also fallen victim to numerous paedophiles, rapists, murderers and the aforementioned kidnappers. Poor kid.

She was born after a dramatic three-day birth that ended in an emergency caesarean. I had been awake for the majority of the time. Through lack of sleep, I had pretty much convinced myself that every joint I'd ever sparked in my life, every line I'd snorted and every cork I'd popped had warped my sperm, and my baby would emerge somehow messed up, the universe's revenge for me having too much fun.

As it happened, she was pulled out feet first, and I reeled back in horror, moaning a long 'No!' as she emerged. I thought her feet were her hands and her bum was her face, poor little thing. You can imagine my relief when they flipped her over and her tiny fat head came into view.

Lulu was a dream baby, sleeping through from six weeks, eating well, off to daycare at one. She and I would watch *The Simpsons* and *Family Guy* well before she was old enough. We'd sing rock and blues loudly in the car. We still do. I told her that Nick Cave's song about the 'no pussy blues' was about a man who lost his cat.

Lulu is whip-smart, with a killer vocabulary and big, agile brain. She's also inherited my traits of being vague and forgetful. The kid can't find the toaster.

As a child, she drew beautiful, strange pictures, with technique and meaning way beyond her years. Once she got her hands on a laptop, from the age of about eight, she began writing voraciously, banging out story after story, just for fun. By the time she was in late high school she'd written hundreds of thousands of words and hundreds of stories and poems. Her Year 10 English teacher gripped my hand and whispered prophetically, 'I can't wait to read Lulu's first novel—she's that good. I've never said that to a parent before.'

She also has an analytical and scientific mind, loves design and architecture, and delights in long, esoteric discussions on philosophy, ethics, racism, sexism, books and film. She bakes cupcakes with oozy centres.

She's on her green P-plates, and she approaches cornering with smooth track-technique—brake, turn in, nip the apex, power out—because I taught her. Well, she does it when she's concentrating.

She is also—and this has been independently documented—quite physically beautiful. So the world should be her oyster.

But, like so many teen girls around her, she's dogged by anxiety, her big brain overthinks things, and she's been more wiggy around food than I would have liked. I'm amazed when she's described as quiet, but that's what she is in some situations, lacking the confidence to be herself.

As she gets older, in a stable relationship with her first serious boyfriend, in her third year at uni, she's growing into the woman I hoped that, for her sake, she would become.

Like me, and like her aunt and uncle, she's obsessed with hardcore exercise. My brother once ran the Coast to Coast race, from one side of New Zealand's South Island to the other, which involved biking, kayaking and running over the Southern Alps. It took two days. My sister teaches yoga professionally and visits real-deal retreats in India and Thailand. She has just returned from Pune, in India, with an aggressive bout of gastro for her troubles.

Lulu's chosen sport is cheerleading—not the rah-rah on the sidelines kind, but the *Bring It On* movie kind, with pyramids and flips and cool chants. Her 'crew' of fierce warrior cheerleaders is as tight a bunch as any football team, and as dedicated to their sport. Lulu proudly shows off her bruises after each practice and trains like a demon. She achieved her goal of becoming a 'flyer' in her second year.

She also points out that she's very aware of the feminist issues around wearing a small skirt and lots of makeup, but it's so much fun she's happy to let that slide for the moment.

Any sport that involves high-level teamwork, strength, balance, flexibility, bravery and skill is okay by me. I'm glad she's found her thing. And to be fit and strong you've got to eat. Being a powerful athlete is more important than being a fragile butterfly.

She is an undeniably quirky young woman with a quick, dry and naughty sense of humour. I tease that her developing adult intellect is like a pair of 'gorilla gloves'—very powerful, but not all that subtle at the moment. We're working on changing the gloves for a scalpel.

•

So that's my dad and my daughter, my world of fatherhood. The keys to making these deeply important relationships, where who you are sets another person up for life, are the same as for all other relationships.

Be brave enough to show your true emotional self. Show sadness. Be caring and soft. Be silly. Laugh with joy. Love deeply enough to show your son or daughter you'll love them always. Always be there, without judgement, to listen. To gently advise. To sympathise. And maybe, from time to time, you'll get to fix a thing.

Ultimately, I know that Lulu knows her deeply flawed, chaotic father loves her desperately and unconditionally, just like I know my father loves me.

I'm writing this now with happy tears splashing onto my keyboard. I have written myself into quite an emotional state, but it's a good one.

Thank you, Lulu. Thank you, Dad.

I love you both.

# Chapter 11

# DYING HAPPY

An old man lies in a hospital bed. Machines beep. Liquids seep into his grey, hairy body through lines down his throat and into his veins.

His massive, heaving belly bears witness to the many excessive appetites that finally felled him. He's been here three weeks, slowly suffocating in his own phlegm. The sound is terrible—not so much a death rattle as a death chainsaw. He is in agony. The only thing keeping him alive is a deep bucket of black and oily willpower.

Nurses check him from the door if they can. He's nasty. When he can talk, he's raging against death and the injustice of finding himself here, at the end of his life—already.

'Fuck . . .' he hacks. There's a long silence before another gurgle and a shuddering, torturous breath—'. . . this.'

Or maybe a man is driving a sports car fast on a country road. The engine bellows and spits, the twin turbos hissing between gear changes. A high, wide drone shot would show the car eating the kilometres, snipping the apex of each corner, making the winding road straight.

The man doesn't see the brown countryside whipping past. His concentration and pleasure are equally extreme as he revels in the feeling of being at one with the wonderful machine. It's talking to him through his hands and the seat of his pants.

This moment is about as perfect as it gets.

He mounts a thrilling crest at over 180 kilometres per hour, and there it is—a farmer lumbering across the road in an ancient truck. There's nowhere to go. Time expands as he considers his options. For the first time in his life, there are none. He desperately aims for a gap between the truck and a tree, but he knows it's too small. The rear of the sliding car clips the tree and it flies out into a paddock, flipping end over end, then roof over wheels. There's so much energy from the speed that the crash takes a long time. The car finally flops to rest in a gorge. So violent were the multiple impacts that the engine is torn from its mounts, petrol hosing onto a red-hot exhaust manifold.

The man, somehow still conscious, is dangling upside down. Blood is already in his eyes. When the fire starts he has just enough time to understand what's going to happen before the fireball washes over him like a breaking wave. 'Oh, fuck it,' he whispers.

That's how I imagine my top two death scenarios. You?

•

I joke to Jayde that, for her, there's a fantastic bonus in our twenty-year age difference. When I shuffle off this mortal coil, she will be able to find some hot bloke twenty years younger than her and go around again.

She does not think this is as funny as I do.

Unfortunately, I'm probably right. In 1825, the British actuary Benjamin Gompertz discovered the phenomena that came to be known as the Gompertz law of mortality. It is, frankly, more than a little unsettling.

It states that your probability of dying in a given year doubles every eight years. For a 25-year-old, the probability of dying in the next year is about 0.03 per cent, or about one in 3000. By the age of 33, it's about one in 1500. By 41 it's one in 750. If you're 100, you have a 50 per cent chance of getting to 101. I'm 53 right now . . .

The Gompertz law holds true across countries, time periods and even species. Your probability of dying doubles every so many years, depending on your species' lifespan. It's an incredible fact, made even more amazing because no one can say why the effect occurs.

So our mortality rate increases exponentially with age, and there's nothing we can do about it. It's got nothing to do with the random things around us that might kill us; our bodies are just hardwired with an expiration date. Gee, thanks, gods.

We usually think of death as random, sudden and unexpected—like getting hit by lightning, or a train. If this were true, it would produce mortality rates that look nothing like reality. Your probability of dying during any given year would be a constant, not increasing across the years, as the stats show it does.

I'm no statistician, but if the lightning bolt theory were true, the average lifespan would still be 80, but out of every 100 people, 31 would die before the age of 30, and two would go on to live more than 300 years.

Actually, when you think about it, the Gompertz law might be the best argument ever for the existence of God. Is it just the big fella in the sky calling us home after our all-too-brief excursion in life?

The Theoretical Physics Institute at the University of Minnesota—their Christmas party is mad—published a paper explaining it. It's jammed with completely incomprehensible mathematics (I wish I knew more about algebra) but let's try to break down the theory.

Imagine that, in your body, there's an ongoing battle between cops and robbers. The cops patrol your body, and when they find a robber, they shoot him. Luckily, there are a lot more cops than robbers. They pass every single spot in your body fourteen times a day. This is known as the Poisson distribution. Look it up. If you understand it, you're smarter than me—but that's nothing to get excited about.

If the cops do miss a robber and he gets enough time to create a hideout too well defended for the cops to break in, you die. But don't worry. The cops are driving past everything fourteen times a day.

As you get older, some of your cops retire. Or die. Or crash their patrol cars. (This is what headaches are.) When your cops drop to twelve drive-bys a day, statistics say your probability of dying jumps seven times. And because the strength of your police force drops in a linear manner over time, your mortality rate rises exponentially.

By the time you've lost so many cops that they're only driving by seven times a day, you're 95 years old with only a two-in-three chance of making it through the year. There may be exceptions to the rule, but this is the rule. Science can be an uncaring bastard.

When they were keen on decapitating people by guillotine in revolutionary France, they did some fun experiments on the severed heads. On 17 July 1793, a woman named Charlotte Corday was executed for the assassination of journalist and politician Jean-Paul Marat.

When good Charlotte's head dropped into the basket, an executioner's assistant (I didn't even know that was a job) fished it out and slapped its face. In what must have been a disturbing moment, according to numerous witnesses, Charlotte's eyes looked at the man and her face changed to an expression of outrage, like Bob Katter.

French doctor Gabriel Beaurieux witnessed the beheading of a man named Languille. He wrote that 'the eyelids and lips . . . worked in irregularly rhythmic contractions for about five or six seconds'. Dr Beaurieux shouted Languille's name, and saw the man's eyelids 'slowly lift up without any spasmodic contraction', and 'the pupils focused themselves'. He did this twice. It was only on the third attempt that he got no more response from Languille.

Whatever the answer, science is still working on finding out the moment death actually occurs, and what defines it.

'Clinical death' is the medical term for the cessation of blood circulation and breathing, the two necessary criteria to sustain human life. This occurs when your heart stops beating in a regular rhythm—cardiac arrest.

At this point, you can still be resuscitated. On clinical death, you lose consciousness in several seconds. Measurable brain activity stops within 20 to 40 seconds.

Brain death, on the other hand, is the complete loss of brain function, including the body's involuntary activity necessary to sustain life. To be absolutely, certainly, dead, this needs to include the brain-stem, which can keep your heart and lungs going, even though at this point there's about as much going on in your cerebrum as a cabbage. Once you're brain dead, they can take your organs out. Then you're really dead.

There's little doubt that the leading cause of death is life.

When we came down from the trees, started eating burnt meat and our brains grew, we realised a horrible truth: we are going to die.

*Homo sapiens* is the only species on the planet with this knowledge. And, wow, does it ever mess with us.

•

That's why we need our gods. That's why we dreamed up the idea of a soul. How could it possibly be that when I die, I'm just gone? I mean, I'm living, breathing, thinking, wonderful me. I can't possibly just . . . stop being.

If our gods turn out to not exist, then we have another very powerful reason to lead our best lives, for us and those around us. We're only getting one chance.

Our old friend Chuck Palahniuk puts it wonderfully in *Fight Club*: 'You are not special. You are not a beautiful and unique snowflake.' It's because we believe we are so special that we love to believe, or hope, that a magic part of us will separate from our bodies when we die and live on for eternity in peace and joy, with a harp on a cloud, protected for eternity by our other father in heaven. All we have to do is ask. Sounds nice, actually. Nicer than worms eating your dead eyes in the cold ground.

What might it be like after death? Well, you remember that longest time before you were born? You don't? Well, being dead will be just like that.

Terror management theory (TMT) was developed by the cultural anthropologist Ernest Becker, in a bloody good attempt to explain the core motivations of human behaviour. *Scientific American* describes it in this gorgeous sentence:

> Although self-awareness gives rise to unbridled awe and joy, it can lead to the potentially overwhelming dread engendered by the realization that death is inevitable, that it can occur for reasons that can never be anticipated or controlled, and that humans are simply corporeal creatures—breathing pieces of defecating meat no more significant or enduring than porcupines or peaches.

What a burn. As a species, we'll do anything we can to avoid looking death in the eye.

A professor of psychology at the progressive Skidmore College in New York, Sheldon Solomon, told *Scientific American*:

> TMT posits that humans ingeniously, but quite unconsciously, solved this existential dilemma by developing cultural worldviews: humanly constructed beliefs about reality shared by individuals in a group that serve to 'manage' the paralysing terror resulting from the awareness of death. All cultures provide a sense of meaning by offering an account of the origin of the universe, a blueprint for acceptable conduct on Earth and a promise of immortality (symbolically, by creation of large monuments, great works of art or science, amassing great fortunes, having children; and literally, through the kinds of afterlives that are a central feature of organized religions) to those who live up to culturally prescribed standards.

An amusing aside to all this is that TMT also opens us up to worrying about spooks, ghosts, spirits and other nasties from the spirit world that we've convinced ourselves exist. The force always has a dark side.

If you're a believer, what kind of ghost you see depends on your religion. Buddhists, Muslims, Christians, Jews, Hindus and the adherents of the couple of thousand other religions on the planet all see different things. That's a pretty good indication it's all in our heads.

People, like me, who reject the idea of a spirit realm due to the total lack of evidence, never see anything. Feel free to rattle a chain outside my door tonight, or possess me like Linda Blair—I dare you, creepy dwellers of the spirit realm. (As I revisit parts of this book in the final edit, it's been six months since I wrote that line. I can report that I remain unhaunted.)

Fairies, witches, poltergeists, astrology, psychics, spirit guides, auras, the flat Earth theory, the approximately 3000 different gods we worship, and all the rest of the mindless rubbish conveniently unable to be proven by science fall into the same category.

Sceptical societies all over the world have millions of dollars in prizes available to anyone, anywhere, who can prove any sort of psychic or spiritual phenomenon. It just has to be clinically verifiable. That doesn't seem too much to ask, does it?

Just zap a quick video of a ghost on your phone, run it by some independent digital image specialists, and you're a millionaire. It's never happened, and I suspect it never will, no matter how sophisticated our recording equipment becomes. The good news, however, is that if you're being chased by a ghost, you should run into a laboratory. Ghosts apparently hate laboratories.

Mind you, maybe I've got it all wrong, and when the inevitable fireball comes I'll be in for a surprise.

But let's assume for a moment that our heavenly father does exist, and think about how death might go. Let's use a big fan of organised religion—say, Australia's Catholic cardinal, George Pell, as an example.

**God:** 'Morning, George.'

**George:** 'Morning, God. It appears I am dead. I'm quite excited to be here. Which is my cloud?'

**God:** 'We'll get to that, George. First, how did you go with the test?'

**George:** 'What test?'

**God:** 'The church test. Organised religion isn't really a thing. I just made it up to sort out the dickheads.'

**George:** 'Excuse me?'

**God:** 'Yes. C'mon, George, you don't really think one of your congregation can murder someone, or abuse a child, then say a few "Hail Marys" and we're all good, do you? That makes no sense at all.' *(Laughs loudly and slaps thigh.)*

**George:** 'Well, I . . .'

**God:** 'Good grief, man. I gave you a brain. And what the fuck are you wearing? What's with the hat?'

**George:** 'It's for . . . um . . .'

**God:** 'Oh, hey, here's Jesus, my son. Jesus, meet George.'

**George** *(gasping)*: 'Oh! Jesus!'

**Jesus:** 'Yo, George. Hey, you seem a little surprised that I'm black. I'm also gay. We never said I wasn't, did we, Dad? Anyway, George, where did you stand on the whole same-sex marriage thing in Australia? The Bible says me and Dad love everyone equally, yeah?'

**George:** 'Oh, well, I . . . um . . .'

**God** *(writing on clipboard)*: 'Now, George, I see you were in charge of the Vatican's finances. *(Whistles.)* Wow! You guys amassed quite a percentage of the world's wealth down through history. I assume you passed those trillions on to the poor, weak, sick, sad and needy, as I instructed?'

**George:** 'Yes, well . . . It's just that . . .'

**God:** 'Hey, Jesus, didn't you drive some accountants out of a temple with a whip at some stage?'

**Jesus:** 'Yep, I totally smashed the place up—went nuts. Dad's house on Earth isn't your personal money machine, is it, now, George?'

**God:** 'Oh dear. Now, this is a little embarrassing, but the all paedophiles in the churches . . . that was a test too.'

**George:** 'I, er . . . but . . .'

**God:** 'Oh, stop crying, for my sake. Only a few questions to go. What was all the stained glass and crap art about? I don't remember asking for that. We're big on simplicity up here. Less is more, George.'

**George:** 'We just thought it looked kind of . . .'

**Jesus:** 'Disgracefully ostentatious? You really should have had lots more of the LGBTQI community around the joint. Our people are awesome at interior design.'

**God:** 'Oh my. The orphanages in the nineteenth and twentieth centuries weren't great either. Your religious boys messed up quite a few kiddies in your care, didn't you? In fact, on closer inspection, these blokes murdered quite a few million people in my name down through the centuries. All the crusades and inquisitions weren't really what I was after from my representatives on Earth.'

**George:** 'I . . . Oh my God.'

**God:** 'Hmm . . . indeed I am, George. Go stand on that hidden trapdoor.'

**George:** 'But I . . .'

**God:** 'The stuff about hell was real, by the way. At least you won't be lonely. Quite a few of your mates are there already. Goodbye, George.'

**Jesus:** 'Lol! *(Pulls lever.)*

That seems about as likely as any other scenario, and a lot more fun.

Anyway, whether you believe your magic soul levitates up to the great beyond when you die or not, we have to agree that our lives are but tiny, fleeting moments. The entire existence of the human race, from start to finish, will be like a flea's fart in the cosmic immensity of space and time. If our minds could truly comprehend the size and timescale of the universe, and our position in it, our brains would surely explode, like in the first (and best) *Kingsman* movie.

Since we only have a tiny sliver of time to be, it is commendably sensible to make the best of it.

•

The incredible Harvard Study of Adult Development, which we met in the last chapter—it's the study that's almost 80 years old and still going—has a lot more to say on the subject of dying happy.

Under its first director, Clark Heath, who ran the show from 1939 until 1954, the study mirrored the scientific trends of the time. The researchers believed that a person's physical constitution, intellectual ability and personality traits determined their development as an adult. The study covered an astonishing range of psychological, anthropological and physical traits, from personality type to IQ to drinking habits to family relationships to 'hanging length of his scrotum', in an effort to determine what factors contribute most strongly to people living happy, healthy lives.

Psychiatrist George Vaillant led the study from 1972 to 2004. It was under his tenure that the truth started to bubble up like Texas tea. 'When the study began, nobody cared about empathy or attachment,' Vaillant says, 'but the key to healthy ageing is relationships, relationships, relationships.'

In his book *Ageing Well*, Vaillant wrote about six factors that predicted healthy ageing: physical activity, the absence of alcohol abuse and smoking, having mature mechanisms to cope with life's ups and downs, and maintaining both a healthy weight and a stable marriage.

To be clear—and, to my shame, I dabble with both—alcohol and cigarettes will kill you. 'Alcoholism is a disorder of great destructive power,' says Vaillant.

Alcoholism, for the inner-city 'Grant' group—which, incidentally, included John F. Kennedy—was the main cause of divorce, and strongly correlated with neurosis and depression. Together, alcohol and the inevitable cigarettes were the single greatest contributor to morbidity.

'The more education the inner-city men obtained,' wrote Vaillant, 'the more likely they were to stop smoking, eat sensibly, and use alcohol in moderation.'

It's proven that your genetics are less a factor in your longevity than your level of satisfaction with your relationships in midlife. I consider myself to have changed radically over the last ten years of my life, which is weird for such an old bloke. But the study agrees that our personalities are not 'set in plaster' by 30.

'Those who were clearly train wrecks when they were in their 20s turned out to be wonderful octogenarians,' Vaillant said. 'On the other hand, alcoholism and major depression could take people who started life as stars and leave them at the end of their lives as train wrecks.'

It's not just about living longer, either—it's got to be about living better. The study shows, without doubt, that loneliness will kill you just as surely as a pack of Marlboros and two bottles of wine a day.

Science says that if you want to die happy, you need deep, rich relationships through your midlife.

If I think back to the best moments in my life so far, I see that they're all about relationships. (Well, there have been a couple of track days at Sydney Motorsport Park at Eastern Creek which were also pretty fun, but that doesn't serve my thesis so well . . .) Jayde, the woman I am lucky enough to love, is my equal, partner, lover and best friend. (I dislike the word 'lover'—it belongs in a Karen Carpenter song, but there's little else that suffices.)

We still can't quite believe, years on, that we found each other. She is the most generous, caring, compassionate, funny, intelligent, sexy, naughty, driven and beautiful woman I have ever met.

Even with the age gap between us, there's absolutely no power imbalance. She wouldn't stand for it. She has supported us for the age I've taken to write this book with the profit from her communications business. I help out with the work when I can. Her clients adore her simply because of who she is—they're all her friends. Her professional success is built entirely on relationships.

We are still delighted to see each other at the end of every single day.

If talking were an Olympic sport, we'd win the mixed doubles gold. A typical night will begin in the kitchen, cooking dinner. We'll open a bottle of wine. We'll eat—probably in front of something we've recorded on the TV, I'm ashamed to say. But the whole process of dinner together will take hours. Pans regularly burn on the stove because the conversation is much more interesting. One show will take three hours to watch because we pause it so often.

Our knowledge and skills dovetail neatly. I'm all sciencey and booky, but we share a love of pop culture and music. She's a social media genius and highly skilled on all things in leading-edge communications. I'm not very good at Facebook.

We train together, work together, live together.

We're both shocking show-offs—she a Newtown High School of the Performing Arts baby, and me a pretend rock star in an amateur band for twenty years. In that way we're creepily similar.

There'll never be any kids, because in our time together Jayde has had a number of surgeries for ovarian cysts, cervical cancer and endometriosis. (If you don't know what that is, look the nasty thing up and hope you never have to feel the pain it causes.) At 32, she had a hysterectomy. To know you'll never have kids is a difficult thing for a young woman. So it's been a fun few years for us. But she's got her meds right and has beaten the absolute bastard side effect of removing your body's natural hormone source: weight gain.

We've been through a lot, but we did it together.

You may well be feeling ill on account of all the sweetness above, but my point is this: my relationship with Jayde brings me deep joy.

An annoying by-product of the current environment in sexual politics is the idea that to fight for equal rights and respect women is somehow unsexy—that we men who choose to respect women are somehow 'cucks' or 'white knights'.

The wonderful secret that men must learn is that really great sex happens when you're with a woman who truly knows she's respected as an equal human being on this planet. Then, instead of having to buy a sex doll, she'll dress up as one for you if you want, because she loves and respects you so much. And you'll do anything for her. That's the deal. There's a lot of porny pleasure to be had in a truly open, happy sexual relationship, where the main noise coming from the bedroom is laughter.

I'm not stupid. I'm working to keep my relationship rolling because I know it will keep me alive, young, smart and happy for many years to come. Jayde is my lovely life insurance. Thanks for the heads-up, old and smart Harvard study!

But if you're a man whose life is ruled by the performance of masculinity, and who lets himself be policed into believing women are his plaything, you're going to miss out. A truly great woman will not be attracted to you. And if a woman is unfortunate enough to get stuck with you, she'll be miserable.

Cynically, it's a fact that there's great reward for our penises in respecting, adoring, loving and being an equal partner with a woman.

There's also great reward for our hearts and minds.

In a weird quirk, the study also revealed if your politics is left-wing, you have more sex. Political leanings had no influence on life satisfaction, but conservative men stopped having sex in their late sixties, while the crazy left are bangin' away until their eighties. 'I have consulted uroligists about this,' Vaillant writes. 'They have no idea why it may be so.'

I'd personally guess at something about old hippies.

Vaillant's key takeaway is this: 'The seventy-five years and twenty million dollars expended on the study points to a straightforward conclusion. "Happiness is love."'

What can men do to be better partners to women, to be *true* alpha males—which, in nature, means to be a peacemaker, a caregiver, a 'consoler-in-chief'?

There's no downside to a world in which men avoid the behaviour dictated by the Man Box and policed by other men.

Women win. They won't get bashed, raped and murdered as much.

Our children win. We can become unshakable rocks on which they can build the foundations of their lives.

Men win. We'll stop killing ourselves. We'll experience the life-saving happiness of wonderful relationships and love in our lives.

To be the best partners to the women or men we choose to love, to be good men in our love lives, men must:

- Believe in our hearts that our partner is an equal to us in every way, because we are both human beings.
- Express emotions other than anger. Be vulnerable enough to share your true self, your fear, sadness and worry. That's how those burdens get lifted from you.
- Listen to what your partner is saying. Men are way too good at 'mansplaining' and knowing better. If you stop and listen instead of trying to fix everything, you'll find out what they really need from you, and you can make them truly happy.
- Not hurt anyone. It shouldn't have to be said, because of the first point, but any violence, aggression, unwanted touching, assault, sexual assault and even verbal and emotional abuse is just wrong. It's the opposite of love.
- Know that unless you have received a clear, enthusiastic, unequivocal, 'yes', you do not have the right to have sex with a woman—ever.
- Understand that the sexes are more the same than different. We all want the same things: to love, to be loved and to be happy.

•

It's not only our romantic relationships that are critical to our happy, healthy futures, it's all our relationships.

When I was a kid, a friend of mine, let's call him Barry, lived on a farm nearby; our houses were only kilometres apart, rare in the country. Barry is now a self-described 'biker for God', and travels New Zealand with a terrifying-looking, Harley-riding gang, who spread love and compassion wherever they go.

When we were in our late teens, Barry and I formed a rock band with a couple of other young blokes and played for a year or two in pubs around the student city of Dunedin. Barry was, and is, an exceptional keyboard player, drummer, photographer and human being.

He was speaking on behalf of White Ribbon recently to a group of young men, and his comments about growing up in a 'violent household' were reported in the local paper. His aunt, a good friend of my mother's, was horrified. She was emphatic that he hadn't grown up in a violent household, and couldn't believe he'd actually 'identified the family'.

Well, I remember stopping in at Barry's house in the mornings so we could ride our bikes to the bus stop together. He wouldn't be crying but he'd be angry, with a man-sized glowing handprint on the side of his face.

'The old man,' he'd simply say, and ride on.

His father, let's call him 'Horsefeathers' for reasons best kept to myself, was the most miserable, irrational, explosive and downright mean human being I've ever met. One example: Barry would get physically lifted from his morning bath by his ear, should it be too deep (above his father's thumb if he put his hand in the water) or too hot.

I used my comparative freedom to do wheelies on my motorbike in the paddock in front of their house until steam poured from Horsefeathers' ears. Once, Horsefeathers said to me that when I went off to university, I'd think I was 'too good for the rest of us'. I was sixteen. I remember saying, 'Probably.' Horsefeathers had no power over me because, maddeningly, he couldn't hit other people's kids. But there was no way in the world I'd ever have stayed a night there.

Barry once wrote a letter to his father, forgiving him for the years of abuse. He never got an answer. The beatings and complete lack of love and compassion had a deep effect on Barry down through the years, and inform the man he is today. It was something he had to overcome.

Barry's brother and sister, cousins, friends and relations nearby all knew. It was just horrible to be around the family home when Horsefeathers was into Barry, which was a lot of the time.

So how has life played out for Horsefeathers, who is now in his eighties, now that his beloved farm, machinery and wife—who was as loving and soft as he was hard and mean—are gone?

Not well.

These days, he lives in a little house on his oldest son's property. Everyone he lived with while that house was being built loathed the experience. He was depressed, mean, uncommunicative and miserable to be around. His family couldn't get rid of him quick enough.

Horsefeathers is pissed off because he knows, very soon now, he's going to die. He's not going to be surrounded by distraught family and friends, talking of how he loved and was loved. He's going to die knowing everyone knew what a total arse he was.

His life is a litany of lost moments, words unsaid, children unhugged, deep feelings never expressed. What a waste of 80 years—a tragedy, really. And what a terrible thing to put on someone else. In the end, this man failed in his relationships and failed at his life. There are more men like him than not.

Our relationships with other men, too, are critical to our happiness. We're brilliant at going to the footy or the pub with our mates, hanging out for hours and not talking about anything at all. But the moment anyone starts a sentence with the words 'I feel', everyone else in the room is saying, 'Whoa, dude! This is the Cricketer's Arms, not the *Oprah Winfrey Show*. Jesus!'

I can probably count my true, rich, deep, honest male friendships on one hand. Like all relationships, they take work, and I have to admit that a long time can go by before any threats of 'catching up' become true.

One of the greatest joys of my adult life has been an amateur rock band called the Hellbenders. The band comprises me, doing what can loosely be called 'singing', photographer, designer and guitar virtuoso Aaron Cliff, and bassist, digital strategist and creative executive Charles 'Chuck' Smeeton. We have also had an array of annoying, unhinged and unreliable drummers over the years.

We're basically a tight punk band that plays covers. So if the Clash were to play their interpretation of, say, '. . . Baby One More Time' by Britney Spears, that's how we are.

It works well live, because everyone knows the songs and you can bash out a high-energy show. I have lived my rock-star fantasies on stage in front of a few hundred highly inebriated family and friends, and I can report it's as much fun as it sounds.

For the band, though, it wasn't so much about the final show as the rehearsals. We'd find a studio, make a date and the guys would lug all their equipment in and set up. Talking about guitars and amps and fiddling with guitars and amps would take up the majority of our rehearsal time.

But it was brilliant. It was a safe space. While the banter flowed thick, fast and filthy, we somehow developed an openness and affection that has lasted almost twenty years. We haven't actually played a note together in a couple of years, unfortunately, simply because life gets in the way. But tomorrow I'm going over to Chuck's to record a couple of things in his marvellous home studio. He and Aaron still have a number of projects rolling. If you're a music fan, check out Chuck's music website, *The Cavan Project*. The guy makes his own guitars, and they look cooler than bought ones.

Since we're all in the media business, the Automation Revolution has had a very real effect on our professional lives. All three of us have struggled, at different points, with depression, and with who we are as men and providers, as the job market has contracted.

It's not a big deal. I just check in with a 'How you going, mate?' every so often. It's not like we're super deep or gathered around a fire examining our manhoods. We've just worked it so it's not weird, embarrassing or unmanly to ask how another bloke's going. To say I feel the same. To say, 'Wow—that's shit. You coping okay with that?'

I know that if I called Chuck and said, 'Mate, I've fucked up. I need food/money/a place to sleep,' he'd help me. Well, with the food and somewhere to sleep, and probably with some sage advice about where to get some money. I hope he can say the same thing about me. (And sorry, Chuck, about the unfortunate incident at your wedding . . .)

Although the Man Box still plays a pretty big role in the world of rock, we've somehow managed to shrug off the sense that communicating properly is not somehow feminine or gay. It's made all our lives more fun and significantly better.

•

As human beings, we don't really know what love is, but we know communication makes it work. As much as we'd like to hope it isn't so, we can fall in love with pretty much anyone. The first girl I loved was in one of my primary school classes, one of the only seven girls I'd ever met. If Jayde and I lived in other cities, or other countries, we wouldn't be pining for the moment we finally met. We'd be going out with other people. She would find love in someone else's arms. So would I.

So we aren't waiting for 'the one'—we're waiting for 'the one that will do'.

Giving ourselves up to another person, finding solace, comfort, joy, laughs and sex in a relationship, is part of the human condition. We can't help ourselves. It makes us happy.

I love Jayde. I love Lulu. I also love chocolate, pinot noir and our cat. I love my car, if I have a good one.

The ancient Greek language had up to seven descriptions for types of love:

*Storge*: family affection.
*Philia*: love for your friends.
*Eros*: sexual desire.
*Agape*: unconditional, or divine, love.
*Ludus*: flirting, childish, playful love.

*Pragma*: long-standing love, the love of the married couple. (I am determined that *pragma* and *eros* aren't mutually exclusive. They shouldn't be.)

*Philautia*: the love of self.

So there are actually many different kinds of love. You can say 'I love you' to two different people and mean two completely different things.

I once texted my dad, believing I'd texted Jayde, telling him all the terrible things I was going to do to him that night. He responded that he appreciated the thought, but he didn't think he owned any undies like that. That's two different types of love right there.

It's important to make sure everyone knows what love we're talking about. That's why communication is so important. We're not mind-readers.

Each couple pretty much has only one fight, but they play it out again and again. In my life, Jayde is a volcano. If she needs to go off, she goes off, but then it's all over. My lesson is not to take anything she says in the heat of an argument too seriously. She doesn't really think I'm a 'mean, mean, man', and she's not really packing to move back in with her parents.

I'm a piece of work too, but in a different way; years of Man Boxing has made me stoic.

'That thing you said really upset me,' I'll say.

'When did I say that,' she'll ask.

'Seven months ago.'

'I don't remember a word of that,' she'll say.

'Really? Here's what you said, word for word,' I'll reply. I can remember all our conversations, word for word. It's a curse.

I can see how that would be annoying . . .

For a relationship to grow, all your likes, dislikes, desires, hopes, dreams, problems, dramas and fears need to be said out loud. Relationships aren't static. Like us, they change over time. A relationship is like a third entity between the two of you. Feed it and love it, and it will grow. Starve it and abuse it, and it will die.

We need to be able to change. We need to be able to compromise. We need to be able to work together to stay together. If you're able to safely say, 'I like this. I'd love it if you did X, Y and Z for me,' to each other—from sex to food to living together well—you've cracked it.

Mind you, one does need to be careful. Early on in our relationship, I overheard Jayde saying to female friends that she liked a certain sexual act. So, of course, I started doing it to her . . . repeatedly. Turns out she didn't love it so much, but thought that I did, so she kept doing it too. Good communication eventually got us out of that sticky situation. (And no, I'm not saying what it was. What's wrong with you people?)

Relationships counsellor and consultant Bill Malone puts it this way:

> One of the benefits of a relationship is that we have someone in our corner to support us and affirm our existence. This support adds to the trust that is needed in any relationship. Without mutual support, a trusting relationship will not develop. Each member must have its emotional needs met in order to continue to invest in the relationship. The continued support, and the being there for the other person emotionally, is the way in which trust is developed. If a trusting relationship is cultivated and maintained, the ability to try new adventures and take new risks are enhanced. A supportive, trusting relationship outside the bedroom always increases the activity in the bedroom.

That's an unsexy sentence but it expresses a sexy idea.

We know relationships are the key to a long and happy life. We know communication is the key to all good relationships. And we know the Man Box rules stand in the way of successful, rewarding relationships.

•

A bloke on Twitter with the handle @HomeOpsDad messaged me after reading a column I'd written about calling out your mates if they make sexist jokes.

He'd written a blog post 'Home Ops Dad—Because Leadership Starts at Home' that showed the Man Box at work. If you're still sceptical about how much men police men, here's what happened to this stay-at-home dad at his school reunion. He was the only man with that job in the room that night. One man told him it was the worst job in the world, and walked away. Another told him he could never look after his own children—it was way too hard. Another dad was proud he avoids his own family, and stays back at work for no reason other than to let his wife 'sort out' the kids at home.

Home Ops Dad writes passionately about work/life balance, gender inequality in the workplace, especially in management and executive positions, the gender pay gap and the benefits of fathers spending more time at home and mothers more time at work. Yet here he is being told he is less of a man because he is at home caring for his children.

What the hell is going on?

This blogger is one of a growing number of men who use digital technologies to work from home when possible, while enjoying the privilege of guiding his children as they grow. Eventually I helped him edit his second blog, *Ten Things I've Learned Being a Stay-at-home Dad*.

What was great about our exchange was that we actually could make contact—he in his suburban Melbourne home, and me in Sydney's Dulwich Hill (or 'Double Chill', as I heard a cool kid say on the train the other day). It's always wonderful as a writer to discover that someone likes your work and agrees with your aesthetic and sentiment, and I was pleased I could support him in return. We reached out to each other in the open way women do—it was a little nugget of niceness for both of us, I hope.

I'm not going to let the point go. The man is trying to look after his kids at home. Other men are making it very clear that somehow this makes him less of a man. He experienced hardcore social control, which expressly aimed to forbid his life choices.

This very morning, he tweeted that he'd woken to his first trolling. 'What kind of man stays at home while his wife goes out to work?'

some anonymous arsehole wrote to him. 'A man that can't provide for his family. Sad.'

What's sad is that a man feels he has to say this to another man he's never met, someone who is trying to make sense of the world for himself and other men with his keyboard.

The good news is that more and more men are constructing their own version of what it means to be a man. Masculinity reimagined, if you will.

We can still police each other's behaviour by refusing to laugh at sexist jokes, by calling out our mates for sexist language and behaviour, and so on. We can make abusive men feel like dumb, backward, unsophisticated fools as the cold winds of Siberia blow. (That's an old News Corp term for being out of favour: you're in Siberia.)

My Home Ops Dad mate makes the perfect point that when you're busy expending so much love and care as you wash, clean, cook, feed, wipe, amuse and referee your children, you'll have neither the energy nor the inclination to bash your wife. Instead, you'll be experiencing a deep, rich, equal relationship with your partner, which is the perfect antidote to any Man Box infections. (And no one wants an infection in the Man Box . . .)

In my view, dying happy will mean being able to look back over one's life and adding up all those moments of joy. I can't wait to remember all those moments in the kitchen. In the bedroom. In the car. I want my daughter and partner and friends around me as I die. I want them to be sad, goddammit! Because that will show me that the way I conducted myself in my few short years on this Earth made other people happy. It will show me that other people were happy to be with me.

The only thing that matters in life is our relationships. We need to work on our relationships. We need to enjoy our relationships. We need to be present and real in our relationships. We need to be good men for ourselves and everyone else.

Women deserve a world of better men.

Happiness is love. Full stop.

# Executive Summary

I love a good executive summary. It's the couple of golden pages at the front of a, say, 600-page corporate document full of confusing numbers and market analysis. In a few pages, the executive summary clearly explains what the document is actually saying.

So if you've flicked to the back of this book, and can't be bothered with all the, you know, annoying words in the front bit, here's an easy-to-digest guide to the state of men and being a better man.

## Part One

### Becoming a Man

Three tiny words echo through the hearts and minds of little boys as they start their discovery of what it means to be a man: be a man. Little boys don't get to decide. We are told.

From the moment we look into our parents' eyes, how we are expected to behave is as clear as the difference between pink and blue.

Don't show weakness. Don't express any emotion (apart from anger). Don't cry. Don't be soft. Don't be empathetic. Don't be a pussy. Don't be gay. Don't be feminine. Don't ask for help.

The direct result of this is that men are growing up isolated, lonely, angry and unable to make meaningful human connections.

A direct line can be drawn from the peer-policed behaviour of 'being a man' to the one woman each week who dies from domestic violence in Australia, and the six men each day who kill themselves. 'Be a man' could well be the three most dangerous words, for men and women, ever.

The Man Box is a simple but powerful exercise used by men working with groups of boys, all over the world, to demonstrate how the performance of being a man is strictly policed, from cradle to grave.

In the exercise, men answer the question: 'What have you been taught, and come to believe, about manhood?' Their answers are put inside the Man Box. They say real men are great in bed, financially successful, provide for their family, never cry, are strong, tough and stoic. They're leaders.

If you're not these things, you're not a real man. This is how 'masculinity' is policed.

The agony, alienation and rage men feel at having to pretend to be a big, tough man every moment of the day, and at never succeeding, are real, painful and deeply damaging.

•

Porn will give you a limp dick and make you a bad lover. It's a massive international industry generating US$100 billion and 13,000 films a year. Hollywood only makes US$10 billion and 600 movies a year.

It is an industry built on the ruined lives and bodies of thousands of young, predominantly female, victims from all over the world.

A boy starts consuming porn by the age of ten. By his early twenties he's watched more than 10,000 hours of porn. Just like our brains aren't made to experience food coming out of a drive-through window, we're not supposed to be able to access thousands of erotic images every day.

But we can, and do. So our brains are physically rewired to need more and more extreme imagery to become aroused.

The porn market is changing to reflect our increasingly hardcore tastes, meaning porn stars must do things that are more and more sick to catch our attention.

Where is the laughter? Where is the erotic back-story? Where is the touching?

Porn teaches young men that women are no more than objects, and sex is a performance, not a loving, intimate mutual pleasure. Porn's clammy touch reaches every nook and cranny of society, making our daughters oversexualise themselves for boys who think a fourteen-year-old girl likes being choked with cock.

There is no benefit to mainstream porn, and a massive downside for men, women and the very real people working under the hot lights.

There is porn to be found where there's laughter, fun and respect in the bedroom. It's just not very popular and certainly not what boys seek out when they first start clicking with one hand.

But don't worry: just 120 days of cold turkey, and your penis, and your sexuality, will be back in fine working order.

Porn teaches young men all the wrong things about sex and relationships. Because of this, they, and their unfortunate partners, aren't exploring the full joy of an equal relationship between two people. Porn is one of the major factors preventing young men developing rich, successful relationships with women.

•

Men's rights activists, or MRAs, would be hysterical if they weren't so dangerous. Most mass shooters either identify directly as MRAs or express the rejection, alienation and rage driving this bizarre social movement.

MRAs believe feminism, left-wing politics and the family court system have led to a world so biased towards women that the average man in the street has no chance at a happy life.

The ultimate MRA calls himself an incel, an 'involuntary celibate'. What this means, in his mind, is that life has dealt him such a crappy hand of cards that he has no chance of a real woman actually wanting to have sex with him. These boys believe they are not 'getting sex' from women because they aren't rich, charismatic and handsome, and so are angry at women, and life.

They are excited about the rise of the sexbot, which means they won't need real women anymore—and sexbots won't complain about being raped, strangled, spat on or slapped.

It's the irony of the incel that if you're sitting in your mum's basement in a cloud of bong smoke, typing on Reddit about how much you hate women, there's not going to be a line of women knocking on your front door.

These men have been barred from the Man Box by both men and women, and it's made them bitter, angry and unhinged, their alienation leading them to an extreme group as surely as a radicalised young Muslim.

Sad, angry young men, unable to even pretend to fulfil the expectations of being a 'real man', are only a couple of clicks away from a YouTube rabbit hole where they will find a like-minded community that will warp their minds forever.

There is absolutely no doubt I will get called a 'cuck' (an old English word the MRAs have made popular again), a 'pussy' and generally a non-man when this book is published. It's totally gay to have expressed the 'mangina' sentiments I have here. They may even use social media to stop people buying this book, as they have done in the past. I certainly hope so!

# Part Two

## Being a Man

The numbers around domestic violence are so huge, sad and confronting that we simply can't wrap our heads around them. Once a week in

Australia, a woman will die at the hands of a partner, or former partner. Every year, more than 300,000 women will experience violence—often sexual violence—at the hands of someone other than their partner. One in three women will have experienced physical violence by the age of fifteen. Women are three times more likely than men to experience violence from an intimate partner. Why does this bloodbath keep happening? What is wrong with men that we are killing the ones we love in such extraordinary numbers?

White Ribbon knows why:

Narrow ideas of what it means to be a man harm both men and women. Sometimes, men feel pressure to be dominant and in control. Some people believe men must be strong and powerful. These characteristics are called 'gender norms'. Examining social definitions of manhood will remove the pressure on men to meet expectations that are impossible to satisfy or attain. These expectations of men create the conditions for violence, abuse and control of women to occur.

The pressure to be a man creates the environment for domestic violence to exist.

•

Like those for domestic violence, the numbers around male suicide are so enormous that they virtually have no meaning. Today, this very day, six men in Australia will kill themselves. The same thing happened yesterday. The same thing will happen tomorrow. That's six men who will never see their children again, six men who will never walk through the front door tonight, six men who will never kiss the women who love them again.

Every bloody day.

'All of the men we interviewed, spoke [of] growing up in a culture where the message was implicit that they should not be speaking about their feelings,' says the Black Dog Institute.

Another expert agrees: 'One of the key drivers of suicide is in the "way we define what it means to be a man in Australia".'

'Men are known for bottling things up. But when you're feeling down, taking action to call in extra support is the responsible thing to do,' according to Beyond Blue.

We are, literally, killing ourselves to be 'men'.

•

Both the corporate and blue-collar worlds adore the Man Box qualities of toughness, stoicism, getting on with it and being an aggressive, entrepreneurial larrikin. Apart from the sporting field, there's no area of life where male behaviour is more strictly policed than at work.

In the corporate world, the required behaviour is made so clear that it could be broadcast in an interdepartmental memo.

The more aggression, leadership and power you display, the more successful you'll be. Is the editor crying because she can't make her magazine with two fewer subeditors? Make the cut anyway and deal with the fallout later—she'll be fine. Need a few more heads to roll in order to make budget for the year? Slash and burn like a man. There's no room for feelings here.

The world of sparkies, chippies and brickies is no different. There is a code policing how you speak, what you speak about and even how you dress.

In both worlds, to express emotion, weakness, sadness, bewilderment or tiredness is to be a wimp. To speak out against sexist behaviour and language will see you ignored and, ultimately, just for not being a real man.

The act we have to put on—pretending to be 'real men' simply so our day goes a little more smoothly—is played out in every boardroom and construction site across the country. We're all pretending, and if we're honest with ourselves, we all hate it.

As men navigate the digital workplaces of the future, there will be very little room for the old-school exec, shouting or throwing things, or the sweary, blokey tradie, wolf-whistling from his ute.

Our professional lives are reinforcing the male behaviours that are killing us, and those we love. How we work is making us profoundly unhappy. The only people who can change that is us.

•

The Industrial Revolution started in the mid-1700s and took effect for some 200 years. It changed the face of society forever. The Automation Revolution—the rise of artificially intelligent systems that will take over almost all of our blue-collar and many of our white-collar jobs—will take only around fifteen years, and it's already started.

Machines are driving our cars, writing our news stories, diagnosing our illnesses and making our burgers. They can do it at high speed, 24 hours a day and at almost no cost, once they're manufactured.

Elon Musk recently scoffed at a Twitter video of a robot jumping onto boxes and doing backflips. 'This is nothing. In a few years, that bot will move so fast you'll need a strobe light to see it. Sweet dreams . . .' Gulp.

What this means is that a man who thought he'd have his job on a diesel forklift for life can't guarantee that anymore. And the same goes for lawyers, doctors, accountants and a thousand other professions.

Men once had a broad contract with women and society: 'I'll earn the money, you look after the house and kids.' However, the goalposts have moved and men are seeing their professional futures whisked out from under them. The system doesn't work anymore. Their rage and disenfranchisement was, in great part, responsible for the Trumpian vote and the appeal of the far-right-wing politician. It's a middle finger to 'the man'.

But with great change comes great opportunity. The most valuable qualities of the job market of the future are going to be creativity and empathy, human traits that make us unique and better than the machines, no matter how fast they can slice a tomato. Machines can do bread but they can't do circuses.

The rub is, of course, that creativity and empathy aren't greatly valued in the Man Box. They are seen as feminine traits, even a bit gay.

So the walls of the Man Box stand between us and the job market of the future—just another reason to smash them down.

# Part Three

## Being a Better Man

If you're taking the care and time to cook for a woman, it means you want to sustain and nourish her. It's an act, and mindset, born of love. Yet many men still consider it a woman's job to feed the family seven nights a week, and many women have been conditioned to believe that's correct.

Apart from the obvious benefits to your wallet and waistline, and the erotic appeal of a man who can cook, the act of feeding people means you won't want to fight with them. If you're being creative in the kitchen, she can be confident that domestic violence isn't coming after dinner.

The super-sexy high-end equipment, the cool techniques, the project-management skills required and the incredible reward for effort make being able to cook a highly desirable art for a man to master.

Add it to your armoury of being a better man. The benefits are legion. And the downside? Nil.

One thing, you can only be a hero in the kitchen once the rest of your half of the housework is done!

•

We have an obligation, as we strut around the planet in our beautiful, big, strong man bodies, to use our powers for good, not evil, like super-heroes. Our strength is our weakness, because it allows us to impose our will over others. The belief that it's okay to do so comes from the Man Box.

Men should hold it as a privilege to protect and provide with their strength. Our physical power enables us to care for those we love. But with that comes the responsibility to resist the corruptible influence of power.

We are only here for a tiny moment of time. We should respect our bodies and look after them well, so that we have so many more joyful moments of deep communication with the people we love. We're all going to die soon. We'll ultimately judge ourselves, and others, by how we lived our short lives in our awesome bodies.

It's not too much to ask for a little self-control, is it?

•

Apart from the love of a great woman, or man, in your life, the deepest, most rewarding joy is fatherhood. There's an easy hack to great father-hood that's easy to write about but incredibly difficult to pull off. Stop trying to fix everything. Just be there for your child in a way that lets them know you'll always be there for them. Open yourself to uncondi-tional love. It's the greatest gift you can give your child, because when a child receives unconditional love, it goes a long way to helping them become a happy, balanced adult. Daughters, particularly, experience a man-sized hole in their hearts if their dads aren't there for them.

You won't achieve this by being the boss, the leader, the enforcer, the problem solver, the provider, the head of the household. You don't get a parenting 'result', a reward for effort, like you might at work.

It's the hardest job you'll ever have, yet it's the most rewarding.

The values of the Man Box hold you back from being a great father. There is no better reason for us to stop 'being the man' and trying to fix everything, and instead simply show our love to our child.

•

They may be a very unscientific sample of two, but if you ever needed to prove the claims of the incredible Harvard Study of Adult Development, you could just look to my parents.

The 80-year Harvard study is unique in the world because of its lifespan. It shows, scientifically, unequivocally, that the only thing that will keep you happy and alive for a long time is the relationships in your life. It's as simple as that. Love does, indeed, make the world go round.

My parents have the happiest marriage I've ever seen. They fell in love when mum was fifteen. They remained happy and grew together, and are now deep into their seventies. They walk kilometres every day. Dad bikes up to 40 kilometres and beyond on his ancient, heavy mountain bike. They have a kayak, for goodness sake! Dad lands trout out of the freezing crystal waters of New Zealand's South Island, and Mum, whose diet is almost entirely plant-based, grudgingly has a little. They're both sharp as tacks, highly energetic and loving this time of life with each other.

They are a shining example of the clear truth that great relationships keep you fit, healthy and happy, long into your life. All around them, unhealthy, unhappy friends have been dropping like flies.

It's the quality of the relationship you're in, and the level of trust you have, that are important.

Of course, there's no trust when you're the stoic, dominant, unemotional Man Box leader, imposing your will on the women around you. Everywhere a man turns, the walls of the Man Box stand between him and the only thing that can make him truly happy: great relationships.

So it's time to free ourselves of the performance of manhood for a better future.

Reimagining masculinity for the new millennium means replacing toughness with tenderness, violence with compassion, pig-headed stoicism with vulnerability and communication. Respect must overcome abuse. All of us, but particularly men, will be happier and healthier if we can create better relationships in the future, and we can do that by being better men.

To die happy means you have lived your life truly, madly and deeply, secure in the knowledge that you have loved and been loved.

In the end, all you need is love. Full stop.

# Acknowledgements

Thank you to my publisher, Jane Palfreyman, for her wisdom, professionalism, calm counsel and bravery. My editors Ali, Julian and Tom also deserve my profound gratitude for taking a mushy manuscript and helping me attempt to apply some intellectual rigour and sensible structure. I have completely ignored their brilliant and insightful advice on more than a few occasions, though, which is why you may be forgiven for asking, as you read, 'Why is it suddenly about chickens?'

I can't thank my partner, Jayde, enough for both her unwavering belief and extraordinary generosity during the writing of this book. She has worked hard day and night to grow her business while, at the same time, supporting us both for way too many months. It's fitting that this book would not exist were it not for the strength of a woman. When we first met I said, 'You're going to be such an amazing businesswoman I'll be able to sit on the balcony and write a book one day.' I'm very glad to have been right.

Finally, thanks to columnist, author, former Wallaby and current chair of the Australian Republican Movement Peter FitzSimons for some crucial advice at a critical moment in the life of this manuscript, which was: 'Fuck 'em!'

# Notes

**CHAPTER 1**

'One study showed that mothers . . .' p. 4

Emily R. Mondschein, Karen E. Adolph and Catherine S. Tamis-LeMonda, 'Gender Bias in Mothers' Expectations About Infant Crawling', *Journal of Experimental Child Psychology*, Vol. 77, Issue 4, pp. 304–316, 2000 <http://citeseerx.ist.psu.edu/viewdoc/download?doi=10.1.1.652.8492&rep=rep1&type=pdf>.

'The fact we often see . . .' p. 5

John Condry and Sandra Condry, 'Sex Differences: A Study of the Eye of the Beholder', *Child Development*, Vol. 47, No. 3, September 1976, pp. 812–819.

'Preschoolers are already aware . . .' p. 6

Lise Eliot, *Pink Brain, Blue Brain: How Small Differences Grow Into Troublesome Gaps—And What We Can Do About It*, Oneworld, London, 2012.

'. . . way of thinking' p. 9

Charis Chang, 'The controversial past of a mother of four who appeared in the advertisements against same sex marriage', *News.com.au*, 30 August 2017 <https://www.news.com.au/lifestyle/gay-marriage/the-controversial-past-of-motheroffour-who-appeared-in-advertisement-against-samesex-marriage/news-story/d9cf1758cc363312e40a0b14603c5d41>.

'A study published in 2017 . . .' p. 9

Andy Coghlan, 'Kids everywhere have damaging gender stereotyping set by age 10', *NewScientist*, 20 September 2017 <https://www.newscientist.com/article/2147963-kids-everywhere-have-damaging-gender-stereotyping-set-by-age-10/>.

'the Mouth from the South . . .' p. 13
'Homosexual Law Reform', *New Zealand History* <https://nzhistory.govt.nz/culture/homosexual-law-reform/reforming-the-law>.

'While women are much . . .' p. 15
Mark Greene, 'The Lack of Gentle Platonic Touch in Men's Lives is a Killer', *The Good Men Project*, 1 June 2018 <https://goodmenproject.com/featured-content/megasahd-the-lack-of-gentle-platonic-touch-in-mens-lives-is-a-killer/>.

'The concept has its genesis . . .' p. 15
Paul Kivel, *Men's Work: How to Stop the Violence that Tears Our Lives Apart*, Ballantine Books, New York, 1995.

'. . . Discussing suicide' p. 18
'Teenage Brothers on Sex, Social Media, and What Their Parents Don't Understand', *New York Magazine*, 5 March 2018 <https://www.thecut.com/2018/03/teen-brothers-on-sex-tech-and-what-their-parents-dont-get.html>.

'The following statement is true . . .' p. 20
Brandon Jack, 'Rape culture is real: spare me your tears for toxic masculinity', *Sydney Morning Herald*, 10 May 2018 <https://www.smh.com.au/lifestyle/life-and-relationships/rape-culture-is-real-spare-me-your-tears-for-toxic-masculinity-20180509-p4zecq.html>.

**CHAPTER 2**

'He argues that young men . . .' p. 25
Philip Zimbardo, 'The demise of guys?', *TED*, March 2011 <https://www.ted.com/talks/zimchallenge?language=en>.

'Today porn is worth . . .' p. 28
Jill Bauer and Ronna Gradus, *Hot Girls Wanted*, Netflix, 2015.

'The porn industry is driven . . .' p. 32
Cindy Gallop, 'Make love, not porn', *TED*, December 2009 <https://blog.ted.com/cindy_gallop_ma/comment-page-3/>.

'Why I Stopped Watching Porn . . .' p. 33
Ran Gavrieli, 'Why I stopped watching porn', *TEDxJaffa*, October 2013 <https://www.youtube.com/watch?v=gRJ_QfP2mhU>.

'runs stories about anal sex . . .' p. 34
Mamamia Podcasts, 'VNSFW: Five things you need to know about anal sex before you try it', 25 July 2016 <www.mamamia.com.au/anal-sex-beginners-tips>.

## CHAPTER 3

'Our current gender zeitgeist . . .' p. 37
Paul Elam, 'An Introduction to the Men's Movement', *A Voice for Men Radio*,
1 March 2011 <http://www.blogtalkradio.com/avoiceformen/2011/03/02/an-
introduction-to-the-mens-movement

'We realised fairly quickly . . .' p. 41
Amelia Broadstock, 'West End bookshop wins against online trolls after promoting a
Clementine Ford book', *The Courier-Mail*, 6 July 2017 <https://www.couriermail.
com.au/questnews/southeast/west-end-bookshop-wins-against-online-trolls-
after-promoting-a-clementine-ford-book/news-story/0e4330dfad4d6fb8023
b1e3526c5846a>.

'Incels are not actually interested . . .' p. 42
Jia Tolentino, 'The Rage of the Incels', *The New Yorker*, 15 May 2018 <https://www.
newyorker.com/culture/cultural-comment/the-rage-of-the-incels>.

'The question is to dwell . . .' p. 42
Amia Srinivasan, 'Does anyone have the right to sex', *London Review of Books*, Vol. 40,
No 6, 22 March 2018, pages 5–10.

'guys who have been frustrated . . .' p. 43
Jeremy Nicholson, 'Why Are Men Frustrated With Dating?', *Psychology Today*,
3 April 2012 <https://www.psychologytoday.com/au/blog/the-attraction-doctor/
201204/why-are-men-frustrated-dating>.

'Samantha was programmed . . .' p. 44
David Moye, 'Sex Robot Molested at Electronics Festival, Creators Say', *HuffPost*,
30 September 2017 <https://www.huffingtonpost.com.au/entry/samantha-sex-
robot-molested_us_59cec9f9e4b06791bb10a268>.

'By July, 2015 . . .' p. 46
John McDermott, 'How the Alt-Right Made "Cuck" the Word of the Year',
*Mel Magazine*, 28 November 2016 <https://melmagazine.com/how-the-alt-
right-made-cuck-the-word-of-the-year-2164dac01e66>.

'I was so confused at that time . . .' p. 49
Edwin Hodge as told to John McDermott, 'I Was a Men's Rights Activist',
*Mel Magazine*, 15 April 2016 <https://melmagazine.com/i-was-a-men-s-rights-
activist-55a0d2eb6052>.

## CHAPTER 4

'Compare that to . . .' p. 58
Bernard Keane, 'The real threat of terrorism to Australians by the numbers', *Crikey*, 4 September 2014 <https://www.crikey.com.au/2014/09/04/the-real-threat-of-terrorism-to-australians-by-the-numbers/>.

'the following key facts . . .' p. 58
'Facts and Figures', *Our Watch* <https://www.ourwatch.org.au/Understanding-Violence/Facts-and-figures>.

'credible information showing . . .' p. 59
Australian Institute of Family Studies, *Report – Australian Family Violence and Death review Network Data Report 2018*, Australian Government, 4 June 2018 <https://aifs.gov.au/cfca/2018/06/04/report-australian-domestic-and-family-violence-death-review-network-data-report-2018>.

'The fact that family violence . . .' p. 59
Jane Gilmore, 'The truth about men and murder', *Sydney Morning Herald*, 2 June 2018 <https://www.smh.com.au/national/the-truth-about-men-and-murder-20180602-p4zj3g.html>.

'The more I stayed with him . . .' pp. 61–64
*True stories*, Domestic Violence Resource Centre Victoria <https://www.dvrcv.org.au/stories>.

'The CEO of . . .' p. 65
Lucie Van Den Berg and Kathryn Powley, 'VicHealth Report reveals Australians turning a blind eye to rape and violence against women', *Herald Sun*, 16 September 2014 <https://www.heraldsun.com.au/news/law-order/vichealth-report-reveals-australians-turning-blind-eye-to-rape-and-violence-against-women/news-story/fcf153e79fe227328c53d5edb64131ef>.

'The feminist linguist . . .' p. 65
Julia Penelope in Jackson Katz, 'Violence against women—it's a men's issue', *TED*, November 2012<https://www.ted.com/talks/jackson_katz_violence_against_women_it_s_a_men_s_issue/transcript?language=en>.

'While researching her book . . .' p. 66
C.J. Pascoe, *Dude, You're A Fag*, University of California Press, Oakland, November 2011.

'In a 2018 article . . .' p. 69
Steve Biddulph, 'Toxic danger to boys when men fail to step up', *Sydney Morning Herald*, 8 June 2018 <https://www.smh.com.au/lifestyle/life-and-relationships/toxic-danger-to-boys-when-men-fail-to-step-up-20180608-p4zkeb.html>.

'61 per cent of . . .' p. 71

'Violence Against Women: Key Statistics', Australia's National Research Organisation for Women's Safety (ANROWS), 14 May 2014 <https://dh2wpaq0gtxwe.cloud-front.net/s3fs-public/Key%20statistics%20-%20all.pdf>.

## CHAPTER 5

'For every suicide . . .' p. 76

'Statistics on Suicide in Australia', Lifeline <https://www.lifeline.org.au/about-lifeline/lifeline-information/statistics-on-suicide-in-australia>.

'Women are twice as likely . . .' p. 81

Konstantinos Tsirigotis et al, 'Gender differentiation in methods of suicide attempts', *Medical Science Monitor*, 17 (8), 1 August 2011 <https://www.ncbi.nlm.nih.gov/pmc/articles/PMC3539603/>.

'It's broken down a little. . .' and 'All of the men interviewed . . .' pp. 81–82

Emily Verdouw, 'Domestic Violence: Can Abusive Partners Change?', *HuffPost Australia*, 29 May, 2017 <https://www.huffingtonpost.com.au/2017/05/28/an-uncomfortable-conversation-with-two-men-who-terrorised-their_a_22092568/>.

'Men are known for bottling things up . . .' p. 82

'Who does it affect', Beyond Blue <https://www.beyondblue.org.au/who-does-it-affect>.

'So I've sort of . . .' p. 83

Gavin Larkin, 'Our story', R U OKAY?, <https://www.ruok.org.au/our-story>.

## CHAPTER 6

'Fox has settled . . .' p. 87

Tom Porter, '21st Century Fox Paid Out $45 Million Over Fox News Harassment Settlements', *Newsweek*, 5 November 2017 <https://www.newsweek.com/fox-news-roger-ailes-sexual-harassment-607211>.

'A number of lawsuits were outstanding . . .' p. 87

Lisa Ryan, 'What Will Happen to the Sexual Harassment Lawsuits Against Roger Ailes', *New York Magazine*, 18 May 2017 <https://www.thecut.com/2017/05/roger-ailes-lawsuits-death-sexual-harassment.html>.

'Things were nasty at the top . . .' p. 87

Ashley Lee, '21st Century Fox Renewed Bill O'Reilly's Contract Despite Knowing of $32M Sexual Harassment Settlement', *Hollywood Reporter*, 21 October 2017 <https://www.hollywoodreporter.com/news/21st-century-fox-defends-bill-o-reilly-contract-renewal-new-sexual-harassment-settlement-1050944>.

'I know part of me died that day . . .' p. 89
Louise Milligan, 'I am that girl', *Four Corners*, Australian Broadcasting Corporation,
    7 May 2018 <http://www.abc.net.au/4corners/i-am-that-girl/9736126>.

'for working in the media . . .' p. 89
Tracey Spicer, *The Good Girl Stripped Bare*, HarperCollins, Sydney, 2017.

'I was inundated . . .' p. 90
Tracey Spicer, 'More to come from #MeToo', *Australian Financial Review*, 15 February
    2018 <https://www.afr.com/lifestyle/arts-and-entertainment/tracey-spicer-more-
    to-come-from-metoo-20180215-h0w4sn>.

'millions of potentially damaging emails . . .' p. 92
Nick Davies, 'Rebekah Brooks "ordered the deletion of millions of News International
    emails"', *The Guardian*, 28 November 2013 <https://www.theguardian.com/
    uk-news/2013/nov/27/rebekah-brooks-news-international-emails>.

'Fraser, in his first interview for years . . .' p. 99
Zach Baron, 'What Ever Happened to Brendan Fraser', *GQ*, 22 February 2018
    <https://www.gq.com/story/what-ever-happened-to-brendan-fraser>.

'like a groom picks up the bride . . .' p. 99
Erin Nyren, 'Kevin Spacey Accused of Sexual Misconduct by "Star Trek Discovery"
    Actor', *Variety*, 29 October 2017 <https://variety.com/2017/biz/news/kevin-
    spacey-anthony-rapp-sexual-advance-1202602082/>.

'We essentially found . . .' p. 101
'Women and Men Report Similar Levels of Work–Family Conflicts' (press release),
    American Psychological Association, 27 July 2017 <https://www.apa.org/news/
    press/releases/2017/07/work-family-conflicts.aspx>.

'I had a good excuse . . .' p. 101
'Male CEO Quits Job After His 10-Year-Old Daughter Reminds Him That Family
    Always Comes First', *The Huffington Post UK*, 26 September 2014, <https://
    www.huffingtonpost.co.uk/2014/09/26/male-ceo-mohamed-el-erian-quit-job-
    daughter-work-life-balance_n_5887592.html>.

'This is what it looks like . . .' p. 102
Karen Maley and James Eyers, 'Cameron Clyne breaks up with NAB', *Australian
    Financial Review*, 3 April, 2014 <https://www.afr.com/business/banking-
    and-finance/financial-services/cameron-clyne-breaks-up-with-nab-20140403-
    ix8jp>.

'I just cannot reconcile . . .' p. 102
'Federal Member for Perth Tim Hammond quits politics for family, triggering WA by-election', *ABC News*, 2 May 2018 <http://www.abc.net.au/news/2018-05-02/member-for-perth-tim-hammond-resigns-from-politics/9718606>.

'The big problem is . . .' p. 104
Caroline Smith, 'BOOK REVIEW: *Father Time* still a clarion call for more involved', *The Record*, 1 September 2016 <https://www.therecord.com.au/blog/father-time-still-a-clarion-call-for-more-involved/>.

'Beyond Blue reports that work stress . . .' p. 108
'Men in the workplace', Beyond Blue <https://www.beyondblue.org.au/who-does-it-affect/men/what-causes-anxiety-and-depression-in-men/men-in-the-workplace>.

## CHAPTER 7

'Last year, for my Fairfax . . .' p. 112
Phil Barker, 'The old school image of Aussie males is now out of fashion', *Executive Style*, 7 May 2018 <http://www.executivestyle.com.au/the-old-school-image-of-aussie-males-is-now-out-fashion-h0zppu>.

'Bobby and Lesley . . .' p. 115
Alex Morris, 'It's a Theyby!', *New York Magazine*, 2 April 2018 <https://www.thecut.com/2018/04/theybies-gender-creative-parenting.html>.

'almost 40 per cent . . .' p. 119
'More than five million Aussie jobs gone in 10 to 15 years' (media release), Committee for Economic Development of Australia (CEDA) <https://www.ceda.com.au/News-and-analysis/Media-releases/More-than-five-million-Aussie-jobs-gone-in-10-to-15-years>.

'All the world's general knowledge . . .' p. 120
Lauren F. Friedman, 'IBM's Watson Supercomputer May Soon Be the Best Doctor in the World', *Business Insider Australia*, 23 April 2014 <https://www.businessinsider.com.au/ibms-watson-may-soon-be-the-best-doctor-in-the-world-2014-4>.

'Even what seems the most very human . . .' p. 120
Celeste Lecompte, 'Automation in the newsroom', *Nieman Reports*, 1 September 2015 <https://niemanreports.org/articles/automation-in-the-newsroom/>.

'Momentum Machines . . .' p. 121
Melia Robinson, 'This robot-powered restaurant could put fast food workers out of a job', *Business Insider Australia*, 13 June 2017 <https://www.businessinsider.com.au/momentum-machines-funding-robot-burger-restaurant-2017-6>.

'bookstores were full of books like . . .' p. 123
Ben Beaumont-Thomas, 'Fight Club author Chuck Palahniuk on his book becoming a bible for the incel movement', *The Guardian*, 20 July 2018 <https://www.theguardian.com/books/2018/jul/20/chuck-palahniuk-interview-adjustment-day-black-ethno-state-gay-parenting-incel-movement>.

'These things don't destroy jobs . . .' p. 125
Mindi Chahal, 'Rise of the machines: Are robots after your job?', *Marketing Week*, 12 January 2017 <https://www.marketingweek.com/2017/01/12/rise-of-the-machines/>.

'Art lifts our species . . .' p. 125
'Circa's Yaron Lifschitz slams the major arts companies as funded by "a government entrenched oligarchy of privilege"', *Daily Review*, 30 November 2016 <https://dailyreview.com.au/circas-yaron-lifschitz-slams-major-arts-companies-funded-government-entrenched-oligarchy-privilege/53024/>.

'The outcome will depend . . .' p. 126
Lucia Peters, 'Stephen Hawking's Last Reddit AMA Focused On What The Development Of AI Really Means For Our Future', *Bustle*, 15 March 2015 <https://www.bustle.com/p/stephen-hawkings-last-reddit-ama-focused-on-what-the-development-of-ai-really-means-for-our-future-8495822>.

'I think we will have to have . . .' p. 126
'Elon Musk on why the world needs a universal basic income', World Government Summit, March, 2018 <https://www.worldgovernmentsummit.org/Observer/list/elon-musk-on-why-the-world-needs-a-universal-basic-income>.

'With phenomenal advances . . .' p. 129
Professor Ross Harley, 'Creative thinking vital for future industries', UNSW Art & Design, 2 October 2014 <https://artdesign.unsw.edu.au/whats-on/news/creative-thinking-vital-for-future-industries-professor-ross-harley>.

**CHAPTER 8**

'And the brain is a total energy hog . . .' p. 134
Jordan Gaines Lewis, 'We Use Way More Than 10 Percent of Our Brains', *Psychology Today*, 17 July 2014 <https://www.psychologytoday.com/au/blog/brain-babble/201407/we-use-way-more-10-percent-our-brains>.

'When our ancestors first . . .' p. 135
Clare Kingston, 'Did the discovery of cooking make us human?', *BBC News*, 2 March 2010 <http://news.bbc.co.uk/2/hi/8543906.stm>.

'Data from the 2016 Census . . .' p. 137
'Census reveals the "typical" Australian' (media release), Australian Bureau of Statistics, 7 April 2017 <http://www.abs.gov.au/AUSSTATS/abs@.nsf/AUSSTATS/abs@.nsf/mediareleasesbyReleaseDate/5E54C95D3D5020C6CA2580FE0013A809?OpenDocument>.

'The maker decides . . .' p. 144
Catherine Pryor, 'Four Australian chefs and the knives they love', Blueprint for Living, Radio National, Australian Broadcasting Corporation, 7 February 2017 <http://www.abc.net.au/news/2017-02-04/chefs-and-their-knives-a-love-story/8238272>.

'the Earth affords them . . .' p. 146
William Dampier, *A New Voyage Round the World*, James Knapton, London, 1697.

'After World War II . . .' p. 146
Michael Symons, 'Australia's cuisine culture, a history of our food', Australian Geographic, 27 June 2014 <https://www.australiangeographic.com.au/topics/history-culture/2014/06/australias-cuisine-culture-a-history-of-food/>.

## CHAPTER 9

'In other weird male body news . . .' p. 155
Anna Schaefer, '12 Surprising Facts About Erections', *Healthline*, 14 September 2015 <https://www.healthline.com/health/erectile-dysfunction/surprising-facts>.

'A 2007 study . . .' p. 157
Anne Harding, 'Men's testosterone levels declined in last 20 years', *Reuters*, 19 January 2007 <https://uk.reuters.com/article/health-testosterone-levels-dc/mens-testosterone-levels-declined-in-last-20-years-idUKKIM16976320061031>.

'The average erect . . .' p. 157
Dr Justin Lehmiller, 'Scientists Measured 15,521 Penises And This Is What They Found', *Sex & Psychology*, 11 March 2015 <https://www.lehmiller.com/blog/2015/3/6/scientists-measured-15521-penises-and-this-is-what-they-found>.

'The number of times . . .' p. 158
JF, 'I'm Tired of Being Ashamed of My Micropenis', *Cosmopolitan*, 5 October 2017 <https://www.cosmopolitan.com/sex-love/a3619161/living-with-a-micropenis/>.

'So exercise could prevent . . .' p. 162
Helen Petrovich, 'Exercise and cognitive function', *The Lancet Neurology*, Vol 4, Issue 11, 1 November 2005 <https://www.thelancet.com/journals/laneur/article/PIIS1474-4422(05)70203-9/fulltext>.

'It's no-holds-barred . . .' p. 165
'Metabolic Strength Training: Tone Muscle And Torch Fat At The Same Time!', 360 Fitness <http://360fitkeller.com/metabolic-strength-training/>.

'New study suggests . . .' p. 166
Phil Barker, 'New study suggests that men are failing when it comes to performance in the bedroom', *Executive Style*, 28 August 2017 <http://www.executivestyle.com.au/new-study-suggests-that-men-are-failing-when-it-comes-to-performance-in-the-bedroom-gy5mgw>.

'Men make up . . .' p. 169
Safe Work Australia, *2015–16 Annual Report* <https://www.safeworkaustralia.gov.au/book/safe-work-australia-annual-report-2015-16>.

'Men's health and gender politics . . .' p. 169
Mary Stergiou-Kita et al, 'What's gender got to do with it? Examining masculinities, health and safety and return to work in male dominated skilled trades', *XYOnline*, 10 September 2015 <https://xyonline.net/sites/xyonline.net/files/Stergiou-Kita%2C%20What%E2%80%99s%20gender%20got%20to%20do%20with%20it%202016.pdf>.

'Each year, 3300 of us . . .' p. 171
'What Is Prostate Cancer?', Prostate Cancer Foundation of Australia, <http://www.prostate.org.au/awareness/general-information/>.

**CHAPTER 10**

'need to provide better . . .' p. 174
Tim Winton, 'About the boys: Tim Winton on how toxic masculinity is shackling men to misogyny', *The Guardian*, 9 April 2018 < https://www.theguardian.com/books/2018/apr/09/about-the-boys-tim-winton-on-how-toxic-masculinity-is-shackling-men-to-misogyny>.

'We know a lot more . . .' p. 174
Steve Biddulph, 'Steve Biddulph's "incredible new findings" on raising boys today', *The Weekend Australian Magazine*, 28 April 2018 <https://www.theaustralian.com.au/life/weekend-australian-magazine/steve-biddulphs-incredible-new-findings-on-raising-boys-today/news-story/4d25b14e4905bfcb0baee894fb5c8521>.

# NOTES

'There's more and more research . . .' p. 175

Susan Scutti, 'Why The Father–Daughter Relationship Is So Important', *Medical Daily*, 12 June 2013, <https://www.medicaldaily.com/why-father-daughter-relationship-so-important-246744>.

'Children with absent fathers . . .' p. 175

Mark Trahan, 'What Makes A Great Father', *TEDx*, 14 December 2016, <https://www.youtube.com/watch?v=omxZvI32yhU>.

'creating an awareness in fathers . . .' p. 178

The Father Effect: Changing Lives & Legacies with Hope & Healing <www.thefathereffect.com>.

'If a daughter knows . . .' p. 178

Dr Meg Meeker, 'Good dads—the real game changer', *TEDx*, 15 October 2014, <https://www.youtube.com/watch?v=pQ3Dkrt-8O4>.

'to identify the . . .' p. 179

'History of the study', Harvard Second Generation Study <http://www.adultdevelopmentstudy.org/grantandglueckstudy>.

'[W]hat if we could watch . . .' p. 179

Liz Mineo, 'Good genes are nice but joy is better', *The Harvard Gazette*, 11 April 2017 <https://news.harvard.edu/gazette/story/2017/04/over-nearly-80-years-harvard-study-has-been-showing-how-to-live-a-healthy-and-happy-life/>.

## CHAPTER 11

'Although self-awareness . . .' p. 200

Sheldon Solomon, 'Fear and Politics: What Your Mortality Has To Do With The Upcoming Election', *Scientific American* <https://www.scientificamerican.com/article/fear-death-and-politics/>.

'In his book *Ageing Well* . . .' p. 204

George M. Vaillant, *Ageing Well: Surprising Guideposts to a Happier Life*, Little, Brown, London, 2002.

'One of the benefits of a relationship . . .' p. 214

Bill Malone, 'Love Is Not Enough – The Making of a Relationship', 1991 <https://www.canville.net/malone/lovenotenough.html>.

# Resources

If you are struggling with depression, anger or any other issue affecting men, please reach out for help.

## Australia

- Lifeline Australia 13 11 14 or www.lifeline.org.au

- Suicide Call Back Service 1300 659 467 or www.suicidecallbackservice.org.au

- Mensline Australia 1300 78 99 78 or mensline.org.au

- No to Violence 1300 766 491 or www.ntv.org.au

- Relationships Australia 1300 364 277 or www.relationships.org.au

- Beyond Blue 1300 22 4636 or www.beyondblue.org.au

- R U OK? www.ruok.org.au

## New Zealand

- Lifeline Aotearoa 0800 543 354 or www.lifeline.org.nz

- Depression and Anxiety New Zealand 080 111 757 or depression.org.nz

- Men's Health 09 973 4161 or menshealthnz.org.nz

- Family Violence: It's Not OK 0800 456 450 or www.areyouok.org.nz

- Relationship Ateroa www.relationships.org.nz

- Mental Health Foundation of New Zealand 09 623 4812 or www.mentalhealth.org.nz